LIKE *a* RÔCK

LIKE a ROCK

Laying the Foundation for the Rest of Your Life

ANDY STANLEY

OLIVER
NELSON
™

THOMAS NELSON PUBLISHERS®
Nashville

A Division of Thomas Nelson, Inc.
www.ThomasNelson.com

Published in Nashville, Tennessee, by Thomas Nelson, Inc., Publishers, and distributed in Canada by Word Communications, Ltd., Richmond, British Columbia.

Unless otherwise noted, Scripture quotations are from the NEW AMERICAN STANDARD BIBLE ®, © copyright The Lockman Foundation 1960, 1962, 1963, 1968, 1971, 1972, 1973, 1975, 1977. Used by permission. Scripture quotations noted NKJV are from the NEW KING JAMES VERSION. Copyright © 1979, 1980, 1982, Thomas Nelson, Inc., Publishers.

Library of Congress Cataloging-in-Publication Data

Stanley, Andy.
    Like a rock : becoming a person of character / Andy Stanley.
       p. cm.
    Includes bibliographical references.
    ISBN 0-7852-7612-2 (hardcover)
    ISBN 0-7852-6579-1 (paperback)
    1. Character—Social aspects. 2. Moral development. 3. Personality development. I. Title.
    BJ1531.S73 1997
    158.1—dc21   96-339920
                                                      CIP

Printed in the United States of America

02 03 04 05 06 PHX 7 6 5 4

For Sandra,
The finest woman I know.

CONTENTS

FOREWORD

Undeniably, character is the foundation of all true leadership. The apostle Paul placed such emphasis on unblemished character that he listed it as the first qualification for Christian leadership: "An overseer, then, must be above reproach . . ." (1 Timothy 3:2 KJV). Out of character have such great leaders as Winston Churchill and Billy Graham been born. And out of a life of character has this book, *Like a Rock,* been born.

For quite a while I've watched Andy Stanley grow as a leader and pastor. In the last couple of years, I've gotten to know him well. The more I see, the better I like him. And I can say without a doubt that he lives out the solid character principles that he shares in this book.

Like a Rock will lead you through the process of discovering things about your beliefs and your values. The impact of a personal value system is comprehensive, encompassing everything in our lives from professional achievement to the way we relate to our children and spouses. And it affects that most important of relationships—the one we have with God.

Step by step, you will be encouraged to target specific character qualities and to discover your true values. You will learn to evaluate your relationships, occupational goals, and even entertainment in the light of character issues. And you will discover whether your goals are character-oriented or achievement-oriented. As you read, you may find yourself in a particular chapter for days as you reflect on your own response to its challenges. You will uncover obstacles to personal character development that you did not realize existed. You will also learn to accept responsibility for your own deficiencies. Most importantly, *Like a Rock* provides you with specific strategies for change, strategies that will help you to develop unwavering character.

This world desperately needs people of vision and personal

conviction. It needs mothers and fathers, employees and managers, citizens and officials who will do what is right regardless of the personal cost. It needs people willing to become more like Christ and lead by example. *Like a Rock* can help you become one such person.

John C. Maxwell
Founder, the INJOY Group

INTRODUCTION

It was another enchanting morning in the tiny Welsh village of Aberfan. October 21, 1966. As dawn broke across the shimmering emerald valleys of South Wales, the people were beginning to stir in the slate-roofed homes that speckled the hillsides of this coal-mining town. A stream of ashened figures flowed steadily into the colliery that had given birth to the quaint community. Not far away, ten-year-old Dylis Powell made her way down the cobblestone streets and gathered with classmates in the Pantglas Junior and Infants School on Merry Road. On a typical day, the stately red-brick building was home for some 250 children of the village.

To the weathered men who bore the scars of a lifetime in the coal pits, the village was not without its faults. But through the untainted eyes of a child, every scene added depth to a colorful tapestry called home. Through the dusty windowpanes along the back of the school, the verdant hills were vibrant with color. The one exception was the tall, foreboding black mountain that stood at the edge of the village.

To the casual observer, it appeared as an unusually shaped monolith—a single piece of rock piercing the earth's crust and serving as the foundation for the entire region. But the people of Aberfan knew better. For them, it was a monument to the years of labor that had made Aberfan home. And in the following moments, that monument was about to capture the attention of children and adults the world over.

Since 1870, the pile of mining debris had been rising ever so gradually from the valley floor. Huge bins, carted by overhead cables, had been dumping loads of coal waste continually for nearly a century. For the people, the slag heap had become a natural part of the landscape. Now it stood literally hundreds of feet high.

October had seen abnormally heavy rains fall upon the valley, turning the coal mound and the surrounding earth into a giant sponge. Ironically, on the morning of October 21, David John Evans, a maintenance worker at the local colliery, climbed the hill near the waste pile to look into reports that the giant mass was moving. Without realizing it, he had just assumed a front-row seat for one of the worst mining disasters in history.

By 9:30 A.M., Dylis Powell and her friends had taken their seats. "We were laughing and playing among ourselves waiting for our teacher to call the register," she recalled later. "We heard a noise, and the room seemed to be flying around. The desks were falling, and the children were shouting and screaming." Across the street, Mrs. Pearl Crowe heard a low rumble and glanced out her window. "I saw a black mass of moving waste pouring steadily into the school, and part of the school collapsed. I was paralyzed." When Mrs. Gwyneth Davies heard the noise, she turned in time to see that "the mountain had covered the school."

In a matter of seconds, the face of Aberfan had changed forever. Liquefied by the heavy rains, two million tons of coal, rock, and mud flowed like a river down the mountainside and into the valley. The school, along with a cluster of homes, was crushed. More than two hundred people, mostly children, were killed. An entire generation of Aberfan had been virtually wiped out. And all because of a mountain that wasn't really a mountain at all.

For years, the people of Aberfan had worked to build their community. The giant coal mountain stood like the centerpiece of a city carved out of the Welsh landscape by years of diligent labor. It was a growing legacy left for each passing generation. But in the course of one day, all of that changed. Not because of the events of a particular day. No, it was a day that had been in the making for some time.

ABERFAN REVISITED

As a pastor, I spend a substantial amount of my time with people who are digging themselves out from personal environmental catastrophes—circumstances that were often years in the making but "took them by surprise." A broken marriage, an unwanted pregnancy, a financial crisis, problems at work. As I listen, two questions race through my mind: Why is it that we have such a difficult time recognizing the traps we lay for ourselves? and What could this individual have done to avoid this situation?

In almost every situation, the answers to these questions boil down to the same issue: *character.* Compromised convictions.

Reshuffled values. Selfishness. Somewhere the people veered off the path of rightness. But nothing happened. At least nothing they were aware of. That was the beginning of their personal slag heap. And it stood within striking distance of the soul.

Another group of people with whom I have dealings on a regular basis includes those who have faced, or are facing, storms of life that are not of their own making. Storms created by the character deficits of others. Storms that are a natural part of a fallen world.

There, in the midst of unjust treatment and seemingly undeserved pain, the true character of a man or woman is revealed. Pretense is peeled away. Inherited, untested belief systems crumble. Religious and social correctness are jettisoned. What you see in such moments is what was really there all along.

Although many break, swept away by the winds of anger or despair, there emerges from the severest of storms a unique breed of people whose perspective and attitude remain intact. Like a rock, their foundations are deeply established. Clearly, there is more to them than meets the eye. These men and women invested years of their lives not in what is seen, but in what is unseen. These are people of character.

THE INSIDE PERSON

Your character is who you truly are. It will affect how much you accomplish in this life. It will determine whether or not you are worth knowing. It will make or break every one of your relationships. Your character is instrumental in establishing how long you will be able to hold on to the fortune afforded you by hard work and good luck. Your character is the internal script that will determine your response to failure, success, mistreatment, and pain. It reaches into every facet of your life. It is more far-reaching than your talent, your education, your background, or your network of friends. These things can open doors for you. Your character determines what happens once you pass through those doors.

Your good looks and net worth may get you married. Your character will keep you married. Your God-given reproductive system may enable you to produce children. Your character will determine your relationship with them. Your character either paves the way or obstructs the way for the possibility of one day relating to your children as friends.

A STRATEGY FOR CHANGE

When you look at a rock, you probably don't think about change. The fact that it's constantly transforming in shape, size, and density isn't the first thought that comes to mind because it's happening so slowly. Nevertheless, it's happening. Some rocks are hard and durable, while others are brittle. What they're made up of determines their strength, their longevity and, ultimately, their value. Sandstone crumbles easily in your hands. But take the right materials and subject them to the right conditions over time, and you get a diamond—the hardest element found in nature.

This book is about change. It's about the process of taking raw materials and molding them, shaping them, and refining them into a finished product. Whether you know it or not, that process is happening in you. It began the day you were born. And it will continue right up until the day you die.

Many of us as children planted trees. They appeared to be the same size the day we left home as they were when we planted them. Not until years later when we returned to the old homestead were we able to measure the growth. But something was happening during those childhood days. A process was under way that eventually produced a mature tree. And years later we stood and marveled at the change.

What is true of every living thing is true of your character. Your character is either developing or deteriorating. It is not stagnant. You are not the same person you were yesterday. I know, I know. You can't sense any change. You aren't aware of a difference. But I assure you, if you were to leave and return ten years from now, you would be amazed, shocked, overjoyed, perhaps saddened, or disappointed at the difference.

Just as your outer person slowly moves through the unavoidable changes brought on by time, so your inner person moves through similar, yet not so unavoidable changes brought on by the world you live in.

In a few years, what do you anticipate finding? I don't mean how many kids or grandkids you hope to have. For just a moment, lay aside the dreams that involve your career or net worth. I'm talking about what you hope to find on the inside. What kind of person do you hope to become?

Today, you took a step. You moved closer to or farther away from what you hope to be. Too many people moved farther away. A handful overcame the negative inertia of this fallen world and moved forward. But nobody stood still.

I have been to and conducted many funerals. It is not the most pleasant aspect of my job. One thing is unmistakably clear, however. There are good funerals, and there are bad funerals. At a good funeral you celebrate a life. You hear stories about love, kindness, selflessness, faithfulness, friendship, sharing. At a bad funeral you hear stories about golf and decorating.

There is certainly nothing wrong with golf or decorating. But when your assignment is to take three minutes and share with friends and family members what you remember most about old so-and-so and to fill the time with golf stories, come on.

What is my point? Your character, not accomplishments or acquisitions, determines your legacy. If you don't believe me, try a few word associations:

> Richard Nixon.
> Pete Rose.
> Leona Helmsley.

You get the picture. Talented, capable, rich, sought-after people. It doesn't matter. Their character determined their legacy. So will yours. So will mine. Is that important? Yes, it is very important. And the older you get, the more important it will become. The problem is, character is like a tree. It doesn't develop overnight. It develops over a lifetime. You can't wait until the last minute, do an all-nighter, and expect to pass. The measure of a man's or a woman's character is not determined by a fill-in-the-blank or true-false exam. It is an essay test, and the essay takes a lifetime to write.

Today, you wrote a section. It wasn't a long section. By itself it wasn't even a significant section. Today's section was only a slight variation on yesterday's. But look back on it in ten years, look back on it in twenty years, and you will be surprised. Whether it is a pleasant or an unpleasant surprise is completely up to you.

You may protest, "Hold on. Completely up to me? I don't think so. A lot of things affect my character that I have no control over!"

You are right if you are talking about your starting point: where you began, who you began with. Certainly, some events, experiences, and abuses put people at a disadvantage in the starting blocks of life.

But we are not talking about *now*. We are talking about *later*. You do not choose your starting point. You have your parents and others to thank or curse for that. But you do have the opportunity and responsibility to choose your ending place because character is not so much about what you are as it is what you are becoming. It is not so much an issue of where you are as it is where you are headed.

One more thing. This is not a solo flight. This is not a "be all you can be" kind of thing. The truth is, most of us are being all we can be. That's the problem. Being all we can be is not enough. We need to be what we *can't* be.

And so our merciful heavenly Father smiles—and in some cases shakes His head—and offers a very large hand: "For whom He foreknew, He also predestined to become conformed to the image of His Son, that He might be the first-born among many brethren. . . . What then shall we say to these things? If God is for us, who is against us?" (Rom. 8:29–31).

Simply put, God plans to be intimately involved in the process of moving your character in a positive direction. He has an agenda: It is your inner person, your character. The part of you that will share eternity with Him. The part of you that, more than any other, determines who you really are.

This book presents a strategy for character development. Every day of your life you go head-to-head with a master strategist, one who is intent on depleting your character of anything that in any way reflects the nature or fingerprint of your heavenly Father. This book offers a time-tested strategy to aid you in the struggle.

More and more I am convinced that Christians don't *plan* to get into trouble; we just fail to plan *not* to. It is my prayer that God will use this book to help you develop a personal character development plan. And that with God's help you will become a *conformist* in every positive sense of the word.

Part One

A DIAMOND IN THE ROUGH

As I wade through all the success propaganda written today, again and again the focus of attention is on one's outer self—how smart I can appear, what a good impression I can make, how much I can own or how totally I can control or how fast I can be promoted or . . . or . . . or. Nothing I read—and I mean nothing—places emphasis on the heart, the inner being, the seed plot of our thoughts, motives, decisions. Nothing, that is, except Scripture. Interestingly, the Bible says little about success, but a lot about heart, the place where true success originates.

—Chuck Swindoll
The Quest for Character

Chapter One

THE INSIDE PERSON

He who walks with integrity walks securely.

—Proverbs 10:9 NKJV

I grew up in a home where terms such as *values, goals, purpose, destiny,* and *character* were commonplace. My father has always had a deep sense of destiny and purpose. Consequently, he instilled into my sister and me the same paradigm for interpreting the decisions and events of life. Everything has meaning. Everything has a purpose. Our responsibility as God's children is to hone in on our purpose, to discover our destiny, and to follow through with all our might!

It was not until I was in my late twenties that I felt the significance and force of his words. At that time I found myself asking basic questions such as, Why am I here? What is my purpose in life? What has God commissioned me to do?

I know it sounds a bit melodramatic, but that's where I was. Standing on the precipice of my most productive years, I had finally focused on some of the most important questions a man or woman can ask. Understand, I was looking for answers in the arena of career, ministry, accomplishment. I wanted a challenge or a task worthy of throwing all the energy of my life into. I was looking for a mountain so high, it would take me a lifetime to climb. And I was confident that the answer would come in the form of some momentous task I was to accomplish, an organization to begin, a ministry to lead, a national crisis to solve.

My dilemma shouldn't come as much of a surprise. After all, I grew up with a father who had accomplished quite a bit. He wore big shoes. He left big footprints. His standards weren't just high; they were pretty much out of sight. I'm not exaggerating when I say that my dad took the Great Commission personally. He lives his life as if the weight of that task rests on his shoulders alone. Through the use of television and radio, he has taken the gospel into every country of the world every day of the week! That was going to be a pretty tough act to follow. After all, he didn't really leave too much for the rest of us to do. At least, that's the way I felt sometimes.

On the other side of the equation, he had instilled in me a deep, abiding confidence that I could accomplish anything I set my mind to. I was beginning to believe that. The problem was, I didn't know what to set my mind to. It looked to me as if everything had been done.

In the midst of this soul-searching time of my life I happened upon "an inspiring national best-seller," as the book jacket proclaimed. It was *The Seven Habits of Highly Effective People* by Stephen Covey. I certainly wanted to be a highly effective person, so I joined the rest of corporate America and bought a copy. Ninety-six pages into the book I found precisely what I wasn't looking for.

RERAILED

The second habit of a highly effective person is to *begin with the end in mind*. Covey opens this section by suggesting that the reader find a place to read where he can be uninterrupted and alone. Ordinarily, I never do what a writer asks his readers to do. I assume that the writer has never done what he is asking the reader to do. But on that occasion I followed instructions and went up to a spare bedroom to read.

The following paragraphs derailed my train and set me on an entirely different track. Now I know this looks like a long quote to wade through. But it is essential for where we are headed in the rest of this book.

In your mind's eye, see yourself going to the funeral of a loved one . . . as you walk inside the building, you notice the flowers, the soft organ music. You see the faces of friends and family you pass along the way. You feel the shared sorrow of losing, the joy of having known, that radiates from the hearts of the people there.

As you walk down to the front of the room and look inside the casket, you suddenly come face to face with yourself. This is your funeral, three years from today. All these people have come to honor you, to express feelings of love and appreciation for your life.

As you take a seat and wait for the services to begin, you look at the program in your hand. There are to be four speakers. The first is from your family, immediate and also extended—children, brothers, sisters, nephews, nieces, aunts, uncles, cousins, and grandparents who have come from all over the country to attend. The second speaker is one of your friends, someone who can give a sense of what you were as a person. The third speaker is from your work or profession. The fourth is from your church or some community organization where you've been involved in service.

Now think deeply. What would you like each of these speakers to say about you and your life? What kind of husband, wife, father, or mother would you like their words to reflect? What kind of son or daughter or cousin? What kind of friend? What kind of working associate?

What character would you like them to have seen in you? What contributions, what achievements would you want them to remember? Look carefully at the people around you. What difference would you like to have made in their lives?[1]

At this point Covey asks his readers to do something else. Again, I don't usually follow these kinds of instructions very well. But I was so moved by the exercise that I put my book down, pulled out my journal, and did as he instructed. I wrote down exactly what I would have wanted to hear from each of the four categories of people mentioned above. I wrote down what I would hope Sandra, my wife, would say. I penned the words I would hope to hear from my oldest son, Andrew. I recorded the imagined words of my friend Louie, whom I've known since the sixth grade. I worked through what I would hope to hear from church members, students I had taught, and associates at work. It took me almost an hour to complete the exercise.

Then I picked up the book and read a sentence that dramatically altered my perspective: "If you carefully consider what you wanted to be said of you in the funeral experience, you will find *your* definition of success."[2]

My definition of success. I had never thought of such a thing. Career, accomplishment, profession—these had been my focus as I thought about my future. I was looking for something worthwhile to throw my life into. The assumption was that in those tasks, through those accomplishments, I would experience success. But none of what I had written down had anything to do with any particular outward accomplishment.

Yet, I knew that *this*—and at that point I wasn't exactly sure what *this* involved—was what I had been looking for. I had discovered what I wanted to become as a person, and the process that would get me there was going to take a lifetime. There was no getting around the fact that the words staring me in the face represented the most important things in the world to me.

Without meaning to, I had been wrapping my hopes for a fulfilling future around the common and mundane. Granted, I should have known better. After all, I was, and still am, a professional Christian. I make a living telling people how to live their lives. People expect me to help them make decisions and set goals in keeping with a divine set of values and principles. And yet I believed that my most pressing need was to find the *task* or *project* that would give my life meaning.

As noble as my aspirations might have been, I was looking for a target that did not even reflect my core values or definition of success. I thought I was asking the right questions. But I had never stopped to think through what success was, that is, success for *me*.

AN INSIDE JOB

The comments I had written down were all related to my character—who I was rather than what I had done or achieved. I wanted my son Andrew to be able to say that he always felt his father's love. I wanted Sandra to say that she always felt that she was the most important person or thing in my life next to God. I wanted the people from my church to say that I was a leader worth following. I wanted the high school students I had taught to say, "Andy walked his talk."

I didn't imagine anyone at my funeral saying, "He was such a good communicator." Neither did I envision anyone bragging about the size of my ministry. At that point, who cares?

I experienced a real change in priorities. My personal ambition and drive were still intact. But now I felt compelled to channel them in a different direction. Suddenly, my inner man became much more of a concern than my outer man. If I was going to be successful by my own definition, some things had to change.

THE PLAN

I knew I needed a plan. I have considered myself a growing Christian since my college days. But the truth is, I was growing by default. I had no real strategy. I had always believed that the goal of every Christian was *Christlikeness*. But that always seemed a bit out of my league. In fact, the idea of being like Christ was so unrealistic that it really wasn't motivating. At times, it was discouraging.

As happens with most people, some aspects of my character were improving without much attention. But other aspects were lacking. And a couple of areas were, well, embarrassing.

The discovery that my number one pursuit in life was to be character-related rather than performance-related sent me scrambling for a strategy. That was not something I could leave to chance. The imaginary journey to my funeral had clarified my desired destination. Now I needed a map or possibly a compass.

In the following weeks, I developed a strategy. To begin with, I came up with nine words that summarized what I wanted to become. The nine character qualities surfaced as a result of carefully examining what I wanted to be said of me in the end. The nine words became both a target and a protective fence for my soul. My conscience became sensitized to these crucial concepts. The slightest move outside the boundaries of these newly discovered core values, and I was smitten with conviction.

PERSONAL PROGRESS

For example, one term I wrote down was *honest*. I want to be known as a man who can always be trusted to tell the truth, even when it costs me. I am ashamed to say that up until that time, I found it easy to tell little, convenient lies if they served my purposes. After all, why sacrifice my reputation or risk losing a friend when a small "fact adjustment" would easily smooth things over? I knew it was wrong when I did it. But at times it seemed appropriate. At least more appropriate than the potential embarrassment that came with telling the truth.

But after I clarified my core values, a little lie was no longer a little lie. It was evidence of failure at the deepest level. It was a big red flag signaling me that I was moving in a dangerous direction, a direction that would eventually take me far away from where I wanted to be.

Lying is usually a means to an end we believe is more important than the end of knowing we told the truth or being known as someone who always tells the truth. Not until I understood my personal definition for success did I realize that anything achieved through dishonesty is of far less value than being honest. Honesty is success for me. To sacrifice honesty for something of lesser value is a poor trade. It is no bargain. In doing so, I give up what I value most.

Another term on my list was *available*. I want to be known as somebody who is there when needed. Everybody is so busy. My tendency is to be so busy trying to help everybody that I am not really available to help anybody.

The Monday after I made my list, I walked into my office at church and heard something I had heard a thousand times before. But on that particular Monday it stopped me in my tracks. "I'm sorry. Andy is unavailable. Could I take a message?" *Unavailable*. A dozen times a day people were told that I was unavailable—the opposite of what I considered personal success.

When the time was right, I sat down with Sallie, my secretary, and brainstormed about how to remove the term *unavailable* from the office vocabulary. Then we evaluated my weekly schedule to determine how available I really was. I shared my concerns about being unreachable. She understood and went to work on the problem. We reworked my schedule to give me more people time. Sallie agreed to help me monitor my availability. She promised to bring it to my attention when she saw me slipping. Instead of telling people that I was unavailable, she began saying, "Andy is with someone right now, but he is available this afternoon. Would that be a good time for him to call?"

SOMETHING TO THINK ABOUT

These experiences illustrate a significant principle of character development: *Once the destination is clear, the way to get there will eventually become clear as well.* Most of us are more aware of *where we aren't* than *where we ought to be.* Consequently, we spend a good bit of time and energy focusing on what we should not be rather than what we should be. Such an approach is self-defeating. We tend to move toward what we focus on the most. Focusing on what you wish you were *not* just about assures you of moving farther in that direction.

This is one reason the biblical writers continually admonished us to "set our minds on" or "think about" certain things. The apostle Paul wrote, "Finally, brethren, whatever is true, whatever is honorable, whatever is right, whatever is pure, whatever is lovely, whatever is of good repute, if there is any excellence and if anything worthy of praise, *let your mind dwell on these things*" (Phil. 4:8, emphasis mine). Why? Because where our minds dwell, our hearts go. And as our hearts go, so go our lives.

YOUR TURN

Now it's your turn to discover what is most important to you. If you are truthful, you may discover that issues of character are not the most important thing. You may want the people at your funeral to brag about your accomplishments, your records, your trophies, your quotas, and your acquisitions. If that's the case, then that's the case.

The main thing at this point is to dig beneath the surface and discover what you really want to be. And if you discover that your goals are achievement-oriented rather than character-oriented, then you have made an important discovery—one that merits evaluation and thought.

But many people discover that *doing* is often their way of trying to *become* something. And once people learn *who* they are trying to become, *what* they do takes on a new significance and often assumes a lesser priority.

Someone may ask, "But isn't there more to success than character?" That depends on whose definition of success you use. For you, there certainly may be. For someone else, character may be the most important thing. We will talk more about that later. Now it is time for you to discover your personal definition of success.

Chapter Two

THE DISCOVERY CHAPTER

The integrity of the upright will guide them.
—Proverbs 11:3 NKJV

In this chapter, I am going to lead you through an exercise similar to the one described in the previous chapter. For this to be meaningful, you need to find a quiet place where you can think and write. If you are a speed reader, this chapter will frustrate you. If you are trying to squeeze in another chapter between scheduled activities, the next few pages will not have their intended effect.

Chances are, the process of self-discovery began for you as you read my experience with the Covey material. Maybe you even jotted down a few of your own insights. Whatever the case, grab a pen and a pad, and find a place where you can concentrate. This exercise involves three steps.

STEP #1: WRITE THEIR SCRIPTS

It is one o'clock in the afternoon. You enter the funeral home from the front. A man in a dark suit greets you and directs you to the chapel. After a quick glance in the hall mirror to check your appearance, you enter the funeral chapel. The ceremony has already begun. You slip in unnoticed and find a seat on the back pew. Those in attendance seem to be reflecting as the organist begins to play. Then a soloist, possibly someone you have known for a long time, stands and begins to sing. It is one of your favorite songs. She sings as if she knew you were listening.

This is your funeral. It is not exactly as you would have planned it. But then, you didn't really have an opportunity to give your input. How far in the future this takes place is irrelevant. The point is, your opportunity to leave a mark on this world, your chance to add value to the people around you, is over. Your legacy is determined. Only the memories of people who knew you remain.

The soloist finishes, and the pastor walks up to the lectern. He reads the date of your birth and the date you died. He reads a list of survivors—your spouse, your children, your siblings. And then he explains what is about to take place: "Instead of a sermon, I have asked several people who knew the deceased to share with us what they appreciated most about his (her) life. To start us off, I have asked . . ."

At this point, the pastor introduces your spouse. Your spouse comes slowly to the platform and in a calm, confident manner says . . .

This is where the discovery begins. If you are not married, don't skip ahead. You have the unique opportunity of discovering ahead of time what you hope to be as a husband or a wife.

Write down what you would want to hear your spouse say about you during this tender moment. Don't worry about what you *think* your spouse would say. Write what you *want* him or her to say about you as he or she thinks back over your life together. What do you want him or her to believe about you, to see in you, to have observed about you? What emotions would you want him or her to express in reminiscing about your years together? How would you want your spouse to feel about you?

Take your time. Try to get past facts or details he or she might share. What quality of person do you want him or her to describe? What will be the focus of recollections about you? If it helps, start with adjectives. Then incorporate the adjectives into sentences. Write their scripts. Go!

Next, the pastor introduces your firstborn. Even if you don't have children at this time, you should complete this part of the exercise. This is a fact-finding mission. Assuming for the moment that you are a parent, what would you want your oldest child to remember about you? What would you want the child to believe about you? What would you want him or her to say about you if you could write the script and you knew he or she would mean every word? Your answers to these questions will surface some of your deepest held values.

As your son or daughter finishes, there is not a dry eye in the place. Your pastor thanks your child as he steps back up to the lectern. Next, he introduces the person you considered to be your best friend. Outside your family, you were closer to this person than anyone else. How do you want to be remembered as a friend? What kind of friend do you hope to be?

Your friend shares a couple of rather humorous anecdotes. After hearing from your family, some comic relief is certainly in order. Things are lightening up a bit.

Then, almost as an afterthought, the pastor asks if anyone else would like to share a few words. To your amazement, up stands a fellow who lives in your neighborhood. You hardly know this guy. In fact, you are surprised he showed up. You've shared a few conversations together through the years. But it was mostly chitchat. Nothing deep. Nothing significant.

At times you got the impression he was watching you to see if you were for real, if your faith really made a difference in your life. Interestingly enough, he went out of his way on several occasions to let you know that he is not a religious person. At one point you thought about inviting him and his family to church, but you never got around to it.

We all have people like this in our lives. Maybe it is not a neighbor. It could be someone you work with. It could be someone you aren't close to, but someone who has had ample opportunity to watch you, to listen to you, to see how you respond to good news and bad. She knows you are a "church person." At least that's the way she describes you. The Bible refers to her and others like her as "outsiders" (Col. 4:5). They are outside the faith.

If someone fitting that description were to say something about you at your funeral, what would you want her to say? What kind of impression would you like to have made? What would you want her to conclude about you and your faith as she has watched you from a distance? Go!

The last person to speak is someone who benefited from your volunteer service at church or perhaps through a community service project. It could be someone you taught in Sunday school or a

Good Leader • *Told me about Christ* • *Good Teacher* • *Friend* • *Caring* • *Good Listener* • *Sensitive* • *Dependable* • *Humble* • *Not a complainer*

camper you bunked with at youth camp. It might be a member of your church who is grateful for your leadership in general.

How do you want to be remembered by the people you led? What do you want them to believe about you? What do you want them to appreciate most about you? What do you want them to recognize about your leadership and service? What would you want to hear them say about you as they reflected on your leadership and your impact on their lives?

STEP #2: TARGET SPECIFIC CHARACTER QUALITIES

If you have taken your time and completed this exercise thoroughly, you now have a rough draft of your personal definition of success. Buried in the sentences in front of you are the values and accomplishments that define personal greatness to you. If you didn't already know, you have just discovered what is most important to you.

The next step is to read through what you have written and identify the specific character qualities and accomplishments you have referenced. Look carefully. As you identify them, write them out in the form of a goal. For the sake of this exercise, a character quality can be any attribute you believe would help you be successful in the roles and relationships we just described.

For instance, let's imagine that one thing you envisioned your child saying was, "My mom (or dad) always listened to me." Then you would write down, "I will become a good listener." If you imagined your best friend saying, "He was there for me when I needed him," you may write, "I will be available," or "I will be dependable." If you want to be remembered for a particular achievement or an award you won, write that down as well. Obviously, it is important to you.

Here is the list of goals I developed from my imaginary funeral. Initially, I put mine in the form of a list of character qualities rather than a series of sentences. The characteristics are in alphabetical order rather than order of importance:

Accountable
Available

• Content

Dependable
Generous
Honest
Loyal
Pure
Sensitive
Transparent

• Loving   • Friend
★ • Servant of God   • Helpful
   • Evangelist/Messenger
★ • Patient   • Joyful
★ • Prayful   • Honest
   • Available   • Sensitive
   • Reliable   • Good
★ • Good Listener   teacher
   • Emphathetic ★ Humble

Notice there are nine, not seven. And the first letters of each word don't spell anything. Don't worry about being creative. Be honest.

Coming to Terms

As you develop your character goals—whether they take the form of a list or a paragraph—keep the following things in mind:

1. When writing out a goal for your character, avoid associating a particular character quality with a specific person. For example, don't write, "I will be a dependable friend." If you become dependable, you will be a more dependable friend. Character is a bit like water. It tends to seep. Your character will eventually seep into every relationship and aspect of your life.

The converse is true as well. Your character deficiencies will become evident across the spectrum of your life. That is why a man who tells lies at work will eventually lie at home. Character is not something you can compartmentalize. You probably attempt this from time to time, but in the end, what's on the inside surfaces in every department of your life.

2. Avoid setting goals that depend too heavily on things you cannot control. For instance, don't say, "I will be the best manager our company has ever had." This goal is comparative in nature. It compares your skills against those of every other manager in your company. The fact is, other managers may have better skills. To achieve this goal, you would have to secretly hope that your company never hires anyone with skills greater than yours. Such a desire would indicate a lack of character. Instead, you should say something like, "I will be a dependable and competent employee." That's different. You can influence your dependability and competency.

3. Never set goals for other people. For example, don't write, "I will be appreciated by my spouse." It's fine if your spouse expressed appreciation for you in the script. But now you need to narrow it

down to a specific quality that you can pursue. You may be the best spouse in the world, but you have no control over how your spouse will respond to your efforts. Instead, you should say, "I will put the needs and wishes of my husband (or wife) ahead of my own." You can make decisions about selflessness and unconditional love. They flow from your character. Your spouse's response to them is out of your control.

Whenever we set goals for other people, the result is always the same—frustration and discontentment. Often, I talk to men who have implicit and explicit goals for their wives. There are things about their wives they want changed. And they do everything in their power to bring about change. Of course, the reason they come to see me is that their plan isn't working. Such plans rarely do. The only person you can change is yourself. Consequently, your goals, both personal and professional, must be centered on your character and performance, not somebody else's.

Assuming Responsibility

Character is probably the most appropriate area for setting goals. It is the one area, other than our diet, where we are truly in the driver's seat. This brings us to one of the foundational truths related to strengthening character. It is one that many people wrestle with and some reject outright: *To blame is to choose to remain the same.*

To blame others for deficiencies in your character only enables you to maintain patterns that will rob you of opportunities and relationships. Until you take responsibility for who you are and what you are becoming, progress is impossible. Your circumstances influence but do not determine your character.

The pivotal issue is not so much where you start as it is where you are headed. You have no control over environmental factors that influence your character. But you have absolute control over the direction you choose to take.

Narrowing the Focus

Once you have completed your goals, you need to separate out the character qualities from the accomplishments you hope to achieve. This book will not be a direct help with the things you want to accomplish outside the realm of your character. I say "direct" because your character ultimately affects everything you attempt to do. But if you want to be remembered for developing an organization or building buildings, other books will be more helpful. Look over your list now and cross off each item that is overtly achievement-oriented.

Assessing Current Reality

As you look over your goals, you will no doubt feel some tension. For most of us, what we are is noticeably different from what we want to be. Peter Senge refers to this as creative tension: "the juxtaposition of vision (what we want) and a clear picture of current reality (where we are relative to what we want)."[1]

This realization allows you to sharpen your focus on exactly what needs to happen for you to become what you want to be. Furthermore, it enables you to get on-line with what God is up to in your inner person.

The changes He wants to make in you probably don't coincide point for point with your list of goals. But there is enough in common for you to get a sense of where He is presently at work in you. You see, whether or not you took the time to work through this little exercise, God is at work in you. The apostle Paul said it this way: "For it is God who is at work *in you,* both to will and to work for His good pleasure" (Phil. 2:13, emphasis mine).

God has an agenda for your character. He is constantly at work chipping away at the rough edges and carefully sanding the areas where progress has been made. He is at work even if you are not aware of it. He is at work, regardless of whether or not you cooperate. My hope is that this book will equip you to work intentionally with the Holy Spirit as He labors to conform your character to that of the Lord Jesus.

STEP #3: IDENTIFY *WHY*

The third and final step is to answer the question *why* as it relates to each goal you have listed. Why should you be honest? Why should you be pure? Why should you treat your spouse with respect? Why should your children feel that they are a priority in your life? Why should you always be fair with your employees?

This exercise is extremely revealing. Answering *why* is no easy task. But by forcing yourself to wrestle with the *why* question, you increase your odds of discovering what is truly most important to you. The answer to that question will tell you a lot about your definition of success. Love for others and greed are issues of character. Answering *why* often leads in one of these directions. In most cases, when you answer *why*, you will find yourself facing issues of character.

Having a Moment of Truth

The pursuit of character involves bowing to a Master other than ourselves. Some of us who have been Christians for many years have become quite proficient in the art of self-deception. We truly believe we are living for God and His kingdom. Discovering that we're not so kingdom-centered or others-centered after all is painful. However, it's also transformational because we must know who and where we are before we can make any progress. We have to know our present location on a map before we can move with confidence toward our desired destination.

Knowing where you are in the pursuit of character is crucial. But facing up to reality can be disheartening. Sometimes the truth hurts. In fact, many believers will choose the path of self-deception rather than face the truth about their character. But progress requires an honest evaluation.

To discover the true condition of your character, look through your goals and ask *why*. The *why* behind the *what* reveals where you are in your pursuit of Christlikeness. This part of the exercise will probably take you longer than any other. The answers may not come easily. But you owe it to yourself to give it a shot. At least try to understand why you value the things you do. After all, you may very well spend the rest of your life pursuing them.

Providing Incentive

One more thing to remember about asking *why: Why =* Motivation.

Deciding that you want to be remembered as someone who was sensitive to people's needs is not very motivating in and of itself. To some, it may sound passive. What makes the pursuit of sensitivity compelling is the reason behind it, the *why*.

For example, I want to be remembered as someone who was sensitive to people and their needs. Discovering that about myself was a little surprising. Sensitivity isn't one of my strengths. And I have been exhorted in the past to work on becoming a more sensitive person. I took each exhortation to heart. But nothing really changed. I wasn't motivated to change. Why? I never sat down and thought about *why* I should be more sensitive. But once I did, I had incentive. Here is my answer to *why* I want to be sensitive to others:

> Sensitivity paves the way to influence. People, including myself, do not allow themselves to be influenced in a positive way by those who are insensitive to their feelings, desires, and needs. In order to influence others, I must express sincere sensitivity. For this to be genuine, as opposed to a form of manipulation, I must become an authentically sensitive person. In order to fulfill God's calling of ministry on my life as a husband, father, and pastor, I must allow Him to create in me the sensitivity of my Savior. (See John 11:35–36.)

Answering *what* connected the abstract concept of sensitivity with my overall calling in life. Sensitivity became a do-or-die issue. The thought of my natural, insensitive ways diluting my influence over my sons is terrifying to me. It would kill me to discover that my insensitivity had driven my daughter away at a time when she needed more than ever to feel her father's love and approval. We have all seen fathers who lost their influence with their children over this one issue of character. How many times have we heard it said, "People don't care how much you know until they know how much you care"? Sensitivity is not a passive nonessential. It could be the difference between success and failure in my role as a father.

Did you find the above paragraph somewhat compelling? Mom, Dad, did you think about your own children? Did something stir within you as you thought about your struggle in this area? If so, you just experienced in a small way the value of thinking through and writing down the *why* behind the *what*. *Why* brings life to otherwise lifeless and stale concepts.

Answering *why* infuses emotion into your list of character goals. *Why* adds incentive. You will actually feel something stirring within as you think through and write down the answer to *why*. It adds passion to the process.

Another goal I set for my character dealt with purity in both conduct and thoughts. I doubt seriously that you would argue with me over the importance of being pure. But have you ever thought about *why* we should be pure?

"Well," you say, "because . . . because . . . because the Bible says we should be." True. But that's not a very motivating reason, is it? Have you ever taken the time to discover *why* God commands purity in our thoughts and deeds? God doesn't make arbitrary commands. He has a reason for everything He says and does. There is a reason we're commanded to be morally pure. *Purity paves the way to intimacy.*

Nothing destroys an individual's potential for experiencing true intimacy like impurity. A husband who has impure sexual thoughts is limited in his ability to be intimate with his wife. Like every facet of character, purity paves the way toward richer, more meaningful relationships.

Establishing Principles for Living

As the preceding paragraphs illustrate, discovering *why* will often lead you to principles. Ideally, principles should be the foundation of your values and character goals. Principles are the immutable equations of life. Principles are just the way things are, whether you like it or not, whether you know it or not. For this reason alone, forcing yourself to surface the *why* behind the *what* will be a rewarding exercise.

You owe it to yourself to discover the principles related to the character qualities you have listed. You are going to spend the rest of your life pursuing them, so you need to know *why*. God won't be offended. He will be honored, for at the end of your search you will be humbled by the wisdom of your heavenly Father. You will come face-to-face with His incredible love and concern for you. And you will wonder why you ever doubted the relevance and practicality of His commands.

Determining an Agenda

Clarifying your personal definition of success can serve as a bridge to some changes in lifestyle. The standard you use to measure your success ultimately determines your agenda. If you measure success primarily in terms of financial achievement, then the pursuit of finances will be at the top of your agenda. You will evaluate every opportunity, invitation, and potential relationship in terms of how it will affect you financially.

If you measure success in terms of the relational health of your family, you will evaluate invitations and opportunities from the standpoint of how they affect the family. Whatever you use to measure success will determine your agenda.

If you work through the exercise in this chapter, more than likely, you are going to discover that you really do measure personal success in terms of character. Making that discovery will give you the incentive you may have lacked to become more intentional in your pursuit of character.

If in fact your character is the measure of your success and if you are willing to embrace this discovery, then in all likelihood, you will evaluate every opportunity, invitation, and potential relationship in terms of how it could affect your character. Your character, from a practical standpoint, will be the measure of your success. And what you spend your time measuring, you generally spend your energy pursuing.

Not by money or reward
It's all about who I am as a person

Getting There

Throughout the rest of this book, we are going to focus on *how*. How do we move from where we are to where we want to be? If you have spent some time working through the exercise, you ought to have a clear target. And most important, you have a target that lines up with what is truly most important to you.

One last word of warning: The remainder of this book will be far more beneficial if you have put some thought into what you want to be remembered for. Before moving ahead, take the time to clarify your character goals. Develop a clear picture of what you want to become. Attempting to answer *how* is futile until you have first identified *what* and *why*. *What* is your desired destination. *Why* is your incentive. *How* is your map. Maps are useless until you know where you are headed.

Odds are, one day a group of people will gather somewhere to pay their last respects to you. Someone will say something nice about you. Someone will share a favorite memory. But regardless of what they say, everyone there will have an opinion about you. Because every day of your life, you are writing your epitaph in their hearts.

As you look back over the scripts you have written, there is no doubt some discrepancy between *who you are* and *who you hope to become.* Allow that tension to be a catalyst to motivate you to actively pursue the characteristics and virtues you deem important. For when the pursuit of character becomes a driving force within, there will be a passion and an authenticity about your life that even the casual observer can't miss.

When he was thirteen, Peter Drucker was asked by his religion teacher what he wanted to be remembered for. Like most thirteen-year-olds, he had no reply. His teacher responded, "I didn't expect you to be able to answer it. But if you still can't answer it by the time you're fifty, you will have wasted your life."[2]

What do you want to be remembered for?

Chapter Three

CHARACTER DEFINED

Aim for nothing and you'll hit it everytime.

—Anonymous

It was supposed to be the greatest achievement in the history of astronomy. It cost nearly $4 billion and took more than six thousand men and women nearly a decade to engineer it. It was respectfully named after one of the most heralded pioneers in astronomy, Dr. Edwin Hubble.

The idea was to place a highly advanced telescope into orbit where it could collect data from high above the distorting effects of the earth's atmosphere. Scientists would soon be able to gather and decipher light from a distance of more than 12 billion light-years. Specialists across the country were contracted to oversee the development of its thousands of intricate parts. Solar panels were designed to power the 2,500-pound telescope's delicate maneuvers. A system of gyroscopes was invented to hold precise aim at objects in the endless depths of the universe.

The crowning glory was the telescope's main mirror. More than nine feet in diameter, it took engineers six years to grind the concave masterpiece to its exact specifications. The lengthy process involved polishing the optics in increments smaller than the thickness of a human hair at each pass while keeping uniform consistency across the entire width of the mirror.

Finally, on April 24, 1990, the roar of rocket engines rumbled across central Florida announcing the launch of NASA's space shuttle *Discovery*, which would place the Hubble Space Telescope into orbit some 381 miles above the earth. Back at the Space

Telescope Science Institute in Baltimore, Maryland, crowds gathered around computer screens, waiting for the first images from the world's only orbiting observatory. As the data began to pour in, the air of anticipation gradually turned into bewilderment, then disbelief and, finally, utter shock.

The unthinkable had happened. The optics wouldn't focus. Throughout the construction of the primary mirror, there had been a miniscule error in the instrumentation used for testing its tolerance. Although the error was miniscule, the problems it created were enormous. It would take nearly four years and $628 million to correct the error. In a daring series of space walks, astronauts wielded an elaborate system of corrective lenses into place inside the telescope. Nevertheless, the Hubble Space Telescope will be remembered forever as one of the space program's greatest blunders. All because of a mistake so small that it escaped detection.

FOCUSING IN

I was nearly thirty years old when I discovered that my own "main mirror" was out of focus. Consequently, I was launching out into life without a clear picture of what was really important to me. I had good intentions. I was highly motivated. I was trained. But I was confused regarding my destination. I was looking for something to do. But by my own admission, success was wrapped up in something for me to become.

After I refocused, character, not career, was the issue. The discovery sent me scrambling to learn as much as I could about the subject of character. Sure, I had come up with nine reference points to guide my daily routines. But what was character? Those qualities I hoped to develop were manifestations of character—the outward signs that character was beginning to take root. But if I was going to pursue character with any success, I had to get a clear picture of what it was. I needed a definition of character itself.

That's when I discovered there is no consensus on what it means to have character. All of us can name various traits that a person with character demonstrates. But what is character? You think you know. I think I know. Your neighbor thinks he knows. I had found the most vital ingredient for my success—the main mirror, if you will—and yet no one seemed to agree on exactly what it was. In your pursuit of character, you will find many obstacles along the way. Defining it is the first one.

CHARACTER: A MOVING TARGET

Think for a moment about how character is depicted in our world. We all know that there's an absence of absolutes in the way morality is defined. Unfortunately, character is given the same relative treatment. Everybody has a definition. And for the most part, it's a definition that fits the mood and lifestyle at the moment. In some circles, a person is considered to have character if she is friendly or nice. In other circles, someone is thought to be a person of character if he stands up for his beliefs. Often, the rightness or wrongness of the beliefs is never questioned. The fact that the person took a stand is enough to brand him as a man of character.

This fuzziness of definition poses a direct threat to you personally. As you wade through the clutter of conflicting ideas about character, you may get sucked into the belief that character is anything you need it to be at the time. It will be a moving target that changes from day to day, depending on your circumstances.

Out of curiosity, I approached several people at random and asked them to define character or to explain what it means to be a person of character. Here is a sample of the responses I got:

- "A leader who is firm, yet fair."
- "Someone who never puts people down."
- "Treating people with respect . . . be a good friend."
- "Strive to be the best you can at whatever you do."
- "Being honest."
- "Somebody who goes after a goal and doesn't let anything get in the way of her dream . . . without hurting other people."
- "Somebody who knows what he wants in life and goes after it."
- "Staying out of trouble . . . out of drugs . . . set goals and reach them."
- "A good role model for society."
- "Someone who tries as hard as she can to achieve, without cheating."
- "Always do what you feel is right."

Most of the people I talked to seemed to agree that character is important. Yet they seemed rather unprepared to give a definitive statement about character. Many scratched their heads, searching the recesses of their brains before putting words together. You'd think I had asked them to recall an algebraic formula or to recite the preamble to the Constitution. They knew the answer was in there somewhere, but they couldn't quite piece it together.

People aren't prepared to give a definition because no single definition is being emphasized. The world encourages us to exercise our freedom to think and act according to our personal preferences. It doesn't seem necessary to lock in on any single definition of character. Defining character isn't so much a matter of reciting a fixed principle as it is sizing up your current circumstances and putting together a definition on the spot. For society at large, character is a target constantly on the move.

CHARACTER: THE WHOLE TRUTH

The Bible presents an entirely different picture of character. It isn't something that moves at all. To begin with, biblical character finds its source in the nature of God rather than the behavioral patterns of people. Biblical character is a reflection of the character of God. Our heavenly Father and His Son are character personified. They are not simply pictures of the real thing. They *are* the real thing. They are the essence. They define character by their existence.

This approach is difficult to adopt because it is not relative. It's not tied to the ever-changing standards of our society. It is absolute. Character is linked to a standard that exists outside humankind. It is something that does not come naturally. It is something we must pursue.

For this reason, it serves as a judge. It is something to which we find ourselves accountable. Consequently, it is something we may attempt to ignore. And yet every honest student of society will eventually agree that the precepts and principles embodied in a biblical understanding of character work.

When we think in terms of what we want in a friend or a spouse, when we think through how we want our children to turn out, when we contemplate the things we wish we could change about our bosses, we come back to the same baseline every time. We long for virtues such as honesty, loyalty, self-control, faithfulness, patience, kindness. No, we may not want to commit to these things personally, but we certainly want them in the people we associate with.

SURVEY SAYS . . .

James Kouzes and Barry Posner surveyed nearly 1,500 managers from around the country in a study sponsored by the American Management Association. They asked the following open-ended question: "What values, personal traits or characteristics do you look for and admire in your superiors?" More than 225 values, traits, and characteristics were identified, and they were then reduced to fifteen categories. The most frequent response was "integrity, is truthful, is trustworthy, has character, has convictions."[1]

In a subsequent study, they elaborated on several categories and added a few new characteristics not included in the previous study. In a two-year series of executive seminars conducted at Santa Clara University and several corporate locations, more than 2,600 top-level managers completed a checklist of superior leadership characteristics. The number one characteristic they looked for in a leader was honesty. Honesty ranked ahead of competency, intelligence, and being inspirational.[2]

In his insightful book *Boys!*, William Beausay refers to a study sponsored by *Psychology Today* in which a poll was taken to discover who were considered ideal men and what qualities typified an ideal man. By a two-to-one margin, Jesus Christ was considered the ideal man. The qualities listed as those typifying the ideal man were caring, loving, intelligent, moral, honest, sensitive, courageous, and someone with a family orientation.[3]

These findings are supported by a study done jointly by Korn/Ferry International and Columbia Graduate School of Business. Surveying more than 1,500 top executives in twenty countries, the study looked into external threats, strategies for growth, areas of expertise, and personal characteristics of the CEO and the importance of these related topics now and in the year 2000. Here is what they found: "The joint survey reports that ethics are rated most highly among the personal characteristics needed by the ideal CEO in the year 2000. Respondents expect their chief executives to be above reproach."[4]

Time and time again men and women demand behavior from one another that echoes the values and priorities of the apostles and prophets of old. Without realizing it, they long for others to model the character exemplified in our Savior. They recognize the inconsistency of the people they live with. They are uninspired by the moral relativism of our culture, our national leaders, and even our modern-day "heroes." And many struggle with the notion that *right* is defined by whatever fits a person's needs at the moment. There is a greater consensus surrounding the issue of character than first meets the eye. As a society, we are certainly consistent when it comes to the kind of character we expect of others.

CONSTRUCTING A DEFINITION OF CHARACTER

Arriving at an acceptable definition of character is a prerequisite to pursuing it with any accuracy. The definition of character we will use throughout this book is based upon two basic tenets of the faith.

Tenet #1: God Is the Creator of All Things

God's absolute sovereignty is established in the very first words of the Bible. Since He possesses the power to create "the heavens and the earth," it follows that nothing precedes or exceeds Him in power. God is the absolute origin of all things. Or to put it in His own words:

> *"To whom then will you liken Me,*
> *Or to whom shall I be equal?" says the Holy One.* (Isa. 40:25 NKJV)

In addition, as Manufacturer, He has published an extensive User's Manual for us to follow. It gives all the details for proper care and maintenance of His products—namely, us. Therefore, we can conclude that His instructions, too, are absolute. Sure, there are plenty of shade-tree mechanics who would love the chance to offer their advice, but nobody knows these products better than the Manufacturer.

Tenet #2: We Belong to Him

From the very beginning, God gave us the freedom to make choices. We have the freedom to choose good or bad, right or wrong. And wouldn't you know it, every single one of us beginning with Adam and Eve has picked bad over good and wrong over right. There are eternal consequences for these choices.

But God came up with a rescue plan, a way to allow us to miss the ultimate consequence of our sin. We trade in the old life and get a new one absolutely free. Best of all, God agrees to run the new one for us and keep up all the maintenance and so on. In a sense, He maintains ownership while we get unlimited use of the new life. One participant described it this way: "For you have been bought with a price: therefore glorify God in your body" (1 Cor. 6:20).

The problem with all of this is that "glorifying God" in our bodies requires the surrender of control. And we don't like to surrender control, even when we know somebody else can do a better job than we can. But that's part of the deal. The degree to which we surrender control is the degree to which we will benefit in this life and the life to come. Jesus said, "For whoever desires to save [keep] his life will lose it, but whoever loses his life for My sake will find it" (Matt. 16:25 NKJV).

The bottom line for all believers is that God owns us. And in order to become men and women of character, we must surrender to His ownership.

CHARACTER DEFINED

Putting these two basic tenets together—God's sovereignty and His right to ownership—character can be defined in this way: *Character is the will to do what is right as defined by God, regardless of personal cost.*

Notice the two essential ingredients for character. First, character demands a commitment to do what is right in spite of what it might cost us personally. When temptation clouds our thinking or doing "right" creates a temporary setback, we have already made our decision based on a predetermined set of principles. Character involves doing what's right because it's the right thing to do.

Second, we must acknowledge that there is an absolute standard of right and wrong, one that exists independent of our emotions, experiences, or desires. This standard is a permanent, unwavering benchmark by which we can measure our choices.

Josh McDowell echoes this sentiment when he writes:

> When you believe that there exists an objective standard for distinguishing right from wrong—that certain things are right for all people, for all times, for all places—you acknowledge that there are fundamental moral and ethical guidelines that exist independently of your personal opinion. You acknowledge that the distinction between right and wrong is objective (it is defined outside ourselves—it is not subjectively determined), universal (it is for all people in all places—it does not change from person to person or place to place), and constant (it is for all times—it does not change from day to day). When you accept an objective standard for truth, you adopt a moral and ethical viewpoint that guides your choices of what is right and what is wrong. Your truth view acts as a lens through which you see all of life and its many choices.[5]

It is not popular to speak of absolutes in any sense. But C. S. Lewis asserted, "Whenever you find a man who says he doesn't believe in real right or wrong, you will find the same man going back on this a moment later. He may break his promise to you, but if you try breaking one to him he'll be complaining 'It's not fair' before you can say Jack Robinson."[6]

By adopting the standard spelled out in God's Word, we arrive at a definition that is universal. It is applicable in all cultures and societies at all times.

During World War II, Alliance missionary John Wolfinger took a stand that personifies our definition of character. Wolfinger was leading a group of about one hundred Christian converts in Borneo. When the Japanese military took control of the island, they sought to arrest the missionary and execute him. Wolfinger's followers devised a plan to hide him in the mountains until the danger passed. But Wolfinger reasoned that by running from his captors, he would be giving his new converts the wrong picture of God. When they urged him further, he explained that when the Japanese asked where Wolfinger was hiding, his followers would have to lie, and that was not acceptable. So rather than risk leaving his followers with a compromised picture of God's character, Wolfinger stayed, was captured, and was executed. Wolfinger believed that lying, regardless of the circumstances, did not meet with God's approval. At the expense of his life, he maintained the will to do what was right.

In your pursuit of character, the temptation will be to adopt a definition that lacks one or both of the two key ingredients. The world encourages you either to ignore the notion of an absolute system of right and wrong or to avoid the short-term cost of adhering to it.

SUBSTITUTES

We are created with a natural affinity to establish a baseline for character. We all adopt some notion of character, whether it's accurate or not. So by default, we have a tendency to fill the void with the many character substitutes offered by the world around us. The problem is, if we listen to a lie long enough, we'll eventually believe it. Consequently, our minds are being stolen away from us faster than we can say, "Hand me the remote." Messages fill our heads at the speed of light, and our beliefs are subtly twisted and contorted. Without knowing it, we develop a version of character that is a caricature of the real thing. By failing to choose the proper definition of character, we choose to fail in the area of personal character.

Despite the fact that the entertainment industry rarely addresses the issue of character head-on, one glaring example is worth exploring because of its bold claim to define "right" behavior. In 1989, filmmaker Spike Lee won critical acclaim and an Oscar nomination for his movie *Do the Right Thing*. The film depicts a day in the life of the residents of the notorious Bedford-Stuy section of Brooklyn. Tensions are growing in the African-American ghetto area because the only prospering businesses are a Korean minigrocery and Sal's Famous Pizzeria. Meanwhile, African-American businesses in the same neighborhood continue to fail. Sal, an Italian pizza chef, seems an unlikely character to become the center of a race riot since he seems to take pride in serving the locals. However, on "the hottest day on record," minor conflict soon reaches its boiling point. Sal's customers take issue with the fact that no African-Americans are among the celebrities whose photographs decorate Sal's Famous Pizzeria.

Caught in the middle is Sal's delivery boy, Mookie, an African-American male in his twenties who feels called to stand up against racial injustice. Mookie is soon forced to choose between his loyalty to his employer and his convictions about Sal's choice of decor.

The climactic scene shows the increasingly agitated delivery boy, played by Spike Lee, standing in front of his place of employment contemplating the conflict in his community. After a few moments of deliberation, he hurls a trash can through the store's front window, triggering a full-blown riot, complete with looting and fires.

The film concludes by juxtaposing quotes from Martin Luther King and Malcolm X on the justification of violence. The film sends a clear message that doing "the right thing" means stirring up hatred, destroying a man's livelihood, and leveling half the city block—a position no doubt influenced by the late Malcolm X, whose civil rights mantra was "by any means necessary."

But there is a significant problem with this philosophy. As the motto focuses only on the means, all consideration of the end seems to get lost. With no particular standard to guide him, Mookie is left to the random ideas of his imagination. And as we will see, unless uniform principles guide our decisions, chaos results.

Believe it or not, *Do the Right Thing* is a movie about character. But as I stated up front, if your definition of character is off, you miss your mark. And that's exactly what happened to Mookie in the story. His anger was understandable. From his perspective, African-Americans have been suffering from centuries of persecution, beginning with slavery and continuing right up to the present with various forms of discrimination and prejudice.

The crimes against African-Americans are real and insidious. Mookie can't be blamed for wanting to see justice served. In his heart, all he wanted was to see the people of his race treated with the dignity they deserve. And in his eyes, he did the right thing. But without an accurate moral compass, his version of "the right thing" only deepened the rift between African-Americans, Koreans, and Italians. Mookie's sincere attempt to do the right thing resulted in chaos.

FEELING JUSTIFIED

I see this same scene reenacted again and again in real life. But instead of Mookie hurling a trash can through a storefront window, I see husbands and wives walking out on their partners. I see children and teenagers rebelling against authority. I see employees taking advantage of employers. And in every scenario the men and women and teenagers feel justified in their actions. They sincerely feel that they are doing the right thing. In their hearts they have an ironclad, open-and-shut case against the offending party.

If you trace it back far enough, just about every act of "senseless violence"—whether political, racial, or domestic—begins with a genuine motive. But somewhere along the way the perpetrator, lacking an accurate moral compass, trades the genuine motive for an evil one. In this case, Mookie traded a sincere motive—the desire to see justice served—for a destructive one—revenge. And the missing link is always character: authentic, divinely ordered, others-first character.

THE CHARACTER OF GOVERNMENT

Mookie found himself with somewhat of a complicated moral and social dilemma on his hands. It is easy to sympathize with Mookie's internal battle over what the *right* thing to do would be. But even when the correct option seems apparent, there is no guarantee that the right thing will be done. Knowing what is right does not necessarily make a man or woman a person of character. Having the *will* to do what is right is often the problem.

An interesting, yet unfortunate example is found within the pages of the *Ethics Manual for Members, Officers, and Employees of the U.S. House of Representatives*. There you will find a brief document entitled "Code of Ethics for Government Service" passed by the House and the Senate in 1958. This antiquated-looking manuscript contains ten simple statements outlining the expectations for elected officials. It includes basic mandates, such as, "Put loyalty to the highest moral principles," "Give a full day's labor for a full day's pay," and "Expose corruption wherever discovered."

In ten points, this code manages to give solid, ethical guidelines for virtually any situation that might arise in the routines of an elected official. It reads like the code of chivalry for the knights of the Round Table. Its instructions are clear and concise. Its language is noble, yet elementary. It's the type of document that could easily be reduced to fit in the coat pocket of any representative.

Contrast this simple document with the section in the back of the manual titled "Appendices." The appendices consume literally hundreds of times the space of the "Code of Ethics" statement. Here is an endless deluge of elaborate rules and regulations describing tedious, detailed guidelines for the House member's every move.

For example, there are rules for attendance: "Every Member shall be present within the Hall of the House during its sitting, unless excused or necessarily prevented; and shall vote on each question put, unless he has a direct personal or pecuniary interest in the event of such questions." Now there is a novel idea. In other words, every member of the House shall go to work. Isn't that what they were elected to do—represent us? Why the need to spell out such an obvious duty?

Here is another example: "A Member of the House of Representatives shall keep his campaign funds separate from his personal funds." That's not a bad suggestion, either, is it? After all, John Q. Public donated his hard-earned money to help the representative get elected, not to buy a new car. But wasn't this already covered under the "Code of Ethics" rule about putting "loyalty to the highest moral principles"? Why should an esteemed elected official have to be told to open a separate checking account when he runs for office?

Consider this: "A Member may not cast a vote for any other Member or record another Member's presence in the House." In other words, if Congresswoman Jones is absent, another representative isn't allowed to say, "Present," when they call her name from the roll. And the representative can't use Jones's vote whenever she is not around. Wasn't that covered back in third grade? Is this their first experience with a roll call?

These are well-educated people with tremendous leadership skills, a polished demeanor, and a keen understanding of government workings. And yet they have to be told that they must actually be Congresswoman Jones in order to cast Jones's vote.

These examples aren't even the tip of the iceberg. There are rules about rules about rules. Many of them were added during the last three decades. That little document passed in 1958 was a reminder to government employees to conduct themselves with character and integrity. And among people of character, those instructions are sufficient.

But the original "Code of Ethics" isn't clear enough for some of the members of Congress anymore. These days, it's hard to be sure exactly what is meant by "the highest moral principles." And statements such as "a full day's labor for a full day's pay" need further explanation when people aren't doing what they were hired or elected to do. Where people once had a general understanding of what character is about, they now lack that understanding. Today, their definition is off.

Somewhere along the way, a crack has been developing in the actual character of this governing body. And as enough individuals fail to follow the basic guidelines for character, it becomes necessary to implement tighter and tighter restrictions to direct their actions. Take away character, and you take away the ability to conduct everyday affairs in a free and responsible manner. Take away character, and gradually, ten simple statements are replaced by a complex system of intricate rules and regulations, woven together like strands of barbed wire in an attempt to control behavior and maintain some semblance of order.

Apparently, there was a day when elected officials understood and heeded the call to character. But obviously, Capitol Hill has not been spared the gradual erosion of America's integrity. If everyone followed the ten rules of the "Code of Ethics," there would be no need for the appendices.

Once again, the root of the problem is that there is neither a consensus regarding the definition of character nor a sincere commitment to the concept. The past three decades have seen freethinking emphasized as in no other period of American history. In 1958, the authors of the "Code of Ethics for Government Service" had a certain picture of ethical standards in mind. And for the most part, their peers seemed to have a very similar picture. Words such as *morality* and *ethics* meant pretty much the same thing to everyone. But that is certainly not the case anymore.

CHARACTER: LIKE A ROCK

Fortunately, there is a single definition of character—one that can survive the attacks of Hollywood, Washington, or Wall Street. This is an issue about which God has spoken. And He has not stuttered. Neither has He changed His mind. When we open the pages of Scripture, we discover that character is not the moving target Hollywood would have us adopt. It is not a product of the "every man for himself" philosophy that prevails in Washington. And character is not defined by what is viewed as common practice in the marketplace. True character is defined by the very nature of Jesus Christ—a stumbling block for some, a rock-solid foundation for others.

> Character is the will to do what is right
> as defined by God, regardless
> of personal cost.

You could use a variety of other words and phrases to define the term. But this will be our working definition. The two basic tenets that shape our concept of character are: the belief in an absolute system of right and wrong, and the will to do what is right regardless of personal cost.

At the core of every character struggle is the issue of lordship. Are you willing to make Christ the Lord over your life when it costs you personally? If not, then you'll pay a greater price later. It's just a matter of time. Being a person of character isn't always easy. The requirements may seem like prison walls. The guidelines like bars. But that is always the case when you invest in something that doesn't pay off immediately. And character is definitely a long-term proposition. But not all its benefits are reserved for some distant, nebulous time in the future. As you are about to discover, you can experience some benefits almost immediately. And to many Christians, these are considered to be the greatest rewards for pursuing character.

Chapter Four

CHARACTER AND OUR RELATIONSHIPS

Change from the inside out involves a gradual shift away from self-protective relating to strongly loving involvement.

—Larry Crabb

It's morning in America. Millions of men and women are about to partake in what has become a daily American ritual. In garages, carports, and driveways, they load up their cargo: briefcases, schoolbooks, overnight bags, and cups of coffee. They close the doors of sedans, pickups, sports cars, and minivans. Then without a second thought, they initiate one of the most intricate and elaborate sequences produced by the industrial age. Beyond the din of screaming children, rambling radio personalities, and slamming doors, a quiet miracle of physics is about to take place. Literally hundreds of complex operations will be performed in a span of less than one second. The choreography of moving parts will make a military parade look like a Chinese fire drill. With one turn of the key it begins.

The ignition switch makes contact, sending an electrical current snaking through a tedious network of twisted wires. Instantly, dozens of individual circuits spring to life. An electromagnet propels a whirling gear into contact with the teeth of the engine's flywheel. The crankshaft accelerates to more than 300 revolutions per minute. A delicate timing system opens and closes valves, regulating the flow of materials through the cylinders. The first piston begins to compress the oxygen and vaporized fuel trapped in its chamber. Simultaneously, an electrical coil sends a steady charge to the distributor, which monitors the activity in each cylinder and releases a spark at the precise moment of full compression, igniting the fuel like a well-timed lightning strike. Meanwhile, the valves open in the other cylinders, releasing the exhaust and inhaling a fresh supply of oxygenated fuel. So far, approximately four-tenths of a second have elapsed.

Long before the seat belts are buckled, hundreds of explosions have taken place. Each one packs enough force to propel a .22-caliber bullet a distance of more than five miles. Neatly contained within the thick walls of the engine block, and muffled by a sophisticated exhaust system, they are scarcely audible to the passengers.

Throughout the engine, hundreds of form-fitted metal parts begin to grind against one another as the explosions continue. Cam lobes spin against push rods. Piston rings race back and forth along cylinder walls. Rocker arms toggle against their retaining springs. Each part performs a specialized role in a delicate ballet of engineering. Now surpassing 1,200 revolutions per minute, the friction they create causes the engine temperature to rise at a rate of seven degrees per second.

The oil pump rushes to bathe the vital components with a fresh supply of oil. In the eleven seconds it takes for the lubricant to race through the arteries of the engine and saturate the parts, the engine endures a critical transition period. During these eleven seconds, it will experience the equivalent of five hundred miles worth of wear as its components assume an abrasive relationship with their counterparts. With only the leftover residue of oil to protect them, they wear against one another with increasing hostility. Without oil, the same parts that were designed for such precise compatibility would destroy one another in a matter of minutes. If you don't believe me, just ignore that little red light on your dashboard.

THE OIL OF OUR RELATIONSHIPS

Your character is showing. It is showing to the people around you. It is especially evident to the people who know you, who live with you, and who work with you. These are the people who wish someone would sit you down and tell you what you either don't want to hear or can't seem to understand. These are the people who have attempted this from time to time. You looked at some of them and said with all sincerity, "You know, you are right. I really need to work on that." To others, you politely smiled and thought, *What right do you have telling me how to live my life?*

Like it or not, your character is showing. And it is showing because of the unique and unavoidable role character plays in the world of relationships.

Character is the oil of our relationships. The world is a complex machine made up of millions and millions of people interacting with one another. Uniquely positioned for specific functions, they perform individual operations vital to the efficiency of our social machine. Just as the pieces of an engine form an elaborate puzzle of interlocking parts, people interact to make society run in families, friendships, marriages. To run smoothly, they must work in concert with one another. But without character, the parts will soon destroy one another. Eventually, the friction of our differences will take its toll. And individuals who at one time seemed to be made for each other destroy each other.

Every day, men and women who seemed perfectly suited for each other cause irreversible damage to their marriages. Once compatible business associates find themselves unable to survive the friction between them. Likewise, fathers and mothers, sons and daughters, neighbors and friends, watch their relationships fall completely apart over seemingly insignificant matters. Others quietly withdraw to avoid the conflict altogether. All because of deficiencies in their character.

TUNING UP OUR RELATIONSHIPS

Another day begins in the machinery of society. A switch is thrown in a bedside alarm clock. An electronic noise fills the bedroom. The sound triggers a groping hand to fumble for the snooze button. An elbow gently nudges the slumbering heap on the other side of the bed. Within seconds, lights are burning throughout the house. Valves are opened, sending hot water spewing through sputtering shower heads. A feeble groan indicates a request for coffee. Another sequence of unintelligible mumbles sends a reminder that it's time to wake the kids. With barely a second thought, the relationship machine churns to life.

At the traffic light, an uncooperative radio distracts the lead motorist as the light changes to green. After the obligatory pause of 1.5 seconds, anxious hands pound the horns of nearby vehicles, issuing a startling wake-up call. The motorist responds with a cutting glare into the rearview mirror and an antagonistic hand gesture. Steadily, the friction increases.

A phone rings in a window office, bringing news of increasing demands on the department. The supervisor kisses his weekend good-bye, then turns and barks the information to the middle managers. A dispute breaks out over the legitimacy of the promises sales reps are making to their customers. In turn, the sales staff questions the efficiency of the production department. The temperature inches upward.

A crying baby provides the background music as a husband announces that he must get away for a weekend of fishing with the guys or he will go crazy. Suddenly despondent, his wife spills a five-pound bag of flour across the counter. She points out the obvious schedule conflict created by his sudden change of plans. A lengthy dialogue ensues. He threatens to leave without her consent. She simply threatens to leave. Both are bluffing. Maybe.

As the heat slowly rises, the parts move about, grinding against one another, inflicting wear and tear. With only a slight residue of oil, they interact with increasing hostility. In businesses, in families, and in communities, the situation is the same. Without the oil of character, the parts will soon destroy one another.

THE PRICE WE PAY

Wherever there is a deficit in character, we pay the price in our relationships. Show me two people who are madly in love and have everything in common, but lack character, and I will show you a breakdown just waiting to happen. Show me a good company that is managed by someone who has no character, and I will show you a group of employees who find it difficult to do their best. Show me a community leader who is gifted and charismatic, yet without character, and I will show you a community where conflict is inevitable.

The longer two parts interact, the greater the chance of friction between them. And the closer the relationship, it seems, the greater the potential for catastrophe. That explains why the people closest to us always seem to hurt us the most, why husbands and wives sometimes become the bitterest enemies. Siblings grow up in classic rivalries. But the friction doesn't stop at that level. An alarming 55 percent of violent crime in America is domestic violence. More than 90 percent of murder victims are slain by someone they know, 45 percent by someone related to them.

MISSING PARTS

The closer you get to the people around you, the greater the chance that conflict will surface. Likewise, things tend to cool down when you back away. You send your bickering children to their rooms until things settle down. You storm out of the house in the middle of an argument. Or you reach into the medicine cabinet for a few hours of temporary relief. Down the street, your neighbor has just been fired again because he can't get along with his coworkers. And somewhere in your town, criminals are thrown into prison and removed from society altogether in order to prevent further problems.

When temporary means are no longer effective, people pack their bags, call their attorneys, and give their children ultimatums. But conflict evasion isn't the solution. As people are removed from key roles in the intricate machinery of relationships, it's just a matter of time before the engine begins to malfunction. When husbands leave wives to relieve conflict, the effort backfires on the children who will face the trauma and insecurity of life without a daddy. When disgruntled employees leave their jobs or are fired, the transition it creates significantly taxes the company and, eventually, the economy in general. And throwing our "problems" into prison only places an ever-growing burden on the rest of society.

Removing ourselves from friction is like removing vital parts from the intricate relational machinery. It leads only to bigger problems. We are created with an inherent need for one another, whether it's meeting the utilitarian needs of daily operations or satisfying personal needs for intimacy. By design, we cannot thrive by avoiding our problems. They must be resolved through the liberal application of a lubricant: *character*.

TOO CLOSE FOR COMFORT

Proximity is directly related to conflict. Spend enough time with anyone, and sooner or later your differences will emerge. If you're like most people, separation is the only solution you ever learned. As a result, we tend to be nonconfrontational. We preserve harmony by putting up false appearances. We bottle up anger and frustration, only to see both turn into a festering bitterness.

We've all been hurt by people close to us. Parents unwittingly cause pain to children. Friends wrong friends. And married couples constantly open old wounds. In every case, the closer we get to someone, the greater the potential for pain.

This principle produces an unfortunate behavior pattern. Over time, you can begin to associate pain with relational intimacy. The tendency is to insulate yourself from the people around you. It may be as subtle as keeping conversations to a superficial level. As long as no one gets close, you think, no one gets hurt. Even on a broader scale, society in general displays the effects of this pattern. More and more, we are a people who value our privacy. We screen phone calls. We quickly close the garage door behind us when we come home at the end of the day. And we pretend not to notice when we recognize an old acquaintance we would rather not talk to. We entertain many relationships but carefully keep them at arm's length.

In an effort to avoid hurt, we miss opportunities to help. Attempting to elude pain, we deny ourselves many of life's deepest joys. As philosopher Viktor Frankl summarized it, "The smallest package in the world is a man all wrapped up in himself."

Separation can be a valuable tool for avoiding heated conflict, but it is by no means a substitute for resolving it. At best, it is only a temporary solution. And if we never advance beyond this pattern, we spend our lives moving from one relationship to another wondering what's wrong with everybody else.

RELATIONSHIPS: WINDOWS INTO CHARACTER

The health of our character can be measured against the health of our relationships. Healthy, long-term relationships are evidence of strong character. Conflict-ridden, short-term relationships are evidence of character deficiencies. Conflict-ridden, long-term relationships are often the products of character deficiencies as well.

The character of the people involved directly affects all interaction. Consequently, we shouldn't be surprised that relationships are the first things to suffer when there is a character deficit.

At a Promise Keepers men's rally, founder Bill McCartney relayed a challenge he had heard that had penetrated his defenses and turned his method of self-evaluation upside down:

This past summer a guest speaker came to our church with a message that challenged my whole way of thinking. He began with a simple question: "Are you a man of character?" Yet it was the way he defined character that especially convicted me. He explained, "When you look into the face of a man's wife, you will see just what he is as a man. Whatever he has invested in or withheld from her is reflected in her countenance."[1]

He went on to explain that when he turned to look at his wife, he saw a tired woman who had given everything to her husband's career with little in return. With one glance, McCartney saw a crystal-clear reflection of his character, not in a mirror, but in the weary eyes of his closest companion. In that instant, he realized the powerful role character plays in our relationships.

As we subscribe to God's absolute standard of right and wrong, we are directed to focus on the needs of others instead of ourselves. Let's face it. God's character is others-oriented. Remember, it was "He who did not spare His own Son, but delivered Him up for us all" (Rom. 8:32).

One writer summarized it this way:

In a social or academic system, you may get by if you learn how to "play the game." You may make favorable first impressions through charm; you may win through intimidation. But secondary personality traits alone have no permanent worth in long-term relationships. If there isn't deep integrity and fundamental character strength, true motives will eventually surface and human relationships will fail.[2]

The pursuit of character elicits a genuine concern for the people around us. It requires that we serve them, regardless of what it costs us personally. And taking on the responsibility of looking out for others has a lubricating effect on our interactions.

THE COMPOUNDING EFFECT OF CHARACTER

People with character have an impact on everyone in their sphere of influence. Men and women of character possess moral authority. When you are with someone who has a proven track record in the areas of integrity and concern for others, you feel safe. You drop your guard. You may actually find yourself drawn to him. Instinctively, you may begin emulating his approach to life and problem solving. Without meaning to, you adopt some of his standards. You follow willingly. His character is contagious.

It's that unique woman who walks away when someone begins sharing a juicy piece of gossip. That one-in-a-million friend who never says anything negative about others in their absence. The guy who quickly owns up to his mistakes instead of blaming others. The woman who readily gives credit to the person who originated an idea rather than taking credit herself. The husband who has only positive things to say about his wife in public. The wife who allows her husband to lead when everyone knows she is more gifted in that area than her spouse.

There is something attractive about these people. We want to be like them. We enjoy their company. Relationship comes easily.

Likewise, the absence of character sets off a chain reaction of its own. When people have a reputation for compromising their integrity to avoid personal loss, they not only forfeit your respect, but they destroy your confidence in them as well. It is hard to follow wholeheartedly. An inner hesitancy is always associated with the relationship. A sense of unpredictability looms about them. You know that if they are willing to lie to a stranger, a customer, a client, or another business associate, they are willing to lie to you.

It goes without saying that if they will cheat in one arena of life, there is a good possibility that everything and everybody is up for grabs. So you approach the relationship with caution. You put up walls. You never know when you will be the next victim.

Think about how you feel when someone shares a bit of juicy gossip with you. On the one hand, you feel affirmed that this person has made you a part of the inner circle of people who know the latest scoop. On the other hand, you feel suspicious. If he talks about other people in their absence, what does he say about you when you're not around?

These are a few of the ways we react to other people's character. At the same time, others are reacting to ours. When we put the two forces together, they weave a complex tapestry of relational dynamics. One person's integrity can have a positive influence. Another person may breed animosity. Some of us have been hurt, and we devote ourselves to self-protection. Others amble naively through life. As our integrity meshes with the integrity of others in this way, the effect of character on our relationships is compounded.

If you want to witness the effects of character on relationships, just look around your neighborhood, your office, or your family. If you want to realize the undying potency of God's principles, compare the harmony of the relationships around you with the character of the individuals.

It doesn't take much observation to realize that God's standard for character was designed for the preservation of relationships. Those who follow it, intentionally or unintentionally, will be rewarded relationally. Those who don't, out of either stubbornness or ignorance, will forfeit the joy of authentic relationships. Where there is character, there is compatibility. Where character is lacking, there is conflict.

FOUR VITAL RELATIONSHIPS

Your character will have a direct impact on four levels of relationships: your relationships with God, self, others, and community.

1. Relationship with God

The instant you knowingly compromise your character, a change takes place on the inside. In that moment you become keenly aware of a disparity between God's standard and the one you are living out. You are filled with a gnawing sense of separation. You feel distanced from Him. We call this feeling guilt.

Once you feel distanced from God, your tendency is to avoid Him. So you move even farther away, and the feeling of distance increases. Eventually, you may entertain thoughts that God would never accept you back, which only makes you avoid Him more. Ironically, you begin to treat God with the same avoidance techniques you use on other people. Instead of facing your conflict, you avoid it. You go on with your life—and often your sin—as if He isn't even there.

You may rationalize your behavior. You may even go so far as to re-create God in your image. After all, if the real God doesn't accept you the way you are, why not just create a version of God that does? Of course, that doesn't solve anything. It usually makes things worse.

To avoid the pursuit of character is to jeopardize your walk with your heavenly Father. If the development of character is not an intentional pursuit for you, you should not be surprised that God seems distant and uninterested. Notice I said "seems." God is not at all uninterested. Neither is He distant. But when your purposes and priorities are out of alignment with His, the relationship suffers. God's purpose for you is to bring your character into conformity with that of His Son. That's what He is doing inside you. As you focus on that same priority, you will become increasingly aware of His presence and power in your life.

2. Relationship with Self

Another relationship affected by character is your relationship with yourself. This is a peculiar thought to some people. Usually, we assume that a relationship requires two parties. But self-image constitutes one of the most basic relationships in life. It is a prerequisite for all other human relationships. The way you view yourself determines the way you interact with God, family, friends, loved ones, and even people you may consider your enemies.

The absence of character can have various effects on self. It all depends on the person. But a few characteristics are common to almost everyone. As we said earlier, when character is compromised, most people experience some form of guilt. In some cases, people have assumed for themselves a certain, arbitrary standard of integrity. Guilt is a by-product of their failure to meet their own standard. As if they were two people combined in a single body, one half somehow feels that it has let the other half down. It feels unworthy and unreliable. The result is lowered self-esteem.

Since God's standards are written on your heart, you sense some obligation to live up to them. So even if you don't have a self-ascribed standard, one has been implemented for you. And when you fail to meet it, a part of you feels that you have let yourself down. You feel like a failure to some extent.

In addition, you must always deal with the consequences of your character deficit. When you make bad decisions, the fallout can be devastating. Many conflicts are created not by unavoidable factors but by your unwise choices. Well aware of your contribution to your problems, your self-esteem takes another hit. It is difficult to embrace and accept an enemy. And when you act as your own enemy, you are even more reluctant to accept yourself.

If you are unhappy with yourself, you will find something to be unhappy about in those around you. Generally speaking, your spouse, children, and close friends will be primary targets. Ironically, when you are least happy about the state of your own character, you are quickest to find fault with others. It is human nature to mirror displeasure with yourself in your attitudes toward those around you.

In contrast, when your character is hitting on all cylinders, you enjoy a clear conscience. No matter what hardships you may face, you can rest in the knowledge that you have honored God. You have done your part. As a result, hardships are not punishment for unwise choices but are the valiant price that must be paid by a person of character. Instead of a guilty failure, you feel more like a victorious martyr. Again, it comes down to the priority you put on your pursuit of character, doing what's right.

3. Relationships with Others

The "others" category includes—you guessed it—others. It includes everyone from spouse and family members to business associates and passing strangers. We have already discussed the impact of character on these relationships. But we haven't discussed the source of almost all interrelational conflict: unmet expectations.

We live in a world where compromise is the ruling principle. You'd think by now that we wouldn't be surprised when someone does us wrong. Nevertheless, we are. We can accept the general notion that the world is full of evil. But somehow, it never ceases to amaze us that someone would treat *us* unjustly. The audacity! We deserve better.

One reason we respond this way is that we operate from a position of expectations. If we demonstrate a reasonable measure of character at work, we expect a certain response in return. Likewise, we have expectations for our families, our friends, and even people we don't know. Some expectations are based on past experience. Others might be based on what we've been told. But as we waltz through life with our delicate system of expectations, we're just begging to have them shattered. We build china shops for a world full of bulls. And when the glass starts breaking, conflict results.

Everyone has a set of expectations. Unfortunately, as we interact with one another, there is no way we can all emerge unscathed. It's like trying to fit two gunfighters into one little town. There is just not room enough for both of them. Sooner or later, somebody is bound to get hurt.

At the bottom of all our self-designed expectations lies a self-centered motive. We agree to be people of integrity as long as we receive reasonable treatment in return. This small qualification turns the issue of unmet expectations into a character issue. Larry Crabb went right to the heart of the matter with this statement: "The greatest obstacle to building truly good relationships is justified self-centeredness, a selfishness that, deep in our souls, feels entirely reasonable and therefore acceptable in light of how we've been treated."[3]

Character involves the will to do what is right even when we have been wronged. Being a person of character means extending the grace of God to those who wrong you. Character is all about loving your neighbors as yourself, even when they don't reciprocate.

Of course, that's a lot easier said than done. But once character becomes a real target, once becoming a person of character becomes your life's ambition, you perceive mistreatment by others as an opportunity to demonstrate character rather than a setback. Once you relinquish your expectations to God, you will be much less likely to be disappointed by others. Consequently, it is easier to resist the urge to back away from those who hurt you or to retaliate. As you develop the will to do what is right, regardless of personal cost, you will experience the rewards of character in your relationships. After all, there is much to be gained from every relationship, whether friend or foe.

4. Relationships Within the Community

The impact of your interaction with others does not stop with personal relationships. It has a ripple effect on all the relationships within the community. Eventually, your character surfaces in the dynamics of your home, your work environment, your place of worship, and every other arena where you're involved.

The collective integrity of a group of people determines the success or failure of that community. In order for our communities to remain functional, the individuals within the community must be functional. Godly character must not only be present; it must be predominant. This is the basic tenet behind the principle of self-government.

The principle of self-government rests on the premise that when a person or entity fails to govern itself internally, it will eventually be governed by outside forces. When a child cannot obey household rules, the parent steps in and implements control. Likewise, when an adult fails to govern himself according to the laws of the land, the appropriate authorities are called in. On a larger scale, when a country fails to govern itself effectively, it becomes ripe for revolution or hostile takeover by another country. Regardless of the size or type of community, the key to success is the character of its individuals.

The two fronts on which I see this principle played out on a regular basis are the home and the local church. Character deficiencies are at the heart of every divided home or divided church. Wherever two or more people are gathered, there will be conflict, tension, friction. But that, in and of itself, is not the problem. In many cases, these things are healthy. After all, the same could be said of your car's engine. But when there is friction and no lubricant, problems develop. When there is no oil, there is eventually a breakdown. When men and women gather as a family or church congregation, there will always be differences. But men and women of character can always find a way to work through differences without division.

In dealing with differences, there is always a way to demonstrate respect for all parties. But that assumes adherence to a standard that values respect. It assumes that both parties are committed to doing what's right, regardless of the personal cost. Successfully dealing with differences and even conflict requires all parties to place a premium on integrity, honesty, fairness—in short, character. Men and women pursuing character know that conflict is another opportunity, and they approach it as such. In their minds, a win-win situation is always possible if both parties put a premium on doing what's right.

THE COMMITMENT TO CHARACTER

These principles are unfailing because they flow from the nature of our unfailing, unchanging heavenly Father. Our ability to understand ourselves is limited to the capacity of our minds. Our day-to-day problems surpass our problem-solving abilities with overwhelming regularity. And when our efforts fail, we often feel frustrated, confused, or just plain burned out. Sooner or later, we must come to the conclusion that we are incapable of facing life on our own with our own methods. We don't have what it takes. We can no more be expected to survive the rigors of life on our own than a newborn baby can take on the challenges of life in the city of Atlanta on her own.

The instructions God has given us are critical to our survival. Without godly virtue, we cause immediate harm to our self-image. Without integrity, it's just a matter of time before we destroy one another. Without character, we inflict untold damage upon our communities. The cornerstone of our entire social structure is the condition of the inner person. By subscribing to the belief in an absolute standard of right and wrong, we can begin to reverse the subtle encroachment of conflict into our relationships. If we commit to do what is right, regardless of personal cost, our relationships will prosper.

Ted and Margaret Cook know this to be a fact. On September 17, 1996, the happy couple celebrated their seventy-fifth anniversary. When asked the secret of their marital success, Ted answered, "If

you do right, you can get along. . . . I tried to do right all along."
When asked if that included flowers and candy on Valentine's Day,
Margaret responded, "None of that stuff matters. Being good to
me, nice to me, is what I liked."

Margaret is not the only one who likes that. We all do. Character
is about doing what's right. Relationships are about getting along.
And in the words of Ted Cook, "If you do right, you can get along."
By doing "right," we create opportunities for our heavenly Father
to advance our relationships from where they are to where He
knows they need to be.

Chapter Five

THE PROMISE OF CHARACTER

O LORD, who may abide in Thy tent?
Who may dwell on Thy holy hill?
He who walks with integrity, and works
    righteousness,
And speaks truth in his heart.

—Psalm 15:1–2

At the edge of a rocky overlook in the Appalachian foothills stands a lone two-hundred-year-old evergreen tree. At first glance, the scene looks like a snapshot taken during a violent storm. Bent by two centuries of strong winds blowing up the steep ridge, the thick, gnarled trunk leans hard to one side. Its heavy branches, too, stretch longingly toward the mountain's peak. Botanists call this phenomenon the Crumholtz Effect. Constant winds from one direction have left the tree frozen in this distressed posture. Like an oversized Japanese bonsai tree, it appears half dead as it clings to the ridge. Only the soft, golden glow of the afternoon sun and the playful twitching of its delicate needles reveal that the old tree is thriving peacefully.

Through the years, it has defied heavy snows, hailstorms, and the steady, westerly winds rising off the valley floor. From its vulnerable view of the endless ridges and valleys, it has seen conditions that would snap most trees in half. Nevertheless, it stands strong.

What's the secret? How can anything face such relentless opposition and survive? The answer lies below the surface. For literally two centuries, the elements have hurled their assaults against the tree. But while storms raged on the outside, the tree was quietly developing an inner support system to sustain it. Every gust of wind sent the roots sprawling deeper into the soil, expanding the tree's tenacious grip on the mountain. Its roots reach deep into the rich mountain soil, producing a steady supply of nourishing sap. The boughs, though severely bent, are positioned to absorb the brunt of nature's blows without incident. Year after year, the weight of ice and snow caused the strained boughs to grow thicker and stronger. On the outside, it may be an oddity. But inside, it's a picture of health.

We are all like trees subjected to the stormy elements of life. And when they come, we either snap or grow stronger. What makes the difference is not the ferocity of the storm but the depth of our character. The outcome depends on the condition of the inner person. Like the old tree, we need a system capable of sustaining and nurturing us through the relentless cycles of life.

SPECIAL PRIVILEGES

I could go on forever talking about the tangible, observable benefits of character. But in addition to these external advantages, character adds value to our lives in two internal ways: (1) spiritual intimacy and (2) emotional stamina.

Godly character is within itself a system that sustains and nurtures the inner person. It enables us not only to survive the storms of life but also to thrive. Although both benefits are referenced throughout Scripture, perhaps they are best summarized in Psalm 15.

> *O LORD, who may abide in Thy tent?*
> *Who may dwell on Thy holy hill?*
> *He who walks with integrity, and works righteousness,*
> *And speaks truth in his heart.*
> *He does not slander with his tongue,*
> *Nor does evil to his neighbor,*
> *Nor takes up a reproach against his friend;*

In whose eyes a reprobate is despised,
But who honors those who fear the LORD;
He swears to his own hurt, and does not change;
He does not put out his money at interest,
Nor does he take a bribe against the innocent.
He who does these things will never be shaken.

SPIRITUAL INTIMACY

There is a correlation between our personal righteousness, our character, and our ability to know God intimately. The psalmist promises that the person who pursues character gains the privilege of experiencing a special closeness with the heavenly Father. The issue here is not eternal salvation. Salvation, in both Old and New Testaments, came by way of faith in the revelation of God. Psalm 15 describes the difference between those who know God from a distance and those who know Him intimately.

You might not think of yourself as a person who longs to know God. Using the term *intimacy* to describe someone's relationship with God may even seem somewhat strange. It may conjure images of praying all day or living in a state of deep spiritual meditation.

But chances are, something in you longs at times for the privilege of intimacy with your heavenly Father. If you have ever faced a crisis and wanted to ask, "Why, Lord?" then you've longed for it. If you've ever prayed for peace and perspective during a time of uncertainty, you've wanted it. If you've ever been afraid or lonely and just needed comfort, you've wanted the benefits that come from knowing God better. Just a word, an insight, an assurance that He was there, would make all the difference in the world. You want an inside track.

This desire is most pronounced when you face the inevitable, unanswerable, perplexing questions that are a part of life. And the longing to know paves the way to knowing Him. Seeking answers to your deepest and sometimes unspoken questions is often the catalyst for seeking Him.

An Inside Track with God

The writer asks, "Who may abide in Thy tent? Who may dwell on Thy holy hill?" The assumption is that these are two things to be sought after. However, neither sounds appealing. After all, who wants to live in a tent? And what's the big deal about living on a holy hill?

The tent referred to the place where God resided. And the holy hill was the hill in Jerusalem where the permanent temple was eventually built. To have access to these places was to have access to God.

The Israelites of that day thought of God as dwelling in the ark of the covenant inside the sanctuary tent. God gave them that picture as a tangible reminder of His presence. In their way of thinking, the closer they were to the ark and the tent, the closer they were to God. The farther they were from the ark and the tent, the farther they were from God. They believed this so deeply that they took the ark of the covenant with them into battle. And who could blame them?

So when you take these questions, steeped in ancient Jewish culture, and translate them into our language, this passage asks and answers one of the most relevant questions imaginable: Who gets an inside track with God? The implication is that intimacy with God is a real possibility.

The psalmist makes it clear that this privilege is reserved for men and women of character. Look again at his description:

- They walk with integrity.
- They do what is right.
- They tell the truth.
- They don't gossip.
- They don't mistreat people.
- They side with those who are right.
- They keep their word.
- They lend money to those in need without interest.
- They don't take advantage of people for financial gain.

That's quite a list. Clearly, character paves the way to intimacy with God.

Anatomy of a Great Relationship

Initially, this idea may sound somewhat pretentious. Unchristian. But that is not the case at all. Throughout Scripture, God is described as having a personality. Again and again, we see Him relating to humankind much the same way we relate to one another. In fact, the rules that govern human relationships are very similar to the rules that govern our relationship with the Father.

Three elements are always present in a healthy relationship: (1) respect, (2) trust, and (3) communication. To have a quality relationship with someone, you must respect her, trust her, and communicate with her. The same is true about your relationship with God.

The pursuit of character entails all three. When you acknowledge that God's standard is *the* standard, you demonstrate respect. When you commit to follow God's standard, regardless of what it costs you personally, you demonstrate trust. And as you seek to understand His standard more thoroughly, and as you run up against your inability to live out His standard consistently, you communicate with Him.

The pursuit of character inevitably becomes the pursuit of God, for the standard by which you judge your life flows from the nature of the heavenly Father. You may begin your pursuit with a list in mind. But eventually, you discover that you are pursuing a Person, not a standard.

Putting the Shoe on the Other Foot

Turn it around for a minute. You've probably known someone in your past who pursued a relationship with you for all the wrong reasons. Once you got close to him, you realized he had a hidden agenda. Do you remember how that felt?

How do you respond internally to a person like that? Do you open up and become more transparent? Of course not. You become cautious. Everything he does is suspect. You rehearse old conversations and think, *Oh, so that's why he said that.*

Think a minute. If your interaction with God is focused primarily on getting something from Him, what does that say about your relationship? You aren't coming to Him on terms that warrant a relationship of intimacy.

Still, God listens to your self-centered prayers. Sometimes He actually grants your requests. But as long as you see Him only as a means to your ends, you will never experience intimacy. You will never truly know Him. This unique depth of relationship is reserved for those who respect Him, trust Him, and are willing to communicate honestly with Him. It is withheld from those who dishonor Him by treating Him like a vending machine.

There is a correlation between your personal holiness and your intimacy with God. There is a direct relationship between your willingness to obey God and His willingness to reveal Himself to you. This is *the* primary benefit of character. Character brings a heightened sense of intimacy with God, an intimacy available only through the pursuit of Christlike character.

His Closest Friends

During His ministry on earth, Jesus modeled this cause-and-effect relationship. He reserved a level of intimacy for a select group. They had left everything to follow Him. They respected Him. They trusted Him. And they were in constant communication. No, the twelve apostles were not perfect. But they had left their businesses and their families to pursue a relationship with Him. He was their priority.

Further evidence of this is found in an incident that took place immediately following the telling of a parable. The meaning behind Jesus' parables was not always clear. And apparently, that began to bother the disciples. On this particular occasion the disciples pulled Jesus aside and asked Him why He wasn't more direct with His audience. He said, "Because it has been given to you to know the mysteries of the kingdom of heaven, but to them it has not been given" (Matt. 13:11 NKJV).

Jesus was suggesting to His disciples that there would always be people who remained on the fringe relationally. There would always be curious onlookers who had a distant interest in Jesus. But special insights were reserved only for those in His inner circle. Did Jesus love the multitudes? Yes. He died for them as well as the Twelve. But the multitudes did not know Jesus as the Twelve did. He chose to reveal Himself to them at a deeper level. After answering the disciples' question, Jesus took them aside and explained the meaning of each parable. To His special friends, it had been given "to know the mysteries of the kingdom of heaven."

We are not talking here about a relationship that excludes anyone. This exclusive relationship is available to everyone; everyone, that is, whose walk is blameless and who does what is right. In other words, it is available to those in pursuit of character.

Jeremiah echoed this same idea when he wrote, "You will seek Me and find Me, when you search for Me with all your heart" (Jer. 29:13).

The Spirit's Gentle Touch

One summer, in the late afternoon, I was walking down the beach by myself. The tide was out, giving the sensation that the beach went on forever. The only sounds I could hear were the occasional call of the gulls and the distant laughter of children playing. As I walked along, the air was noticeably still. I remember thinking how odd it was that there was not even a breeze. After walking for about a mile, I turned around to head back to the hotel. And when I did, something strange happened.

Suddenly, from out of nowhere, there was a breeze. I didn't feel it as much as I heard it whistling in my ears. Where had it come from? It had been there all along. I just wasn't aware of it. As long as it was at my back, I didn't hear or feel it. But as soon as I faced the other way, my ears immediately sensed its presence.

The same is true of God. As long as we have our backs turned to Him, doing our own thing, living life the way we think it should be lived, we are less aware of His presence. He is there, but we remain unaware. Once we begin prioritizing our lives around His values and principles, it is as if He comes alive in our lives. We have a heightened sense of the reality of God. But again, the sense of His presence is reserved for those who have turned in His direction.

THE IMMOVABLE OBJECT

The second internal benefit of being a man or woman of character is found at the end of Psalm 15. After describing the person of character in detail, the psalmist concludes, "He who does these things will never be shaken."

Now this is a benefit you don't experience immediately. It's something that comes from weeks, months, or years of investing in your character. It's the result of adopting a lifestyle. The image the psalmist paints is that of two trees in a storm. And while the same storm sweeps over both trees with the same force, one tree is destroyed while the other is left standing.

So it is with men and women of character. They are not delivered from the storms of life. But they are delivered through them, for their roots go deep. Their faith is strong. Their resolve is unwavering.

Their pursuit of Christlikeness has gained for them the unique privilege of saying to God, "God, I'm just doing what You told me to do. You got me into this. It's up to You to get me through it." And so they deliberately and sincerely cast their deepest and most intimate cares upon God. And they live with confidence that He is going to care for them (1 Peter 5:7).

No place in the world is more secure than the middle of God's will. It's the only real security. In that way, to pursue a life of character is to prepare for the storms of life. Remember, "he who does these things will never be shaken."

Unshaken

In 1984, my father was elected president of the Southern Baptist Convention. In the weeks leading up to the election there was a great deal of controversy surrounding his candidacy. One particular press conference will be forever etched upon my memory.

He had just finished speaking for a chapel service at one of the denominational seminaries. Immediately following the service, he was whisked away for a press conference. I squeezed into the packed conference room and stood against the wall to watch.

What made the press conference unique was that a fellow who had taken a public stand against my dad was being interviewed as well. There they were, sitting shoulder to shoulder as the reporters and writers pelted them with questions, taking every opportunity to drive the wedge deeper between the two of them.

I will never forget two things about this event. The first was my father's calm demeanor. The other fellow being interviewed was adamant regarding my father's lack of qualifications for the position of president. There was nothing friendly or cordial in his tone or mannerisms.

My dad sat there unshaken. He never raised his voice. He never accused. He calmly, graciously, and thoughtfully answered the questions. Meanwhile, I was ready to wring the other fellow's neck!

The other thing that stood out was my dad's answer to one particular question. "Dr. Stanley," the reporter asked, "do you think you'll win the election tomorrow?" "Well," he replied, "if I win, I win. And if I lose, I win. Because my responsibility is simply to be obedient to God and trust Him with the outcome."

No matter how hard the storm raged around him, Dad wouldn't be moved. He knew that when a person is in the center of God's will, he has the privilege of leaving all the details with God. And God takes them willingly.

Hanging in my dad's office at home is a quote from one of his sermons that someone reproduced in calligraphy and framed. It reads, "God assumes total responsibility for the life that's yielded to Him." That's why men and women of character will never be shaken. Navigating the storms of life is not their responsibility.

Compare and Save

The greatest tragedy of missing this process isn't that your marriage might fall apart. Or that you'll flounder in your career. Or that you'll be lonely the rest of your life. As tragic as these things may be, the greatest tragedy of refusing to pursue the character of Christ is that you'll miss God. He will be right there at your back, but you'll miss Him. There is a price for becoming a person of character. But it's not nearly as high as the price of pursuing other things.

Character paves the way to intimacy with God. To know Him is to trust Him. To trust Him is to live with the confidence that He will not allow you to be shaken. That's the ultimate promise of character. It is the promise of His presence, a presence you cannot possibly miss.

Part Two

GETTING OUR BEARINGS

When I was nineteen, I went to the Bahamas with my father for a month of rest and relaxation. There I met a fellow named Michael who has been a friend ever since. When it was time to leave, I asked if I could stay behind. My dad said it would be all right, and thus began one of the most memorable months of my life. It was just me and my new friend Michael, a resident of Man of War, the tiny island where we were staying. Together, we passed the days sailing, fishing, and snorkeling.

One day, Michael had the job of picking up a houseboat from a nearby island and delivering it back to Man of War. Since the task required two drivers, he asked me to come along. To Michael, it was a routine island chore. To me, it was a rite of passage. I was nineteen years old, alone at the helm of a twenty-foot houseboat.

Even by island standards, Michael was a pretty laid-back guy. I don't know if it was because he was a teenager or because he grew up in a place where the closest thing to rush hour is when high tide forces people to move their chairs up the beach. Either way, he didn't place a lot of emphasis on preparation. By the time we reached the other island to pick up the boat, the sun was already setting. And when we finally made our way out of the harbor, it was dark.

With five miles to cover in the black of night, Michael's navigational strategy caught even me by surprise. "Here's what you do," he said. "The boat I'm driving doesn't have any lights." (I tried not to flinch.) He went on, "I've set up a little white light on the back for you to follow. Your boat has lights, so follow me, don't get too close, and we should be fine. Just keep your eye on the white light."

The trip was awkward at first. I wasn't accustomed to driving from inside an enclosed cabin, so I was a little out of my element. But after a while I regained my confidence. I was feeling like an islander again as I followed the white light out on the horizon. Everything was going great—until we started getting close to our destination.

As night was falling on the island of Man of War, the residents began to turn on the lights in their homes. And as we got closer and closer to the island, the growing backdrop of white lights began to camouflage the light from Michael's boat. Soon, I was losing him completely. Needless to say, radios were not a part of Michael's boating vocabulary.

With our destination closing in fast, I shifted my strategy. I wasn't just looking for a white light anymore. I was looking for one that moved. From time to time, a light would seem to leap off the backdrop, and I'd focus on it for a while. Then another would catch my eye, and I'd aim for it. I turned to the left and tried to gain ground on the little white light way ahead of me. Then I turned right, still trying to close in on Michael's boat.

Should I speed up and try to catch him? Or should I slow down in case I came upon some obstacle or hit a sandbar? I was getting scared, but I did the best I could. I'm not sure what caught Michael's attention first—the way my houseboat was tacking back and forth like a sailboat, or the fact that I was headed straight for the reef off the island's shore. Just in the nick of time, though, he saw that I was in trouble and circled back. Cutting across my path, he managed to get my attention. I was startled but relieved. After a moment of reorientation, I was back on course, headed for home.

COMPETING LIGHTS

Most of us can think back to a time when the light we were to follow was clearly in sight. We were younger. We were idealistic. We were sure of ourselves. We weren't going to make the mistakes others had made. Some of us were determined not to follow in the footsteps of our parents. Others of us were committed to being just like them.

Then gradually, other lights appeared on the horizon. Lights of opportunity. Relational lights. Educational lights. Promises of quick financial gain. Promises of pleasure. Suddenly, our original point of reference was gone. We were lost.

In a world where so many things are competing for our attention, it is easy to lose our bearings. It is easy to become distracted by the good things this world has to offer. And it is easy to get distracted by the not-so-good things as well.

LOST AND FOUND

Individuals are not the only ones who lose their bearings. Nations are prone to wander as well. In the next two chapters we will look at two nations that started off with a clear sense of moral direction but lost their way. This brief journey through history will give us valuable perspective as we navigate our way around the obstacles to becoming a person of character. Furthermore, these two national examples remind us of the unavoidable consequences of abandoning what is right as God defines right.

Chapter Six

ONCE UPON A TIME IN AMERICA

When you have eaten and are full—then
beware, lest you forget the LORD.

—Deuteronomy 6:11–12 NKJV

A snapshot of America today depicts a people fragmented into small factions, lobbying for their interests, arguing for their rights, and fighting for recognition. Meanwhile, all around us are the archaic remnants and reminders of a different kind of America. An America united around a common creed, a common worldview, a common conviction.

Our currency is branded with "In God We Trust." Some official buildings are still adorned with placards bearing a list of ten strange commandments. If indeed they once made sense to someone, they certainly don't apply anymore. They no longer fit today's forward-thinking breed of Americans.

Today in America, individuals are demanding the assurance that they won't be force-fed religious doctrine. In fact, the laws seem to form a protective bubble around citizens, ensuring that they won't be confronted with someone else's beliefs, someone else's morals, someone else's understanding of what is right and wrong. After all, everybody knows that there are no moral absolutes. What's right for me isn't necessarily right for you. Morally speaking, America has become an every-man—excuse me—every-person-for-himself-or-herself world. Moral relativism is the norm. In that respect, the definition we are using for character is outdated.

And I'm not just talking about the nonreligious, unchurched element of America. The church is full of people who question the idea of moral absolutes. Research indicates that an entire generation of Christian teenagers is growing up with the assumption that there is no absolute standard of right and wrong.

SO WHAT?

So what does that have to do with you and me? A great deal. It is particularly difficult to pursue character in a climate of moral relativism. Why? Well, it's not because people are against character per se. It's much worse than that. Moral relativism redefines character. Character to the average American means nothing more than being faithful to what you think is right at the moment. Character is a moving target. And no two people's targets are at the same place at the same time.

But it wasn't always this way in America. For the first 150 years, there was somewhat of a consensus concerning right and wrong. And that common understanding had its roots in Scripture. Our founding fathers did not take on the responsibility of deciding what was right and wrong for the nation. Instead, they committed themselves to the task of discovering what the Almighty had to say.

This is how we explain the overtly religious language of our nation's official documents. This is why our currency bears the inscription "In God We Trust." It is for this reason that when we pledge allegiance to our flag, we say, "One nation under God." Our founding fathers did not question the notion of moral absolutes. Neither did they hesitate to make known their beliefs regarding the source of those absolutes.

So why is it so hard for Americans to come to a common understanding of right and wrong today? Why is there no consensus concerning what appear to be simple matters of integrity and morality? What happened?

LOOKING BACK

Political science researchers at the University of Houston asked some of these same questions in 1973. In search of the key to America's political prosperity, they began a project to discover what made this country's foundation different from the rest of the world. They wanted to know why its Constitution had survived for two hundred years while France had gone through seven forms of government and Italy fifty-one during the same period. Their study took ten years to complete. They theorized that the best way to uncover the political philosophy of the founding fathers was to examine the writings they produced. What better way to reveal what they were thinking? Their discovery was astounding.

In all, they collected 15,000 writings from the era of the American Revolution. Painstakingly, they isolated 3,154 direct quotes from the founding fathers. Then they dug deeper to identify the sources whose philosophies had influenced these quotes. When the research was completed, most quotes were traced to a handful of the world's elite statesmen, such as Baron Charles de Montesquieu, Sir William Blackstone, and John Locke. What was most significant about the men was not their renown in world politics or law, but the fact that they were openly Christian in their philosophies.

When it was concluded, the study showed that 60 percent of the quotes of the founding fathers came from evangelical Christian teachings and were strongly influenced by biblical ideals. More astounding is the fact that another 34 percent of the founders' quotes came directly from the Bible.

ESTABLISHING A FOUNDATION

But America's founding fathers didn't stop with citing Scripture in their writings. They went so far as to implement them in their government. For example, congressional records show that the concept of a government with three branches—judicial, legislative, and executive—came from the founding fathers' familiarity with Isaiah 33:22, which depicts God as Judge, Lawgiver, and King. Similarly, Jeremiah 17:9, which portrays wicked tendencies of people and the need for accountability, convinced the architects of the Constitution to introduce the idea of the separation of powers and the system of checks and balances. And tax exemption for churches wasn't implemented just out of generosity; it followed the command of God issued in Ezra 7:24.

THE BIBLE AND LEGISLATION

Today, it's almost impossible to imagine a lawmaker standing before the House or Senate and reading from the Bible to argue a position on a legislative matter. But in the years immediately following the founding of this nation, congressmen often brought to the floor something that they had found in Scripture before an item was voted into government policy.

These weren't just religious outbursts from a handful of America's leaders. National records plainly show that our founding fathers had a clear agenda that the government of this country be unashamedly based on the teachings of the Bible. Consider this statement made by Patrick Henry clarifying the intentions of the founding fathers: "It cannot be emphasized too often or too strongly that this nation was founded, not by religionists, but by Christians; not on religions, but on the gospel of Jesus Christ."

THE REMOVAL OF RELIGION

Today, the U.S. Supreme Court seems to have taken on the responsibility of ensuring that the leaders of government and private institutions refrain from voicing any hint of religious preference. But compare this position to that of John Jay, the first chief justice of the Supreme Court: "Providence has given to our people the choice of their rulers and it is the duty—as well as the privilege and interest—of our Christian nation to select and prefer Christians for their rulers."

FRANKLIN AND JEFFERSON

Fifty-two of the fifty-five founding fathers were members of orthodox Christian churches. Today, historians play up the atheism of Benjamin Franklin and the deism of Thomas Jefferson. But even those two statesmen had very clear intentions for designing the United States government around the instructions of the Bible and selecting leaders who pursued Christian character.

In his famous speech made before the Constitutional Convention on Thursday, June 28, 1787, Franklin brought the following convictions before the delegates:

We needed God to be our friend, not our enemy, and our ally, not our adversary. . . . We needed to keep God's "concurring aid." . . . If a sparrow cannot fall to the ground without his notice, is it probable that an empire can rise without his aid? We've been assured in the sacred writing that, "Except the Lord build the house, they labor in vain that build it."

Franklin went on to call for regular, daily prayer to keep God in the midst of the affairs of the nation. Similarly, Jefferson was outspoken in his belief that government and religion were inseparable:

And can the liberties of a nation be thought secure when we have removed their only firm basis—a conviction in the minds of the people that these liberties are the gift of God? That they are not to be violated but with his wrath? Indeed I tremble for my country when I reflect that God is just: that his justice cannot sleep forever.

BEYOND THE FOUNDING FATHERS

And it wasn't just the founding fathers who held these ideas for America. For more than 150 years, the decisions of our nation's leaders reflected a firm commitment to maintaining the bonds between the laws of the country and the moral absolutes of Scripture. The leaders were familiar with America's heritage, and it showed in their decisions. For example, in 1892, the U.S. Supreme Court concluded the case of *The Church of the Holy Trinity* v. *the United States* with this ruling: "Our laws and our institutions must necessarily be based upon and must embody the teachings of the Redeemer of mankind. . . . It is impossible for it to be otherwise. In this sense, to this extent, our civilizations and our institutions are emphatically Christian."

THE *FIRST* FIRST AMENDMENT

The current understanding is that Christianity was prominent in early U.S. government because it was the unanimous choice of Americans at that time. Popular opinion also holds that while the founding fathers made Christianity their personal choice, they did so with the understanding that democratic rule was the overriding principle. In other words, when Christianity was no longer the clear choice of all the people, it would be de-emphasized. As we have seen, both views are errant.

Although the average citizen today believes the First Amendment was intended to provide a nonreligious environment, a closer look at the founding fathers' motives proves otherwise. Regarding religion, the amendment states, "Congress shall make no law respecting an establishment of religion or prohibiting the free exercise thereof."

During its creation, the First Amendment underwent a dozen revisions as its authors worked to choose the most accurate wording possible. The U.S. congressional records from that period, June 7, 1789, through September 25, 1789, leave no doubt about the intent of the amendment. The concern of the founding fathers was that one denomination should not be running the nation. They didn't want denominational rule, but other writings from the era express their commitment to placing Christianity and its principles at the helm of the country. Christianity was a given; they were drawing the line with regard to emphasizing one *denomination* over another.

Today, the facts have been twisted to say that we are not to emphasize one *religion* over another. In essence, the U.S. has embraced a new version of the First Amendment. Our founding fathers aren't just rolling over in their graves. They're pounding on the lids.

THE MYTH OF SEPARATION

The phrase "separation between church and state" first appeared on January 1, 1802, in a letter penned by Thomas Jefferson. Members of the Danbury Baptist Association in Danbury, Connecticut, had heard a rumor that the Congregationalist Church was about to be named the national denomination of the United States. Alarmed by the breach of First Amendment provision, they sent a letter to Jefferson to voice their concern. Jefferson wrote back, assuring them that it would be unconstitutional to select one denomination out of the Christian faith to guide the nation's religious convictions. He wrote, "The First Amendment has erected a wall of separation between church and state."

American citizens in 1802 clearly understood what Jefferson meant. In the context of the times, there was no avoiding the fact that religion was to play a vital role in both federal and state governments. Jefferson's letter drew the line for how far the Constitution could go in governing that relationship.

DEFENDING THE CONSTITUTION

For the next century and a half, various people stepped forward to challenge the nation's allegiance to the religion of Christianity. In these cases of direct assault we get the clearest picture of what "separation between church and state" didn't mean. For example, in 1844, a school's administration announced that they would teach morality without the Bible. The announcement led to another Supreme Court case—*Vidal* v. *Girard*—in which the Court actually ruled that the school would teach the Bible:

> Why may not the Bible, and especially the New Testament . . . be read and taught as a divine revelation in the [school]—its general precepts expounded . . . and its glorious principles of morality inculcated? . . . Where can the purest principles of morality be learned so clearly or so perfectly as from the New Testament?

In 1853, a group petitioned Congress to separate Christian principles from government. Their plea included doing away with all chaplains in Congress, the military, and every other government institution. To settle the matter, both the House and the Senate Judiciary Committees deliberated for a year before returning on March 27, 1854, with their statement:

> Had the people [the founding fathers], during the Revolution, a suspicion of any attempt to war against Christianity, that Revolution would have been strangled in its cradle. . . . At the time of the adoption of the Constitution and its amendments, the universal sentiment was that Christianity should be encouraged, but not any one sect [denomination]. In this age, there is no substitute for Christianity. . . . That was the religion of the

founders of the republic and they expected it to remain the religion of their descendants.

In addition, the Court exercised the same interpretation of the First Amendment in cases of individual free speech. In 1811, a man named Ruggles exercised his freedom of speech by openly attacking God, the Bible, and Jesus Christ in speeches and in his writings. The uproar he caused resulted in the case of the *People* v. *Ruggles*. With little hesitation, the Court saw Ruggles's renouncing of Christianity as an attack on the foundation of the country. In its ruling, the Supreme Court declared, "Whatever strikes at the root of Christianity tends manifestly to the dissolution of civil government." For his crime, Ruggles was sentenced to three months in jail and fined five hundred dollars.

This case took place just twenty years after the First Amendment was implemented. The Supreme Court's decision reflects an accurate interpretation of both "freedom of expression" and "separation between church and state."

The government had refused to interfere with the religion that served as the foundation of the nation. But it was quick to interfere with religions that conflicted with Christianity. These were seen as a direct threat to public peace and safety. Later Court rulings further confirm this, with laws drafted against human sacrifice, polygamy, licentiousness, bigamy, sodomy, and other forms of immorality. Anytime immorality was practiced in the name of religion, whether atheism or satanism, the courts intervened. After falling into obscurity for several decades, Jefferson's letter was used again in the 1870s, 1880s, and 1890s to affirm the position that it was legal for Christian principles to be vitally linked with government. Today, however, all we hear of Jefferson's letter is "a wall of separation between church and state."

GOVERNMENT BY PRECEDENTS

In the American judicial system, leaders are required to uphold the laws of the country and to defend the Constitution. Every ruling official takes an oath to that effect. Their assignment is clear. It is not to render judgments according to their personal opinions or their political persuasion. Their decisions are to reflect the original intentions of our governing Constitution and its authors. To make sure this happens, our legal system operates on the basis of precedents. That is, whenever there is any doubt about the interpretation of a law, the judge is to consider the way it was interpreted in the past—to see what precedent has been established for that law. The idea is that by going back far enough, a person can discern the law's original intent. For more than 150 years, that policy preserved our American heritage. But one day, the U.S. developed a chronic case of amnesia.

THE DAY AMERICA FORGOT

It was 1947. The U.S. seemed invincible. The nation had been given a new lease on life and on freedom. Citizens were still relishing the resounding victories they had won over the most notorious enemies on the face of the earth. There wasn't a force in the world that posed a threat to them. The atmosphere in the country was festive, prosperous, and full of hope.

Then in what had become periodic routine, another legal case arose to challenge the government's ties with its biblical foundation. Typically, the Court would examine long-standing precedents and reaffirm the nation's commitment to the commandments of God. But something went wrong.

EVERSON V. THE BOARD OF EDUCATION

The case was *Everson v. the Board of Education*. As it happened in many earlier cases, the prosecution argued that a conflict existed between the First Amendment provisions and the Board of Education's role in condoning one religion over another. As the Court made its final deliberations, nine men were about to change American history forever. On January 24, 1947, the Supreme Court of the United States not only misinterpreted the intentions of the First Amendment; the justices literally reversed its meaning. Not a single precedent was cited in the Court's decision. The nine men handed down their ruling based purely on their personal opinions. They even used a phrase from Thomas Jefferson's letter out of context in their final statement: "The First Amendment has erected 'a wall of separation between church and state.' That wall must be kept high and impregnable."

The Supreme Court had spoken. Americans didn't bat an eye. Perhaps the people were too weary and battle-worn to take up another fight. Besides, all in all, America was enjoying some of its finest years. The enemy paled in comparison to those the country had faced since the morning of December 7, 1941. What great harm could possibly come from a slight change in the Court's interpretation of one constitutional amendment? Little did they know, Pandora's box had just been opened.

After 1947, it seems as though the American judicial system quit doing its homework altogether. When it came to the issue of religion and government, the concept of precedents was virtually ignored.

Repeatedly, the courts failed to quote the founders or identify the context of the rulings. Finally in 1958, in the case of *Baer* v. *Kolmorgen*, one frustrated judge warned that if the courts continued to throw around the phrase "separation of church and state," people were going to start believing it was part of the Constitution. Alas, his prediction has come true. Just as Dr. William James, the father of modern psychology, suggested, "There is nothing so absurd but that if you repeat it often enough people will believe it."

THE TIDAL WAVE

Once the door was open allowing opinion to rule over precedent, a flood of challengers rushed forward to redefine American policy. In the years that followed, case after case chiseled away at America's moral foundation. On June 25, 1962, the case of *Engel* v. *Vitale* resulted in the removal of prayer from public school. Once again, the Court quoted no precedents. On June 17, 1963, the case of *Abington* v. *Schempp* and *Murray* v. *Curlett* reaffirmed the ban on school prayer and banned school Bible reading, offering this explanation: "If portions of the New Testament were read without explanation, they could be and . . . had been psychologically harmful to the child."

With prayer and the Bible officially banned, the watchdogs moved in, removing every semblance of religion. In 1965, a ruling held that a student could say a prayer over lunch as long as no one could tell it was a prayer.

In 1980, the Court ruled that the Ten Commandments could remain posted in school because they were displayed passively, not forcing anyone to look at them. But the justices added: "If the posted copies of the Ten Commandments are to have any effect at all, it will be to induce the school children to read, meditate upon, perhaps to venerate and obey, the Commandments . . . [which] is not a permissible . . . objective."

THE AMERICAN REPORT CARD

When our nation gave up on moral absolutes, it lost its conscience. What we have now is a nation that doesn't really feel that bad about anything other than taxes and the economy. How often do you hear a newscast or read a headline that expresses concern about the moral climate of the nation? Other than an occasional article about teenage pregnancies or crime, there aren't many.

We have lost our bearings. We are lost and don't know it. Other lights have caught our attention, and we are moving full speed ahead in an unknown direction to an unknown destination.

I realize I haven't told you anything you don't already know. And I imagine you are as frustrated by the current state of affairs as I am. So why rehearse it all again? Because this is the world we live, play, and work in. This is the climate in which we are called upon to be men and women of character. And we need not kid ourselves into thinking that our efforts will be applauded or appreciated. The opposite is true.

Men and women of character in a moral climate such as ours will be passed off by many as judgmental, compassionless, narrow-minded, and uninformed. You aren't going to get much help or encouragement in your pursuit of character. It is not generally considered a noble pursuit. For many people, it doesn't even make sense.

FROM BAD TO WORSE

After 1963, when prayer and the Bible were banned from public schools, virtually every moral measurement that exists for students spiked violently upward. Since 1962, pregnancies for girls ages ten to fourteen have gone up 553 percent. Sexually transmitted diseases are up almost 300 percent. Premarital sex among teenagers has also risen by nearly 300 percent. The number of unmarried couples living together has jumped by 550 percent. For decades, the divorce rate had been declining, but between 1963 and 1981, the number of families splitting apart tripled every year. And maybe most disillusioning of all, suicide among teenagers has increased by 300 percent in the same time period.

Since 1962, America has become the world leader in violent crime, divorce, teenage pregnancies, voluntary abortions, and illegal drug use, to name a few troubling issues. We also boast the highest illiteracy rate of any industrialized nation.

According to the Barna Research Group, more than three-quarters of the entire Baby Buster generation claim to have had sexual intercourse with another single person. Two out of ten Busters say they have had sex with a married person. And almost half of the babies born to Baby Buster females in 1992 were born to unmarried mothers.[1]

John Adams was correct when he suggested, "We have no government armed with power capable of contending with human passions unbridled by morality and religion. Our constitution was made only for a moral and religious people. It is wholly inadequate to the government of any other." In other words, if there is no moral consensus, no common understanding of right and wrong, the whole system will self-destruct. And it has.

AMERICA'S ETHICAL EARTHQUAKE

The shift in judicial precedent was fueled by another, more covert, shift that was taking place at the same time. The character of America was shifting as well. A study of American literature reveals a change that was taking place in the way Americans were thinking.

One researcher did a study of American self-help literature covering a 200-year span. He observed that literature written during the first 150 years focused on developing what he called the "character ethic" as the foundation of success.[2] In essence, success was defined according to virtues such as honesty and integrity and the golden rule. In sharp contrast, literature written in the last 50 years focuses on what he termed the "personality ethic"; that is, success is defined by a person's ability to achieve, improve performance, and simply get ahead.

This subtle change in the definition of success carries with it some devastating consequences to our nation's perception of character. If honesty and integrity are no longer highly sought-after values, a shift occurs in our moral and ethical framework. If virtue is no longer the objective, then what you are isn't nearly as important as what you do. And how you think means nothing compared to how you feel.

Suddenly, the ultimate goals are position and achievement. The first priority is personal fulfillment. So what we're really saying is that right and wrong are now determined by what helps or hinders our progress. And if we're totally honest, *right* is defined in terms of what moves us toward our goal. *Wrong* is defined as anything that gets in our way.

When achievements take precedence over character, a new code of ethics has been introduced:

- If the family stands in the way of someone's career, then the family is sacrificed.
- If honesty impedes the accumulation of wealth, then deceit becomes the norm.
- It's right to steal if stealing means progress.
- It's right to claim another person's idea as your own.
- If cheating means winning, then cheating is right.

When personal fulfillment takes precedence over character, a new moral standard is introduced:

- If it fulfills me, it's moral.
- If it doesn't meet my needs, it's immoral.
- Self-control is renamed self-denial and is considered unhealthy.
- If cheating on my spouse makes me happy, then unfaithfulness is moral.
- If an unexpected pregnancy threatens my career or social goals, then abortion is not only an option; it is the right thing to do.

Meanwhile, we invent an endless stream of subconscious rhetoric to justify and qualify our actions in our minds:

- "This isn't immoral. I need this because . . ."
- "How else am I supposed to compete?"
- "I just can't seem to stop . . . ."

REVOLUTION IN AMERICA

There was a time in our country when men and women made the development of character a top priority. There was a time when this book would have been totally unnecessary. But somewhere along the way, the focus shifted. We lost our bearings. Americans stopped emphasizing the inner person and began to measure success by what they saw on the outside. It was the second civil war, one that pitted each American against himself, the inner person against the outer one. And as the outer person has prevailed, the outer person is establishing a new Constitution. Slavery is being reinstituted. Only this time, the citizens wear the chains. Daily, they are sold to the master of self-indulgence.

A quick look at history reveals that a shocking revolution has taken place in our nation. It goes beyond the obvious decay of moral principles or the rise in social problems. At its very core, the Constitution has been redefined. The old one hangs as a mockery to a set of antiquated ideals. For all intents and purposes, citizens are governed instead by the diverse array of stickers posted on the bumpers of their cars. "In God We Trust" has been replaced by "Don't follow me. I'm lost, too."

Choosing to take up the pursuit of character in this nation will mean choosing to stand against your culture. You won't fit in. You are not going to get much help or encouragement from the outside. But as you have seen, character has rewards that far outweigh anything you may be forced to give up along the way.[3]

Chapter Seven

ONCE UPON A TIME IN ISRAEL

Then you shall know that I am the LORD,
when I bring you into the land of Israel, into
the country for which I raised My hand in an
oath to give to your fathers.

—Ezekiel 20:42 NKJV

The light began as a soft glow from a myriad of distant stars that filled the night sky. A divine promise that one man would father a great nation. Centuries later, the light grew in intensity, resting on a bush in the form of a flame. A leader had been chosen for the nation. Again the light burned brighter, building into a pillar of fire and smoke to lead the people toward the promised land.

Slowly and methodically, the God of the universe was fanning the flame. Hotter and whiter it grew, gradually approaching the intense radiance that accompanies the presence of a holy God. The Creator was in the process of revealing Himself to the world once again. His mission was to restore the fractured relationship with the rebel race who had been forced to leave His presence shortly after creation. Many years had passed, and they had many other gods. They worshiped His creatures, His creations, and even themselves. But the light He was sending would outshine them all. It was, after all, the Light of the World. Then the world would be able to see that the God of Israel was the one, true, living God.

RIGHT, FROM THE HAND OF GOD

So that His nature might be known to all generations, God established a covenant. It was a system of laws and principles that would, for a time, demonstrate His sovereignty. Wherever His statutes were honored, those who kept them would be honored. As long as the principles were protected, those who guarded them would be protected. By that, the world could know that the God of Israel is the God of all creation.

There, under the scorching eastern sun, God scripted the cause-and-effect relationship that would govern the success of individuals and nations. The individual or nation that adhered to His precepts and commands, the individual or nation that subscribed to His interpretation of right and wrong, would be blessed. And the individual or nation that ignored His standards would suffer. That was it. Plain and simple. The foundation for all that can be said of character was literally set in stone on the day that God spoke to Moses. God called upon the nation of Israel to have the will to do what was right as He determined right from wrong. Today, God calls us to do the same.

Time and time again Moses stood before the people of Israel and reminded them of this equation: "Behold, I set before you today a blessing and a curse: the blessing, if you obey the commandments of the LORD your God which I command you today; and the curse, if you do not obey the commandments of the LORD your God" (Deut. 11:26–28 NKJV).

In the years that followed, God made it evident that His good hand was upon the fledgling, nomadic nation. He protected them from plagues that destroyed their neighbors. He parted seas and rivers as they passed along their way. He fought their battles, defeating fearsome giants and the superpowers of the day. Eventually, they gained a reputation that preceded them. Kingdoms and empires feared Israel because of the God who was in their midst. In all of history, there has never been a nation like it.

THE ROOTS OF OUR ROOTS

When we looked at America's original foundation, we saw a picture of character exemplified. But to discover the roots of our national claim to character, we must dig back even farther into the history books. America's beginnings pale in comparison to the significance of the birth of Israel. Three thousand years before the founding fathers penned our governing document, Israel's constitution was being written by the finger of God Himself. America's founding fathers may have engineered one of the most successful governments in history, but the real genius of their plan was adopting the principles established by the world's original founding Father. As Benjamin Franklin, then ambassador to France, declared in 1774, "He who shall introduce into public affairs the principles of primitive Christianity will change the face of the world."

Franklin had observed that when people willfully place themselves under the government of the principles first revealed in Israel, something mysterious happens. It's something so powerful and supernatural that it has the potential to change the face of the world. Somewhere along the way, even Franklin noticed the connection between human affairs and Israel's ancient commandments. Indeed, from its inception, Israel was created to provide evidence that there is one God, that He is without equal, and therefore, that His commands are absolute. Time after time, the destiny of the unlikely nation faced inconceivable odds, only to be preserved by miraculous intervention.

AGAINST ALL ODDS

Consider that the man who received the promise of fathering the nation was ninety-nine years old. His wife, in her nineties also, had been barren all her life and was well past her childbearing years. And yet, their descendants were to be as numerous as the stars. Sarah laughed in disbelief. Who wouldn't? Nevertheless, God had spoken. And within the year, a son was born. Then a grandson, several great-grandchildren, and eventually the promised nation.

Year after year, subsequent events proved equally astounding. Waters parted to provide a way of passage, then flowed from desert rocks to keep the people alive. The earth split apart to swallow up dissenters from within their midst. On one occasion, a powerful Assyrian army completely overshadowed the city of Jerusalem, preparing to attack with the formidable weapons of siege warfare. However, on the night before the raid, the entire army dropped dead in their tracks. The next morning, the corpses of 185,000 enemy soldiers lay outside the city walls.

Even the casual observer can see that Israel had a divine advantage over its neighbors and enemies. There could be no other explanation. But it wasn't just some arbitrary cosmic force or one of many gods. The events were deliberately orchestrated to form a single, resounding historical theme: There is one God, He is the God found in Israel, and to find favor with Him is to find protection, provision, and security.

I don't want you to rush by that information too quickly. The events were deliberately orchestrated to form a single, resounding historical theme. A theme that God intended for us to adopt as the driving force of our lives. *There is one God. He is the God found in Israel. To find favor with Him is to find protection, provision, and security.*

As the plan played out, it was eventually revealed that God was pursuing a relationship with the whole world, not just Israel. Every generation has the privilege of experiencing His protection and provision. And although a new covenant was announced some two thousand years ago, the principles established from the beginning remain in effect: Wherever the commandments of God are upheld, they will bring blessing, and wherever they are ignored, look out!

"IN THE BEGINNING"

Let's go back even farther for a moment, all the way to the very beginning, in the Garden of Eden. There, people were perfect and innocent, the way God intended them to be. When God gave instructions or made emphatic statements about certain things in the garden, the people didn't question anything He said or did. Adam and Eve simply enjoyed the garden where they lived, along with all the things in it. It was the world's first model of character. People believed God's definition of right and wrong, and they did what was right—regardless.

But what if what God said wasn't true? What if His rules were arbitrary? What if His rules limited human freedom and pleasure? Eventually, Adam and Eve put God's statement about the tree of knowledge of good and evil to the test. They broke the rules. And they lost their freedom. They lost their freedom from fear, pain, loneliness, and death.

THE UNDERLYING PRINCIPLE

As Adam and Eve discovered the hard way, God has established a cause-and-effect relationship between His blessings and our obedience. This phenomenon is governed by the principle of sowing and reaping.

Unfortunately, many people know only half the equation. For many of us, the devastating curses that result from disobedience are all too familiar. We know the ache of loneliness, the sting of failure, and the fear of uncertainty. Moreover, the feeling that comes when we disobey God is almost always accompanied by the belief that there is no hope for us anymore.

Amid the turmoil and confusion of our tattered lives, we forget about the positive side of the principle. As surely as we suffer the consequences of our actions, we can also experience the rewards of godly living. This, too, is part of God's unchanging nature. When we begin to walk by faith in obedience to God's commands, we begin to enjoy the freedom He provides.

For all the enticing options presented us each day, there is no rival for being in the center of God's will. *To find favor with Him is to find protection, provision, and security.* A man or woman who has divine protection and provision is like a rock. Unshakable. Immovable.

Earthly kingdoms rise and fall. But the same principles that God gave to the people of Israel govern all people today. To the degree that we uphold God's revealed statutes, we will benefit from their protection. We will always reap what we sow. For every action, there will follow the accompanying curse or blessing. If we sow seeds of peace, then peace will tend to prevail around us. If we sow seeds of anger, then the fruit of anger will be our harvest. Likewise, honesty has its rewards. And in the end, crime never pays. Through it all, in curse and in blessing, God is glorified as His steadfast nature is forever revealed. Nobody really gets away with anything. And no act of obedience goes unnoticed.

TAKING RESPONSIBILITY

In almost every counseling situation I face, the people are dealing with difficulties that were the direct or indirect result of unwise choices they made. They're reaping the fruit that comes from the seeds they have sown. Although there are certainly cases of bad things happening to good people, much of the time, the people who reap bad fruit planted it themselves, and in many cases, they did it unintentionally.

In the lives of too many Christians, the principle of sowing and reaping doesn't get the consideration it warrants. Despite what appears as an occasional exception, this principle affects the development of character more than any other. The believers who take responsibility for their actions will experience the rewards of character.

PERSONAL ACCOUNTABILITY

If we think back, most of us can identify times when we've experienced the rewards or consequences of our personal choices. Similarly, we've already seen how the decisions of our national leaders affect an entire country. Individuals, as well as nations, reap what they sow. However, nations and individuals sow and reap in different ways.

Quite often as we observe other people, it's hard to see the principle of sowing and reaping at work. We see bad things happening to good people. And even more aggravating, we see good things happening to bad people. Sometimes it doesn't make sense. But just as God issued "a blessing and a curse," He also revealed some additional information to help explain how this principle applies to us as individuals.

Most notably, God reserves the right to decide *when* a matter is judged. And God's timing is almost always different from ours. While we watch the clock, He watches the calendar. For us this is often a tremendous inconvenience and source of frustration. In some ways things would be much easier if we lived in the make-believe world of Pinocchio. Imagine what it would be like if we experienced immediate consequences for every wrong deed or word. How long would your nose be? Actually, it probably wouldn't be very long. I suspect you would be extremely careful about telling the truth. But in the real world, we tell a lie, and nothing happens. We steal an idea or take credit for somebody else's work, and we are rewarded! Or so it seems.

If we're honest, we don't really mind this delayed judgment when it comes to our behavior. But sometimes it drives me crazy when I see what other people seem to be getting away with. I don't want my nose to grow. But I sure think theirs ought to.

Regardless, God proceeds at His own pace in all things. The principle of sowing and reaping belongs to God. He determines the timing. As a result, people might face immediate rewards or consequences for their actions, or they might go for years with no evidence that their actions are making a difference either way. All we really know for sure about this cause-and-effect principle is that God is watching. He is taking notes, and everything will be settled up eventually. Some things in this life. Others in the life to come. But ultimately, nobody gets away with anything. And no good deed goes unrewarded.

The believers in Galatia must have struggled with this idea. So the apostle Paul encouraged them by saying, "Let us not grow weary while doing good, for in due season we shall reap if we do not lose heart" (Gal. 6:9 NKJV).

Jesus also reminds us of the positive half of the equation when He says, "And behold, I am coming quickly, and My reward is with Me, to give to every one according to his work" (Rev. 22:12 NKJV).

It's impossible for us to know when we might experience the consequences or rewards of our actions. All we know for sure is that they are coming. Once again, our best bet is to set a long-term course for character and wait for the rewards to manifest themselves.

A NATIONAL REMINDER

The moral rise and fall of the United States and Israel stand as a divine reminder against the backdrop of history. Unlike an individual, the moral cycle of a nation can span generations. But ultimately, a nation reaps what it sows. The nation that adheres to the absolutes of God's Word reaps the benefits. The nation that abandons them suffers the consequences.

The subject of national accountability was of particular interest when America's founding fathers were designing their government. They saw the arrangement as a direct ultimatum for their survival as a nation. Their explanation was that while individuals will answer for their actions in the future, nations cannot. When a nation dies, it will not be resurrected in the afterlife to face judgment. A nation must answer now, in this life. At the Constitutional Convention in 1787, George Mason, the father of the Bill of Rights, put it this way: "As nations cannot be rewarded or punished in the next world, so they must be in this. By an inevitable chain of causes and effects, Providence punishes national sins by national calamities."

Long ago, God instituted a principle that could effectively condemn or condone a people's actions before the eyes of the world. And the events of history bear strong evidence that it has remained in effect ever since. When the children of Israel served Baal, they were delivered into the hands of plunderers. When Baasha caused Israel to sin, God took away the nation's prosperity. Ahab's wicked rule brought three years of drought upon the land. And when King David ignored Joab's warnings by counting his troops and gloating over all his victories, the result was a plague that killed seventy thousand people in Jerusalem in one day alone.

CLUELESS

As I mentioned before, my purpose in looking at the history of America and Israel is to establish the proper context for evaluating the importance of character in our lives. If you're like me, you read the stories about Israel's rebellion and ensuing captivity and think, *How could they be so clueless? Were they just not paying attention? Could they not put two and two together?* But the truth is, we are equally guilty and equally naive.

We deliberately disobey God and assume that we will get away with it, that there will be no negative fallout. Every one of us bears the emotional, and in some cases physical, scars of past disobedience. And yet we repeat our personal history. We turn our backs on God, break His laws, and ignore His principles. And we do so as if the results will be different from the last time.

SOME THINGS DON'T WORK OUT

As I talked with a young woman about her decision to move in with her boyfriend, she could tell that I disapproved. I'll never forget her defense.

"I know it's not the best thing . . . I mean . . . I know about sex and marriage and all of that . . . but it's what I need right now."

My heart broke for her. Earlier in our conversation she had admitted that similar decisions in the past always complicated her life; they always took a toll on her self-esteem. Nevertheless, she was going back for another round.

In a situation like that, it is tempting to judge. I want to say, "If you are smart enough to recognize that it's not the best thing, then why don't you make a different choice? Why would you intentionally do something you know is going to harm you?"

But I already know the answer. She was hoping that this time would be an exception. She thought that maybe, just maybe, it would work out. But of course, it didn't work out. Violating God's principles never works out.

She chose wrong because she believed wrong. Like so many, she had never settled the issue of basic right and wrong. She had never adopted any absolute standard, much less God's. And her will was at the mercy of her emotions. She wasn't opposed to becoming a woman of character. She just had no context for thinking in the right terms. In a way, she was a victim and example of our culture's drift away from absolutes. She didn't make the "right" decision because there was no "right" decision to be made. She just did what she "needed" to do.

If only I could have made it clear to her that she has a loving heavenly Father. And that to find favor with Him is to find protection, provision, and security. If only I could have convinced her that favor with God is found through faith in His Son. And that an act of faith would ensure for her the will to do what was right. But none of that happened. And she went on to discover once again that the path she had chosen did not lead to the destination she desired.

BECOMING BLESSABLE

There is no denying what has happened in this nation since character took a backseat to achievement. Similarly, the story of

Israel is that of a schizophrenic nation that bounced for generations between faithfulness and unfaithfulness. Each time, the people faced the rewards or consequences of their actions.

What's true for America is true for Americans. What happened to Israel is repeated a thousand times a day in the lives of believers and unbelievers alike. We reap what we sow. We reap later and greater. Obedience sets us up for blessing. Disobedience sends us down the road of consequence. It has been that way from the beginning.

So why aren't we more careful? Why is it so easy to see this principle at work in our nation and in our neighbor but not in ourselves? Part of the reason is that every day, a quiet battle rages for control of our beliefs, the beliefs that form the basis of our attitudes and convictions. But as we're about to see, rather than staging an all-out attack on the front lines, our crafty enemy uses a subtle form of propaganda to soften our defenses. Like an undetected anesthesia, it weakens our discernment. It slows our moral response time. And in the end, we say, "I know it's not the best thing, but it's what I need right now."

Chapter Eight

THE SUBTLE EROSION OF CHARACTER

The safest road to Hell is the gradual one—
the gentle slope, soft underfoot, without sudden turning, without milestones, without
signposts.

—C. S. Lewis

I t makes its home in the dark recesses of America's rural land-
scapes. Of all the neuropteran, there is no predator more fierce
or cunning. Its name is *Myrmeleontidae*, or "ant lion." Never
more than two inches long, it demonstrates a cruel, deadly deception seldom matched in the animal kingdom. With long sicklelike
jaws and a muscular grublike body it sits below a thin layer of
earth, waiting to ambush its prey.

As if its anatomy weren't fearsome enough, the ant lion's hunt-
ing methods are macabre. Locating a sandy, dry section of ground,
it builds a clever trap designed to draw unsuspecting victims slowly
toward their doom. First, it anchors its mandible into the earth.
Then with powerful snaps of its torso, it begins burrowing round
and round, kicking up a hill of sand and creating a steep funnel in
the earth. Finally, the ant lion covers itself at the bottom of the
cone and waits.

Back on the surface, thousands of ants pass by in single file,
working busily to support their colony. Their march is directed by
a trail-marking pheromone, a hormone laid to show the way

between their home and the latest source of food. Though death lurks only a few inches away, the entire colony passes by in the safety of the scent trail. That is, until one ant wanders off the path. Once out of contact with the trail, the drones resort to random exploration.

From the outside, the ant lion's trap appears as a slight rise in the terrain. Inevitably, the foraging ant happens upon the subtle elevation. With only its antennae to guide it, the ant soon finds itself tumbling down the slope of sand inside the trap. The fall is uneventful. The victim quickly regroups and begins the climb back up the steep wall. However, as it nears the top, gravity wins again, sending it back to the mouth of the funnel to start over. Still, there is no cause for alarm. The forager starts over again. And again. And again. All the while, the gentle avalanche of sand rings against the base of the funnel like a dinner bell.

Slowly, the ant lion rouses from its den of leisure. Emerging from the layer of sand, it readies its deadly jaws and awaits the inevitable feast. A few more falls, and the victim begins to tire. Patiently, the ant lion observes while the trap inflicts its venomless bite. Then with surgical precision, the ant lion snatches the meal and devours it.

OFF THE BEATEN PATH

Living in a nation that has lost its way wouldn't be so bad if everybody who subscribes to the philosophy of the day would just leave me alone. But people won't. Their motto is, "You do what works for you, and I'll do what works for me." But my experience is, what apparently works for them is working against me.

I'm thirty-eight years old. I have a wife and three kids. I grew up in a Christian home. My wife grew up in a Christian home. Most of the people we run around with are Christians. And still, I struggle with staying focused on the light I have been called to set my course by. My world, and I assume yours, is full—and I mean full—of competing lights. And as sure as I am that they hold no lasting meaning or fulfillment, they are distracting just the same.

Like the unsuspecting ant, I am tempted at times to stray from the beaten path to get a glimpse of what's on the other side of that little mound of sand. After all, other ants have wandered off in that direction. And whatever is on the other side must be wonderful because they never came back!

REENTRY

Perhaps you can identify somewhat with the ant caught on the slippery slope of the ant lion trap. Perhaps there was a time when everything in your life was falling into place. You had a plan, and you were following it. But then you spotted that intriguing sand hill, that job, that opportunity, that shortcut, that invitation. Something told you to ignore it and keep moving. But it was just too good to pass up. And from that day forward you have been scrambling to get back on track.

In fact, since that day, nothing has been the same. You just can't seem to get back to where you were. No matter how hard you climb, you can't seem to make it out of the pit. And you are smart enough now to know that you dare not give up.

The little things, the harmless distractions, draw your attention away from the straight and narrow. But it takes only one bad choice. A small compromise. At first, there is no cause for alarm. You attempt to scale the walls of minor consequences created by your decisions. Society may offer you political, social, or psychological solutions. But things only seem to get worse. With increasing futility, you attempt to scramble back to where you were. You try to reassemble your life to its original form. But things don't fall into place. In most cases, they continue to fall apart.

THE OUTSIDE WORLD

The odd thing is that none of this is planned. You didn't wake up one morning and say, "Hey, I think I'll get myself into a little trouble today. Maybe I'll make some bad choices, be a bit careless, hurt myself." Like most people, you were just minding your own business, trying to get by, and BOOM, you had a problem on your hands. And you shake your head in disbelief because, after all, you knew better.

THE VOICE OF PROPAGANDA

In his book *1984*, George Orwell depicts a world controlled by a political persona known as "Big Brother." Big Brother sees all, knows all, controls all, and polices all. Through the use of propaganda, the citizens of this tyrant are routinely brainwashed to the extent that they believe, obey, and defend the dictatorial rhetoric of their leader. Their robotic minds bear the imprint of their master programmer. As long as the steady stream of propaganda is maintained, the citizens remain under Big Brother's control.

The year 1984 has come and gone, leaving most of us to write off Big Brother as an entertaining element in science fiction. But the truth is that in your life, and in mine, we are exposed to a mind-altering force of phenomenal proportions. It doesn't have a political leader behind it. And it doesn't watch our every move. But it is designed to control our minds. And for the most part, it's working.

This powerful voice of propaganda offers the clearest explanation of how we moved from being a people for whom character was a primary pursuit to a country where character is not only absent but, in many cases, is openly mocked.

BE ALL YOU CAN BE

For a sample of its subtle potency, turn back the pages of your mind about a decade or so: You're in the living room watching your favorite TV program. Suddenly, a commercial breaks in. You hear an upbeat music track. You begin to tap your feet. You see tough-looking soldiers leaping out of an airplane, one after the other. You're impressed with their bravery. Within seconds, they have assembled a tank and set up camp, and they're drinking their morning coffee. The singers chime in, "Be all that you can be." Then just as you're wondering what it means to "be all that you can be," the spokesman gives the answer: "We do more before 8:00 in the morning than most people do all day." The private smiles at his first sergeant. You feel inadequate but challenged.

Nothing against the army. The creators of the ad were just pushing the motivational buttons we've all been programmed to respond to. Everybody knows that in order to "be somebody" in this life, you have to do lots of significant things. Jumping out of airplanes doesn't hurt your cause, either. And while you're at it, the more you do before 8:00 A.M., the better.

SELLING INSECURITY

A friend of mine in the advertising business tells a joke to describe the purpose of his profession. "Being in advertising is a lot like being a stockbroker," he begins. "They sell securities, and we sell insecurities." Although his tongue-in-cheek job description is laced with cynicism, there is some truth to the joke. To motivate buyers, advertisers highlight the unmet needs in our lives.

But just like the self-help literature of the past fifty years, the focus of advertisements has changed, too. Where slogans used to focus on the tangible benefits of a product, today's strategy has changed. Much advertising today is built around the premise that who we are is determined by whether or not we own a certain product. Often the message is designed to create a feeling of insecurity.

If you want to be attractive, you need the right clothes. If it's companionship you're after, then pop open the right drink and suitors will appear out of nowhere. And if you're on your way to the top, certain cars will get you there faster than others. Success is a matter of accumulating the right possessions and putting together the right "look."

We all know that this race has no finish line. If you're attractive, then you need wealth. If you've got money, then it's time to improve your appearance. A little more is never quite enough. All in all, the messages tell us that our possessions determine our identity. And our physical appearance reflects our value to society. For most of us, that's not a very comfortable thought when we're standing in front of the bathroom mirror at 7:00 A.M.

AN IDENTITY CRISIS

As you can see, self-help literature isn't the only place where we find evidence of the shift in our moral and ethical framework. It's also a predominant theme in contemporary advertising. And like most vehicles of modern media, advertising is a fairly accurate measurement of American thinking and values. But these media are just the beginning. Across the board, whether in the movies, television, radio, magazines, newspapers, or any other communication forum, the message is the same. Your worth and my worth are determined by what we do, what we own, and how we look.

For almost half a century, we've been engaged in an all-out propaganda war. More than five thousand messages a day tell us to dedicate ourselves to the care and preservation of a dying cause called the outer person. Meanwhile, the real object of treasure, the inner person, is withering away. As much as we'd like to invest in the things that really count, our perception of worth is slowly and steadily distorted by this barrage of bad advice.

For the most part, the lies are so subtle that they slip by unseen. Our defenses are never engaged. We just sit and take it all in. So we go to a movie for a night of entertainment, and we cheer along when the bad guy finally gets blown up. After all, it's not really revenge when it's just a movie. And when an off-color joke circulates around the office, we laugh because the premise is humorous, not because it contains so much profanity.

They wear the disguise of humor. They come dressed as entertainment. Like an invisible breeze, they move through our lives with no obvious effects. But underneath their costumes, they are dangerous, perspective-altering *lies*. They are the principles of an alien religion, commandments spoken by a god known by various names.

With stealthy deception, the lies infiltrate our lives and soften our defenses. Spoken in jest, they bait us to entertain beliefs that cause us to reconsider our values and convictions. And given enough time, they slowly wear away at our standards.

NUMBING YOUR CONSCIENCE

This process is dangerously effective because it goes largely undetected. People don't change from upstanding citizens into hardened criminals overnight. The change usually begins with a small compromise that leads to another compromise and then another.

- "I know I should be with my family right now, but it's just one weekend."

- "I probably shouldn't report this as a company expense, but it all comes out in the wash anyway."
- "I know the hero commits adultery, but the plot is supposed to be great."
- "I know this person isn't right for me, but one date can't hurt."

The minute you stop measuring your actions by an absolute standard, you surrender all landmarks. Your reference points for character are simply floating comparisons that you can change on a whim. Eventually, you lose your bearings in a sea of drifting wishes and desires.

And while gradual changes are taking place in the outside world of behavior, the effect on the inner person is even more devastating. Every time you are called upon to compromise your character, you are forced to ignore your conscience. Your conscience is designed to be a divinely programmed early warning signal. Ignoring it is paramount to being awakened in the middle of the night by your burglar alarm, getting up, turning it off without checking for intruders, and going back to sleep!

Over time, your conscience can become calloused. Scar tissue replaces what were once sensitive nerve endings. When that occurs, your defenses are weakened considerably. Over time, what once bothered you doesn't even register.

Again, it is subtle. There are no immediate consequences.

But what looks like a small, insignificant act of compromise can ultimately have a profound impact on your character. It paves the way for a shift to a standard other than that given by the heavenly Father.

DEFENDING THE CAUSE

By nature, we are cause-oriented. A critical stage in the process of establishing our personal identity is associating ourselves with a cause. This is a primary motivation. For some, the cause is selling more widgets than any salesperson in history. For others, it's feeding the homeless. Some people get their identity from raising children. Others take up the cause of implementing a political philosophy.

Throughout our lives, we may switch from one cause to another. Teenagers often dream of becoming collegiate or professional athletes. Later in life, we may pursue a graduate degree or start a business. Human beings are driven by the need to accomplish tasks. We all desire to make an impact on our world. And identifying ourselves with various causes is fundamental to our sense of security.

As with any cause, our human impulse is to defend it at all costs. Our sense of security is at stake. As a result, we possess an incredible tendency to justify our actions rather than conform to something that challenges our cause.

This tendency plays a significant role in the subtle erosion of character. When we abandon the cause of God, along with God's standards, we automatically assume a new cause—our own. When we are confronted with God's standards, our natural response is to justify our actions rather than to realign with His standard. Once we step away from God's absolutes, the road back is filled with obstacles.

SHAMELESS

When we throw in the elements of peer pressure and social conformity, our capacity to justify actions rather than realign with a standard can reach absurd heights. For example, in 1993, disturbing reports began to surface from a middle-class suburb of Los Angeles known as Lakewood. As the story was pieced together, it was revealed that some high school boys had formed a sexual conquest group, calling themselves the "Spur Posse." Members of the group competed for recognition, awarding themselves points for every conquest. Some of their victims were as young as ten.

The members of the posse were shameless in their pursuits, with scores ranging into the fifties and sixties. Many young girls, especially ninth graders, felt pressured into having sex with twenty or twenty-five members of the Spur Posse. Some even pursued the social notoriety of having "done" the whole group.

But the most unsettling part of the story is the response from the boys' parents. Fathers offered explanations such as, "Nothing my boy did was anything any red-blooded American boy wouldn't do at his age." Likewise, several of the boys' mothers placed the blame on the victims, calling them "trash."

Meanwhile, after several of the boys had been arrested on various felony charges and released, they returned to their high school classes and were greeted by the cheers of their classmates. No remorse. No shame. Just a handful of clichés, feebly arranged to form a defense for the hideous actions of misguided children. All because they would rather justify their actions than realign with a standard.

The problem with erosion is that once it starts, reversing the effects is difficult. Water washes away soil in one area, creating a gully. The gully then becomes a natural path for future drainage and further erosion. Gradually, the chasm grows deeper and wider. With every rain, the channel becomes more and more established. Eventually, a creek or riverbed forms. Ultimately, it becomes a canyon.

When you abandon God's absolutes, you default to a system of increasing consequences. One compromise leads to another, then another. Soon, the entire standard is redefined. Like a trickling stream building into a thundering river, the erosion of character is a subtle, gradual process. And the farther you go downstream, the harder it is to turn and face the current.

But when you cling to what is right, when you refuse to ignore your conscience, and when you renew your mind to what God says is true, you can overcome the negative inertia of this fallen world. You can be a person of character.

Part Three

A STRATEGY FOR CHANGE

This final section is focused on specific strategies for change. If you took the time to work through the exercise in chapter 2, you should have a clear picture of what's most important to you. The following chapters will help you move from where you are to where you want to be. You already know the areas that need work. I hope that Part Two made you more sensitive to the factors that will help or hinder your progress.

Now it's time to dig down to some of the core issues that directly affect your character. It will require a level of honesty that may make you a bit uncomfortable. It will mean taking a long, hard look at areas of weakness. But this is no time to feel defeated or overwhelmed. Every successful journey began someplace other than where the traveler desired to be. And besides, you are not in this alone.

Chapter Nine

AN INSIDE JOB

May the inner man and the outer be one.

—Socrates

A canopy of heavy clouds hung just above the airport. Somewhere up in the hovering mist, a fully loaded 747 banked to the right and began its final approach to runway 24R. The pilots could see nothing. The captain anxiously scanned the instrument panels as the aircraft gradually gave up valuable altitude. His moist palms clenched the yoke as he guided the plane along the prescribed course. The sole source of guidance was an airport beacon that emitted a steady radio signal to indicate their position. Without it, they were lost.

The young copilot eyed the altimeter, monitoring their descent: 1,000 feet . . . 900 . . . 800. . . . Repeatedly, he scanned the gauges, checking airspeed, rate of descent, glide path, and glide slope. Then he began the process again. He longed to glance out the window, looking for a break in the clouds and the ground below. But his job required him to focus on the repetitive task of scanning instrument readouts and checking tolerances.

The flight had been long. They had encountered strong, steady head winds. And after more than an hour of circling the airport, they had burned a lot of fuel. Relentless turbulence had rocked the craft for half a day, and the monotony was beginning to wear on the flight crew's nerves. Heavy rains roared against the nose of the plane. The windshield wipers cranked out their steady, deafening rhythm: "whomp, whomp, whomp, whomp." The cockpit felt like a tiny broom closet, and as the intensity grew, the room was getting smaller by the minute.

Though he could see nothing, the captain bore all the confidence of an eagle gliding purposefully toward its target. "Auto go, auto land," he methodically announced to the crew as he scanned the flight data. The aircraft's tracking devices were locked in on the signal of the beacon. Now it was a matter of faith.

Once again, the copilot cross-checked the instruments. He was watching for deviations from any one of the readouts. As the ground closed in beneath them, he had to be ready to initiate a "go around" immediately. The vertical airspeed indicator confirmed the rate of descent. They were on the correct glide slope. Everything looked good. But in the tension of the moment, it didn't feel right. His instincts told him they were headed for an aborted approach. The forecast was dismal, and he reasoned they wouldn't get the visibility they needed to land. But despite all he was feeling inside, he kept silent and continued the landing procedure. After all, the instruments wouldn't lie.

In a moment the captain would have to make a decision. Within a window of only one or two seconds, he would either declare visual contact and take over the landing or abort and begin the process of reversing the heavy plane's downward momentum.

They were at 400 feet . . . 300 feet. . . . Still, the dense clouds prevailed. With his left hand resting on the throttle, the copilot rotated his palm toward the back of the handle until he felt the two buttons that, if pushed, would terminate the approach and initiate an automatic ascent. His index finger quivered slightly as he held it in the ready position. Everything about him was ready to cancel the approach: 200 feet . . . 100 . . .

Suddenly, a loud thump shook the plane as it slammed through a pocket of turbulence. The copilot swallowed the lump in his throat. Then like a whale plunging into the quiet safety of the ocean's depths, the giant aircraft dropped below the ceiling of clouds and into the clear. The air was peaceful and calm. Instantly, they could see for miles. And runway 24R, situated precisely in the path of their approach, seemed to sprawl out for miles awaiting their arrival. "I've got it," announced the captain. The copilot sighed a deep sigh.

CLOUDY VISION

Sometimes all of us find it difficult to navigate through the turbulence of life. Circumstances close in around us, narrowing our perspective. We lose our passion for living. Terms such as *purpose* and *destiny* elicit no emotion. Our goals no longer seem worth striving for. Our surroundings distract us. And to make matters worse, God seems a million miles away.

But in the middle of the dark times a beacon is beckoning for our attention. There is a signal worth locking in on. It is not found in the circumstances or events around us. No, it is found within. It is the beacon of integrity. It is God's still, small voice calling us to become men and women of character. It is a constant signal emitted from the Spirit within us to remind us what matters most, matters of the heart, right and wrong, love, character.

However, like the pilot in the storm, it is our nature to look out at the world around us and to reach for the controls. We feel compelled to take over, to alter our course. Our common sense tells us that pursuing character is great for the blue sky days, but storms are another matter altogether. Storms are exceptions. When life becomes turbulent, it is every person for himself or herself. In crises, pursuing character may not be in our best interest.

Nothing could be farther from the truth. For nothing tests, shapes, and strengthens character like periods of turbulence. And yet in these difficult times, so many people look elsewhere for direction. When the clouds of circumstance close in around them, they lock in on something other than the absolutes God has given as a beacon to guide them home safely. And consequently, they find themselves somewhere they never intended to go.

LOOKING FOR GOD IN ALL THE WRONG PLACES

Just about every week I talk to people who say things such as, "I don't think God loves me," "I don't think God really cares about me," or "God doesn't answer my prayers."

When I ask why, they tell me about the circumstances of their lives. They tell me stories of sickness, death, divorce, prodigal children, financial ruin.

As all of us are prone to do from time to time, these hurting folks are looking for God in all the wrong places. They are evaluating His presence and concern by how well He measures up to their expectations. They are taking their personal agendas and measuring God's faithfulness by how well He meets them.

This works fine until God takes them someplace they hadn't expected. The minute adversity arises, it seems that there is a glitch in the system. In reality, everything is still right on track. The problem is not their circumstances, but how they interpret them.

While we're frantically looking for God on the outside, we can always find Him on the inside. That's where He is hard at work. That's where He does His best work.

Sure, God is concerned about our circumstances. For believers, He promises to meet our every need. But we tend to place much more importance on the outer things than God intended. God's main focus is not so much on the seen but on the unseen. Consequently, if we are going to gain a greater appreciation and understanding of what God is up to in our lives, we are going to have to give some quality attention to what He is up to inside us.

INTRODUCING THE INSIDE PERSON

Kevin was leery of blind dates, and he had the misfortune of being the only remaining bachelor among his friends. He was a magnet for matchmakers. Time after time, he was taken through the same routine. A friend would call and recite a script prepared by his wife. The wife would coach him when he got part of it wrong. A biography would be presented, including hobbies, likes, and dislikes. To close the sale, the friend would promise to bring a picture of the young woman to church. A week later, Kevin would find himself in a restaurant playing "This Is Your Life" with a total stranger.

Then it happened. Her name was Jane. He had read the bio. He had seen the picture. There was nothing to indicate that the date would be any different. But that was before he met her in person. The moment the door opened, he knew. The bio had been wrong. It didn't say anything about how gracefully she moved about the room. It failed to mention the warmth of her voice. The picture, too, was incomplete. Deep in her eyes was a sparkle like that of a dazzling cluster of distant stars. Kevin was spellbound. Jane never let on that the feeling was mutual, at least not yet.

What made Jane so special? What did the picture and detailed descriptions fail to capture? There seemed to be a host of inner qualities that could only be experienced firsthand. Behind Jane's physical appearance and her biographical data, there was an inside person. A person who represented the real Jane.

As Kevin discovered, the body is only a shell. It no more determines the quality of the person than the clothes on it. Inside the shell is a complex system of thoughts, motives, beliefs, styles, and mannerisms that make up the real person. This system directs the shell's movements, shapes its countenance, determines its responses, and gives it personality. It also reflects its character.

When we talk about the inside person, we're referring to that inner part of us where character is developed. The Bible refers to it as the heart. The heart is the true measure of a person. The heart, with all its complexities, drives our behavior and our attitudes.

A CHANGE OF VIEW

We give our best time to the external world. We focus most of our energy on controlling our circumstances. We don't want them too hot or too cold, too poor or too rich, too old-fashioned or too trendy, too old or too new. Whether it's politically correct, socially correct, religiously correct, or whatever, each of us makes a pretty good attempt to be "correct."

Unfortunately, this leaves us little or no time to focus on the inner person. And the tragedy is, as long as we allow the outside world to control our lives, we miss out on what God is up to.

When a student pilot practices for an instrument rating, the instructor often places a veil over the airplane windows to teach her to focus on the instruments. We could all take a lesson from that example. Once in a while, all Christians should put up a veil, so to speak, and practice focusing on what's happening on the inside.

All of us are susceptible to putting our focus in the wrong place. But as long as your priority in life is anything other than the character of Jesus Christ, you will be prone to look for God in your circumstances. When you do, you will miss Him, misunderstand

Him, and doubt Him. And it won't be His fault. Because all the time you feel that way, He is very much there, very much at work. He is still committed to His original plan and agenda for your life. And that is to work inside you and transform you from the inside out.

Until you embrace that paradigm of the spiritual life, you will have a difficult time turning your focus away from what's happening around you. You will continue trying to measure and evaluate God's love and involvement by your circumstances. And you will overlook His most significant activity—the activity taking place inside you.

WHEN THE THRILL IS GONE

Maybe you gave up on church and the Bible sometime in the past because you didn't think God was holding up His end of the bargain. No matter how hard you prayed, nothing seemed to go your way. Basically, God just didn't act right.

Or even worse, when you couldn't find a direct correlation between your prayers and your daily life, church gradually turned into some kind of benign ritual or a social occasion for you. You go through the motions of attending church and praying and giving and serving, but the person of God is no more of a reality in your daily life than Santa Claus.

Perhaps you have become content simply believing that your sins are forgiven and that you'll go to heaven when you die. You don't feel especially compelled to pursue your religious beliefs beyond the traditional church environment. You don't really accept the concept of knowing God in a personal way. His ways seem so much higher than our ways that you don't see any real purpose in trying to get closer to Him.

Maybe you've thought, *If there is a God in heaven, He would have answered my prayers by now. . . . If God wanted us to know Him better, He would reveal Himself more clearly. . . . If God is a God of love, He wouldn't have let this happen to me. . . . If God really loved me, my parents would have . . . If God protected me, my boss wouldn't have . . .* And on and on it goes: *He should have . . . He shouldn't have . . .* Maybe you've spent years secretly doubting the existence of God, all because of what's going on around you, on the outside. And so, in a way, you've ended up avoiding God. You've avoided the idea that God really wants to change you. Or you more or less gave up because you weren't sure what God was up to.

But His agenda has been the same from the beginning. He is relentless. He is working to conform you to reflect the nature and character of Jesus Christ. And for most of us, that's a full-time job.

LEAVING GOD AT CHURCH

In many cases, when Christians can't make sense of what God is doing in their lives, they adopt a worldview known as *dualism*. In this belief system, life is divided into two categories: the religious and the secular. The religious side includes all situations in which God is perceived to be interested or directly involved, such as church activities, acts of service, and benevolences performed in the name of God.

All the other activities are then lumped into the secular category, which can include work, community, recreation, friendships, and family, to name a few. *Secular* then becomes the catchall for everything that is not related to their religion. It is a place where people put the parts of their lives that they determine are not of interest to God. As far as they're concerned, He doesn't want access to them, nor do they concern themselves with surrendering these parts to Him.

A person governed by the philosophy of dualism gives a portion of his life to God but maintains control of the rest. He does his part when it comes to religious duties, such as attending church, but he fails to take an active role in conforming his whole life to the image of Christ.

Life doesn't work that way. God is not satisfied just selling eternal fire insurance. He is actively interested in every aspect of our lives. He wants to transform us from the inside out to reflect the character of His Son. But when a person consciously or unconsciously chooses a dualistic approach to life, he locks God out of portions of his life. As a result, he can never make sense of the circumstances of life. God appears as a distant, uncaring Creator. Life is governed by luck and random chance.

Most people who adopt a dualistic worldview do so by default. Since they can't see evidence of God in their circumstances, they assume He is not there. Why? Because they're looking in the wrong place. They're looking on the outside while He is busy on the inside. That's not to say He is not active in our circumstances or the outside world. But generally, His work externally is a means to an internal end.

Let's face it. It's a lot easier to focus on career, family, and friends. At least we can see how all that works. We can see when we're making progress or when something needs attention. But real life begins on the inside, where God is at work. The danger for you and for me is that we'll miss out on what He wants to do—all because we measure His love and activity by an external standard that totally ignores the focus of His work. And all along, if we're believers, He is inside pushing, pulling, working, to create something wonderful from the inside out.

GOD, THE CONSUMMATE INVESTOR

All of us have wondered at times why God doesn't do more to fix our problems. But our human eyes often fail to see that God isn't rushing to change our circumstances because He is concerned with a much more serious problem—our character.

While you struggle with the woes of this world, God's main occupation is preparing you for the world to come. The focus of what God is doing in your life takes place *in* you, not *around* you. And for good reason.

God is a wise investor. He is not going to waste His investment on a body or a world that is destined to pass away. His money is on the part that's going to last forever, the soul, the spirit, the inside person. But as Christians, we turn it around. We spend our time, energy, and resources on the outer person. Think about it. Most of our prayers have to do with our health, our wealth, and our social life. And when we experience a setback or grow impatient, we ask, "God, where are You?"

At the same time, we fail to pray for the things that will benefit us for eternity. If God answered all of our prayers, our character would suffer because in most cases, our prayers center on the removal of the very circumstances He is using to conform us to His image.

Larry Crabb writes, "When we ignore what's happening on the inside, we lose all power to change what we do on the outside in any meaningful way. We *rearrange* rather than *change*, and in so doing, we never become the transformed person God calls us to be."[1]

Every day, eager investors scope out the trading floor on Wall Street looking for tips. In addition to doing their own research, thorough analysts watch certain key people to help determine if a stock's value will change. Sometimes the least little flinch can cause a flurry of trading. If it looks like somebody knows something, it catches people's attention.

In your life and in mine, the Consummate Trader has spoken. God has purchased a million shares of your inner person. That should tell you something. The question you should be asking is not, Why doesn't God do something? but What is God up to, and how can I get in on it? If God's main concern is your character, that should give you a pretty good idea about where to place your focus. After all, God isn't just going on a hunch. He has insider information.

GOD, THE DILIGENT WORKER

In the following chapters, we are going to look at several things you can do to work alongside God in the development of your character. But the first step is to understand what He has been up to since the day you were born. Once you see what God has planned for your character—and *why*—you'll be more motivated and better equipped to get in on it.

No passage I know summarizes it better than Philippians 2:12–13 (NKJV): "Therefore, [my dear friends], as you have always obeyed, not as in my presence only, but now much more in my absence, work out your own salvation with fear and trembling; for it is God who works in you both to will and to do for His good pleasure."

In this passage the apostle Paul stresses a couple of things. First, he tells his readers that God is working inside them. It doesn't get much plainer than that! Second, he tells them that this work is going on right now. The verb is in the present tense. It's happening now. It was happening when Paul wrote it. And it was still going on when his readers finally received the letter. God *is* at work.

This is noteworthy since Paul wrote to a group of people, many of whom he didn't know. They might have written back, "Hey, Paul, you don't even know me. . . . How do you know what God is up to in my life?"

The fact is, God is at work in all believers. That means you. It's present tense. It's constant. When you're tempted, give in to temptation, or tempt someone else, God is still at work. While you're busy working, juggling your children, or dreaming about your true love, He is still at work. He has purchased His investment at a price, and He is making certain that it goes up in value. He won't give up.

UNAWARE

I remember the first time I really thought about that passage in Philippians. I thought, *I'm not aware of anything going on.* You probably had the same reaction. Most of the time we don't feel any different. We go through dry times spiritually, and somebody says, "Hey, what's God doing in your life?" "Well . . . nothing," we mumble. Every now and then, we may see Him doing something, but most of the time it seems that He is not up to much.

I know a woman named Helen who worked for years in the abortion industry. Before she became a believer, she didn't give much thought to the fetal tissue they discarded every day. To her, it was just tissue. While she was employed at an abortion clinic, she became a believer. The couple who led her to Christ told her to read 2 Corinthians 5:17. They assured her that once she became a Christian, she would become a new creature in Christ. She took them literally. She thought she would look different. After praying the sinner's prayer, Helen looked in the mirror, but there stood the same Helen. She was disappointed and wondered if her prayer had "taken."

It wasn't until the next morning, when she showed up for what would be one of her final days of work, that she became aware of the change that had taken place. For years she had seen only tissue as she witnessed the abortions at her clinic. But on that particular morning she saw dead babies. Something had changed inside

Helen. And the change in her inner person resulted in several lifestyle changes in her outer person.

That is God's way. Every minute of every day He is at work in us.

TRUTH, THE HIDDEN TREASURE

When I was in college, our family went sailing in the Bahamas. One afternoon we all went snorkeling. While everyone was busy dragging up conch shells and pieces of coral, I happened upon a sand dollar. When I showed it to our guide, he was amazed. He explained that sand dollars were extremely rare on that side of the island because of the tides and other conditions. That only fueled my determination to find more. So back in the water I went, scouring every inch of the reef with one goal in mind. After an exhaustive search, I emerged with the world's smallest sand dollar. It was so small, I took off my mask and stuck it to the inside of the glass. I called everyone over to our dingy to show off my prize.

The perfectly formed sand dollar was so small, it barely covered my smallest fingernail. The guide said he had never seen a sand dollar that small. Then came the inevitable question, "How did you even see it?" Immediately, my father replied, "Because he was looking for it, and because it was there."

So often we miss God because we're not looking for Him, or we're looking in the wrong places. We reach a lull and we cry out, "Oh, God, why don't You do something in my life?" But the truth is, He never stopped. And as we grow more familiar with His ways, we will catch Him at work. We must learn to focus on the things that God is focused on *in* us. When we do, it is as if He suddenly comes alive in our lives.

CHRIST, THE PERFECT MODEL

The next thing you need to know about God's work in you is that it's designed with God's purposes in mind. You may ask, "If God is at work in me, then what in the world is He up to?" Remember all those disillusioned people who pass through my office, trying to measure God's involvement in their lives by looking at their circumstances? Here's your chance to avoid that trap.

The end result of God's work is not measured by how smooth your life runs or how rich or how physically attractive you become. His goal is to re-create in you the character of Jesus Christ.

The apostle Paul said it this way: "For whom He foreknew, He also predestined to become conformed to the image of His Son" (Rom. 8:29). That's what God has been working to accomplish in you—to make you more like His Son. This doesn't mean He wants you to start wearing a robe and sandals, grow a beard, and add a "verily, verily" to the beginning of every sentence. His goal isn't to make you smarter and smarter, or to alter your personality. After all, He is a God of variety. He never made any two things alike.

It means that when you became a Christian, there was placed in you a brand-new potential for character. The life of Christ was planted in you. Your potential for good, for character, for change, went up about 1,000 percent. That doesn't mean you're going to be God. I know that comes as a shock. But it does mean that you have been given the life of Christ along with all its potential. And now that you have this potential in you, God wants to fan the flame so that as your character develops, you reflect Jesus' character.

When you think about it, that verse from Paul is a real mind-blower. The God of this whole universe has determined your destiny. And it's not to be His doormat or part of the sole of His shoe. His plan is that you are to be conformed to His image!

NOT ME?

For me, that's hard to believe. I look at some of my attitudes and habits and say, "Not only do we have a long way to go, God, but we're going to run out of time before You ever get me to that point."

Maybe you heard about the fellow who said, "Everybody has been given a certain amount of things to do in this life. Right now I am so far behind, I'll never die." If God's plan is to totally conform my character to that of Jesus Christ before I die, I may never die, either.

Maybe you find it hard to believe, too. You're thinking, *That sounds good, but you don't know me. . . . I've got this temper, and it's out of control. . . .* Or *You don't know about this habit I've got. . . . It practically runs my life.* That may be true. But keep in mind, God did not move in simply to fine-tune your behavior. He moved in to transform your character.

Again, Larry Crabb reminds us, "I understand moral effort, but good patterns of behavior alone, no matter how strenuous, cannot produce those deeper character qualities I admire and properly covet."[2]

GOD, THE RADICAL TRANSFORMER

Sometimes the hardest part of getting in on God's plan is simply believing that it can happen. All of us have areas that we assume are always going to be a struggle. A lot of the time it's easier to say, "Well, that part of me will never change. That's just the way I am! My mother was this way. Her mother was this way. Her mother's mother was this way. I imagine Eve was this way, too. There is no point in even trying to change."

Think about that statement for a minute. Have you ever felt challenged about an area of your life and given that as your response? Many people do. But God doesn't accept that. He doesn't say, "That's just the way you are, eh? Well, okay, we'll just work around that." No, God seeks a total overhaul. And the question is, Are you going to continue to work against Him by making excuses? Or are you going to say, "God, if You're an inside guy, then I want to be an inside guy. I want to be part of what You are doing in me"?

God has the power to change who you are on the inside. Eventually, these changes make their way into your behavior. I'm not talking about imitating Jesus or asking, "What would Jesus do?" No, I'm not talking about a "do" thing at all. I'm talking about a "be" thing. And inside you is the potential to be what God wants you to be. Only then will you be able to do what He wants you to do. And it happens only because God is in you working and working and working.

WHERE DO I SIGN UP?

Are you willing to focus a portion of your time and attention on what God is already up to in your life? I'm not asking you to commit to avoid doing something or to vow to be this or that. I'm asking you to involve yourself in the process of allowing your character to be shaped and conformed to the character of Jesus Christ. That is God's will for you.

In 1984, I was sitting in my dorm room in seminary, studying and listening to the president of the United States give a send-off message to the U.S. athletes on their way to the Olympics. In his speech, he paraphrased a quote from Vince Lombardi that I immediately wrote down: "Men and women, you above all people know that it's not just the will to win that counts. It's the will to prepare to win that really counts."

As I sat there preparing myself for a life of service to God, the overtones of that statement almost knocked me out of my chair. From time to time we all have the will to be good Christians. We all experience moments when everything in us wants to do right. How many times have you vowed, "I'm going to be a better spouse," "I promise, Lord, I'm never going to sin again, and this time I *really* mean it"?

You have the will to be a dedicated Christian. But do you have the will to prepare? The next step in the strategy for character development is all about preparation. If you involve yourself in this process of working along with God in your life, you will come out on the other end with transformed character.

PRIORITY ONE

Before we move ahead, you need to answer a very important question for yourself. Do you need to transfer some time, some energy, some focus, to your inside person? If you are willing to reprioritize, God will fan the flames of that new life in you so that it bursts alive inside and touches every relationship and every facet of your behavior.

As you begin to grasp this concept, as it becomes a part of your worldview, you will notice real change taking place because inside you is a new life. And over time, it's going to influence your behavior.

When this becomes the focus of your life, you will quit blaming God and quit blaming others, and you will start celebrating the really good things He is up to. Jesus came to set you free, not just in the future, but now. He wants you to experience a fulfilling life of knowing Him intimately. And it all begins with an internal focus.

Sure, He cares about your hurts—more than you can imagine. But something more important than your comfort is at stake. And if you're not careful, you'll miss it. God has invested His time and energy in your inner person. And when that becomes your focus, it will revolutionize the way you interpret events around you. It will revolutionize your whole perspective on Christian living.

Chapter Ten

THE RIGHT RESPONSE

Vindicate me, O LORD, for I have walked in
  my integrity;
And I have trusted in the LORD without
  wavering.

—Psalm 26:1

Now that you have a clearer picture of what God is up to, it's time to focus on what you are supposed to be up to. It's time to look at your part in the equation because all the time He has been working and working and working, you've been responding and responding and responding. And as you will see, your response to God's work will either enhance or detract from the process.

OBSTACLES TO CHARACTER

If you're going to be a man or a woman of character, you must overcome certain obstacles in your pursuit. One of these obstacles is referred to in Scripture as a "hard heart."

For many, the term *hard-hearted* denotes meanness or selfishness. But the Bible uses the term differently. Perhaps the best definition of *hard-heartedness* I have heard came from one of my seminary professors. He defined a *hard heart* as "overexposure and underresponse to truth." When your exposure to the truth greatly exceeds your response to it, the result is a hard heart.

When we say no to God repeatedly in a particular area of life, we begin the process of developing a hard heart. When we hear the truth and hear the truth and hear the truth and keep ignoring it and keep ignoring it and keep ignoring it, our hearts grow hard.

A similar thing happens to your hands when you work in the yard or lift weights without gloves. At first the rake or the barbell rubs against the skin, and it hurts. There is a sensitivity to the consequences created by the friction. But after a while, the skin toughens up. Gradually, you develop calluses. Eventually, you feel nothing at all. Your skin gets so thick that it insulates your nerve endings. You can't feel it anymore. The sensitivity is gone.

That's what happens to our hearts. When we say no to God over and over and over, our hearts can become so hard that we no longer detect His voice. He is still speaking, but we can't hear. He is still at work, but we are in no position to respond. We lose our sensitivity.

The tragedy of a hard heart is its long-range consequences. Once we lose the ability to discern the promptings of God's Spirit, we are open to just about anything. The consequences will go far beyond the issue over which we had an initial falling out with God. Saying no repeatedly in one area affects our ability to discern His voice in every other area as well.

NATURAL BORN SINNERS

Whenever God's standard conflicts with our personalities, our lifestyle, and our circumstances, an interesting phenomenon occurs. Our first instinct is to tweak His standard; we adjust it just a little bit to fit our lifestyle. It's not that we have anything against God. It's nothing personal. It's simply human nature. We have a natural propensity to change the rules on God. We tend to change His commands to fit our personalities, our present lifestyle, and our present circumstances. I have never met anyone who didn't struggle with this.

In fact, as Christians, we are masters at this game. We've had years of practice, hearing the truth and dodging the bullets. We've long since perfected our moves. And so subconsciously, we emphasize parts of Scripture that fit our personalities. We give our focus to parts of Christianity that fit our standing in life. And when confronted with truths that conflict with our personalized version of Christianity, we play them down.

Without thinking about it, we assign a value to various issues based on how they fit our present lifestyle and goals. Sure, we know what God has said about the "other things." But over time, we declare that some of them are just not quite as important to God as the ones that come naturally to us.

"THAT MAY BE TRUE, BUT . . ."

You've probably experienced this phenomenon. Every once in a while, you'll hear a sermon that hits close to home; it hurts a little bit. And instantly, you start looking for a way to ease out of it. You think, *Well, yes, that's true, but I have all these other issues to deal with, too.* Or *I know that's what the Bible may say, but that will have to wait because I'm just not ready for that. . . . But my situation . . . but my circumstances . . . but my past . . .* And all the while, you can't wait to get out to the car so you can turn on the radio, tune in the ball game, and forget about what you've just heard.

There is one problem. When you change God's standard, it isn't God's standard anymore. Unknowingly, you create a caricature of Christianity, one that doesn't accurately reflect what God thinks. Instead, it exaggerates certain features, distorts some, and minimizes others.

Most of us are so good at this technique that we practice it without even realizing it. And ironically, the more we do it, the better we feel about ourselves. Maybe one of the following scenarios will strike a familiar chord.

The responsibly minded dad marches up the stairs and bangs on the door of the teenager's bedroom. He opens the door and turns off the CD player and lectures for thirty minutes about his son's music. The teenager can't make out all the words, but it comes across something like this: "You're not going to listen to this music anymore. It's going to tear up your mind and your soul, and it's of the devil and blah, blah, blah, blah, blah. . . . And we're going to leave you up here to think about it while we go downstairs and turn on the television and watch the visual equivalent of what you've

been listening to. . . . But of course, that's different because . . .
because it just is . . . and you just need to get this blah, blah music
out of your life if you know what's good for you . . . blah, blah,
blah. . . ."

It's easy to see what's going on in this family. Basically, the parents in this picture don't like the music. And let's face it, it's easy
to find something wrong with music that we don't particularly like.
But when the crusade is over, these same parents will sit down and
entertain themselves visually with the very things they are against
their child listening to. And we tell ourselves, "Well, that's different. See, that's just how I unwind at the end of the day. . . . I'm an
adult. I can handle that. . . . There was just this one part . . . and
they didn't show anything. . . ."

In another household lives a very disciplined woman. Some people are like that. They don't even seem to have to try. And she loves
all the parts of Christianity that deal with discipline. She is doing
Bible studies and leading Sunday school classes and having quiet
times and memorizing verses. She wouldn't think of missing
church. She is there for the early service, the late service, the candlelight service, the Communion service, the prayer service.

But at the same time, she is disrespectful to her husband. She
doesn't submit to his leadership. She quotes Scripture at him, and
she intimidates him with her "spirituality."

So what's wrong with this picture? Like the rest of us, she has
focused on the things that come naturally. She hasn't looked at the
whole counsel of God. She has de-emphasized the things that don't
come easily, and she feels good about herself.

In another household is a teenager who is gung ho about sharing his faith. He doesn't own an article of clothing that isn't silk-
screened with some kind of Christian slogan. He practices his
testimony in the mirror every morning and shares his faith with
everything that walks. But at the same time, he can hardly speak
two words to his parents without saying something disrespectful. Every other word out of his mouth is a grumble, a sarcasm,
a sneer. And sure enough, if you talked to this teenager, he
would tell you how great he is doing with God because of all the
witnessing and the T-shirts and the persecution he faces at
home.

AN OLD SIN WITH A NEW TWIST

In each of these cases, Christians have managed to put the spotlight on what they're good at while ignoring what they're not so good at. They have edited the program.

We all struggle with this issue. Consequently, many of us live with a distorted picture of Christianity. We remold the Christian life to fit our lives. And when we do, we become guilty of a sin we don't hear much about anymore—idolatry.

One of the most confusing and yet fascinating stories I heard while I was growing up was the story of Moses' going up on Mount Sinai to receive the Law. I can still remember the pictures in the storybook, the clouds surrounding the mountain, the people gathered around a big golden calf. Moses went up on Mount Sinai and the people thought to themselves, *Okay, Moses is dead. We need something to worship.* So they turned in their gold and made a big calf. Then they bowed down and began to worship it.

Even as a kid, I used to think, *How dumb! How dumb to make something yourself, and then worship it. I mean, you made it! You created it!* For years I thought that was the craziest idea. Idolatry didn't appear to be something I would wrestle with as a twentieth-century Christian. But I was wrong.

CUSTOMIZED GOD

As we allow our hearts to harden toward God, we edit His program. We de-emphasize and reemphasize to the point that we end up worshiping a god that doesn't exist. We create him ourselves. He may bear a striking resemblance to the God of the Bible. But our god is custom-made. He is a variation on the real thing. He is an idol.

The bottom line is this: You can worship the God of purity and holiness, or you can worship a god that makes you feel accomplished, affirms all your strengths, and never touches your tender spots. But they aren't the same god. The one, true God is committed to reshaping your inner person. He moved in to strengthen your weaknesses, not your strengths.

We all struggle with sin. We all fall to temptation from time to time. All of us have character flaws we aren't even aware of. A hard heart is not a heart that is necessarily in conscious rebellion against God. It is a heart that no longer feels the conviction of God. It is a heart that has grown insensitive to the voice of God.

CHECKING YOUR CONDITION

How do you determine if you have a hard heart? You may not be aware that your heart has grown hard toward God. After all, hardness translates into numbness. And numbness is sometimes difficult to detect. It is possible to maintain an impeccable, religious routine while your heart is as hard as steel. In fact, it is human nature to try to compensate for disobedience by overachieving in another area. As a result, a surprising number of the world's hard-hearted people can be tremendously religious people.

So how do you evaluate your situation? How do you know if you have grown numb to the promptings of the Holy Spirit in your life? The true test of hard-heartedness is found in a simple equation: *The degree of your hard-heartedness is equal to the disparity between what grieves you and what grieves God.* You need to ask yourself, Am I grieved by the same things that grieve God? Do I feel what God feels? Am I bothered by the things that bother God? Is my heart in sync with His?

SIN: A LAUGHING MATTER

For example, every week through television and videos, Christians entertain themselves with the very sin for which Christ died. And in most cases, these Christians are not the least bit grieved by their sin. Entertaining themselves with the sin for which Christ had to die doesn't strike them as sinful, especially if they are of age. After all, the movie rating system says they are old enough to handle these things. So what's the problem? Consequently, scenes that would break the heart of God elicit laughter and cheers from His children. And worst of all, they rarely give it a second thought.

Perhaps you've never given much thought to how God feels about the things you call entertainment. After all, you were just relaxing with some friends. But it didn't bother you because you aren't sensitive to it. And that is the nature of a hard heart. When what grieves God no longer grieves you, your heart is hard. When what bothers God doesn't bother you anymore, your heart is hard.

Your response to entertainment is just one way to evaluate the status of your heart. There are many others. For example, pick up your Bible and read. What grieved the heart of God in the Old Testament? What grieved the heart of Jesus in the New Testament? How do the same things strike you? Do they elicit any emotion? If something grieves God in Scripture, but it leaves you wondering whether He might have overreacted a little, you may have some work to do. You could be growing numb.

TAKING NOTES

If others were watching your lifestyle—what you laugh at, where you go, and what you allow into your mind—what conclusions would they draw about your God? How would the picture they developed compare to the picture of God found in Scripture? What if they assumed that your priorities reflect His priorities? What if they took their cue about what grieves your God by watching what grieves you? Would there be many similarities between the God of the Bible and the god you follow? Or would there be such a huge discrepancy that they would be forced to conclude that your god is not the God of Christianity?

Sure, I know. Nobody is perfect. But are you aware of and bothered by the contrast? Are you doing anything to close the gap? We're not talking about where you *are*. We're talking about where you are *headed*. The tragedy of a hard heart is that it distorts your sense of direction. You lose your bearings. It causes you to sincerely move in the wrong direction. A hard heart deafens your ears to God's voice. It blinds your eyes to the beacon of Christ's character. In that way, a hard heart short-circuits your pursuit of character.

Character is acknowledging that life isn't about doing what's good for you or what's easy for you or what comes naturally to you. Character is about being conformed to His image, not conforming Him to yours. If you claim to be a God-follower, and yet your lifestyle reflects values and standards different from God's, you need to rethink which one you are really following: God or god.

OFF LIMITS

A hard heart is like an OFF-LIMITS sign to God. A person who has said no to God in one area may be interested in seeing Him work in other areas. A man may limit God's influence over his finances while begging for God's intervention in his family. A single adult may invite God to take control of her career while refusing to surrender to His plan for her social life.

But God doesn't operate that way. God requires an "all-area pass." He is God, not a genie. He is not here to do our bidding. He has a specific agenda—to transform our hearts. And He is willing to wait for our cooperation. In the meantime, our character suffers.

We've already seen how our relationships are affected. But the problem runs much deeper. A hard heart opens you up to a host of self-destructive behaviors, things you have promised yourself you would never do.

Have there been times when you looked at your life and thought, *How in the world did I get into this mess?* Maybe you've felt like a puppet, controlled by some outside force, or an actor, playing the role of somebody you swore you'd never be.

Chances are, it all began when you said no to God. And little by little, you began saying it over and over and over to the point that you started to think God didn't even care about that area of your life anymore. After all, He didn't strike you dead. In fact, things got better for a while. But gradually, you noticed a discrepancy between the person you wanted to be and the direction your life was headed. Such is the eventual outcome of a hard heart.

TRACING OUR STEPS

In his letter to the believers at Ephesus, the apostle Paul outlines a blow-by-blow account of how individuals can go from being people of character to people whose sin surprises even them:

This I say therefore, and affirm together with the Lord, that you walk no longer just as the Gentiles also walk, in the futility of their mind, being darkened in their understanding, excluded from the life of God, because of the ignorance that is in them, because of the hardness of their heart; and they, having become callous, have given themselves over to sensuality, for the practice of every kind of impurity with greediness. (Eph. 4:17–19)

Paul's admonishment implies a couple of significant things. First, it implies that the nonbelievers in the passage, at some point in life, had a good idea what the moral will of God was. But their response was, "No, no, no, no." "Inconvenient. Inconvenient. Inconvenient." "Doesn't fit. Doesn't fit. Doesn't fit." And they developed a hard heart. Having chosen not to take their cue from the Creator, they looked elsewhere. But alas, they had no moral compass. And so they lost their ability to make wise decisions. They were left with only their futile speculations and their uninformed reasonings.

All of us have seen this principle at work somewhere in our society. How many times have you heard political or business leaders present supposed solutions to social problems and you thought, *That is about the dumbest idea I have ever heard in my life?* Remember the first time you heard about the concept of handing out condoms in the public schools as a "solution" to something? Did you wonder, *Where do people come up with ideas like that?*

Or maybe you hear people talk about their marriages. One minute they're talking about how much they love their kids, and then they turn right around and talk about an affair as if it was nothing. And you're thinking, *How in the world can you live with yourself?* That's what Paul is talking about in this passage—having lost all sensitivity.

A second implication from this passage is that believers can fall into the same pattern. We, too, run the risk of losing our bearings morally, ethically, and relationally. We have the same potential as nonbelievers when it comes to bad decisions and misinformed ideas. And it all starts with one little word: *no.* "No, God, You are asking too much."

When we say no to God, we move into dangerous territory. We separate ourselves from the Source of wisdom and discernment. We put ourselves in the unenviable position of having to make decisions without divine input. In short, we set ourselves up for failure.

SOFTENING OUR HEARTS

After years of working with teenagers, nurturing my marriage, and guiding the development of my children, I've learned a basic principle: The more I love people, the less I am able to tolerate the things that hurt them.

When you love others, you don't tolerate the things that hurt them. You don't even tolerate things that could potentially hurt them. The same is true about your love for God. Your love for Christ will be reflected in what you tolerate in your life. Jesus said it this way: "If you love Me, keep My commandments" (John 14:15 NKJV).

Overcoming a hard heart is not about drumming up pseudo-guilt over things you really don't feel guilty about. Your heart is transformed through fellowship with the Savior. Only Jesus can make your heart tender and sensitive again. Pursue that relationship, and your heart problems will clear up over time.

JUST SAY YES

Going back to the passage in Ephesians we looked at earlier, Paul concludes his explanation of hard-heartedness by giving us the antidote: "You did not come to know Christ this way."

Paul is saying, "You didn't come to Christ by saying no. You came to Christ by saying yes. When you became a Christian, you didn't bargain with God. You didn't pick and choose which parts of the gospel were relevant to your particular situation. No, you accepted the whole thing."

When you became a Christian, only one word captured the expressions of your heart. That word was *yes*. And on that day a relationship began, a relationship designed to bring your heart into alignment with His. Remember how you felt when you became a Christian? Remember how willing you were to do whatever God asked? You had a high level of trust and certainty. You felt God could be trusted, so you stepped out in faith and looked expectantly for Him to intervene. God hasn't changed. He can still be trusted. He still has your best interests in mind.

THE TURNING POINT

I know how tempting it is to alter the rules a little. And granted, there are rarely any immediate consequences. But in the long run, you pay a price.

Overcoming this obstacle is critical to your pursuit of character. Facing the reality of a hard heart usually represents a turning point. It is a question of lordship. It boils down to whose rules you're going to play by.

If you sense that you are suffering from a hard heart, there is only one way to move forward. You have to go back. You must return to that time when your heart was pliable and sensitive to His Spirit. You must readdress the specific issue where you drew your line in the sand. You must say an unqualified yes to God. No more OFF-LIMITS signs. You must give Him access to *all* of your heart.

When you get serious about allowing God to transform your character, you can count on Him to come after those off-limits areas first. He has a tendency to take up where He left off. Remember Jonah? When he finally said, "Yes!" God responded, "Nineveh!" God never changed His agenda. But eventually, Jonah changed his.

It is time to search your heart. To develop character amid the numbing climate of our society, you will need a great deal of sensitivity. You cannot afford to develop calluses. You cannot risk operating with blind spots. Before you read any farther, search your heart. Is anything off limits to God?

Chapter Eleven

A PROCESS CALLED RENEWAL

Character is what you are in the dark.
—Dwight L. Moody

The weather was calm over Huffman Prairie on the morning of June 23, 1905. After completing a lengthy checklist, Orville Wright climbed to the controls of the *Wright Flyer III*. It had been nearly two years since the highly publicized flight at Kitty Hawk had captured the world's imagination. Two years since the flood of telegrams requesting exclusive rights to their story. The race for manned flight had been won, and aviation scientists from all over the world were abandoning their exotic prototypes and scrambling to learn about the simple machine created in a bicycle shop in Dayton, Ohio. Orville and his brother Wilbur had been asked to address the distinguished Western Society of Engineers on two occasions. Officials from the U.S., Great Britain, and France had met with the brothers about the possibility of purchasing Wright flying machines for their armies. The two former bicycle makers were recognized the world over as the foremost authorities in aviation.

The Wright brothers had shared the world's fascination with flight since childhood. When Wilbur first sent a letter to the Smithsonian Institution requesting information about flying and aeronautics for himself, he wrote, "[I have been] interested in the problems of mechanical and human flight ever since as a boy I constructed a number of bats of various sizes after the style of Cayley's and Penaud's machines."[1] And now, undaunted by their own success, the brothers continued their work in the same humble fashion in which it was begun.

As Orville prepared for another test flight, the absence of swarming reporters offered a welcome reprieve. While the world was celebrating the dawn of aviation, the Wright brothers were diligently going about the task of improving the controls on their airplane. They completely cannibalized the original version in favor of a new design intended to give the pilot more stability and control. One account of their ambitions notes, "The brothers were concerned about stability problems in turns and resolved to concentrate on this during the following year in a concerted effort to develop a truly practical flying machine for long distance flights." A new engine was delivering almost twice the horsepower of the *Flyer I*. The brothers made several modifications to the wings and stabilizers. And now Orville was anxious to measure their progress.

The engine sputtered to life, and soon the contraption was airborne. But within a matter of moments, it became obvious the modifications hadn't worked. After a few attempted maneuvers, Orville brought the craft back down, where it crash-landed, breaking four wing ribs. Once again, the brothers retreated to their workshop. Almost two years and a hundred test flights since the thrill of Kitty Hawk, they had more work to do. As one biographer put it, "The Wright brothers had flown, but they still needed to learn how to fly."[2]

GETTING OFF THE GROUND

Every day, disillusioned Christians wake up to a new life that seems strangely similar to the old one, and they ask, "Where is the change? Where is the joy? Where is the peace that passes all understanding?" Unable to "mount up with wings of eagles," they grow confused, skeptical, and even uncertain about their salvation. Often, people expect their Christian label to make them spiritually mature overnight. And when it doesn't, they doubt God, their faith, and themselves. These Christians have flown, but they still need to learn how to fly.

When we focus too narrowly on getting our Christian "wings," we may forget what Christianity is really all about: a lifelong process of being transformed to Christ's likeness. That initial experience of floating on air is just the beginning. The success of future flights depends on how well we prepare for them. Although Christianity changes our eternal destiny, it's no guarantee that our behavior will be altered.

ON WINGS OF RENEWAL

A woman was caught in the act of adultery and dragged against her will to Jesus' feet. After granting her acquittal, Jesus issued the following simple instructions: "Go, and sin no more." We have no record of how successfully she carried out His command. But accounts like this one cause many to believe that their own transformation must be instantaneous and final. We have heard so many testimonies of people whose lives were changed overnight. Criminals who leave their lives of crime to follow Christ. Alcoholics who suddenly lose their desire to drink. Husbands and wives who pray "the prayer," and immediately, their marriage is healed. And while I would never doubt the authenticity of these accounts, I know for a fact that these are the exceptions, not the rule. God's timing is not the same for everyone. And for the majority of Christians, the transformation process is a slow, methodical one.

Unfortunately, we tend to assume that if our spiritual experience was real, it will produce instant change. When it doesn't, we are prone to conclude that it must not have been real. Or we think maybe we weren't sincere enough. Or maybe we didn't have enough faith.

The fact is, becoming a Christian doesn't mean an automatic change in your behavior. Being placed into God's family and kingdom does nothing to improve your character. Spiritual growth and the change associated with that growth come as a result of a process called *renewal*. Take a careful look at Paul's instructions to the believers in Rome: "Do not be conformed to this world, but be transformed by the renewing of your mind" (Rom. 12:2).

BEYOND BEHAVIOR

Imagine if Paul had stopped with the first part of the verse: "Do not be conformed to this world." That is certainly an appropriate admonition, but it offers little help. This part of the verse restates what we've heard throughout our lives: "Be good." "Behave." "Get rid of those old habits." "Change!"

As valid as these instructions are, they can be very frustrating. Maybe you're like me. I've never really struggled to know the difference between right and wrong. That part was generally easy. I knew *what* I was supposed to do. I just didn't have the *will* to do it. How do we go about developing the will to do the right thing?

This is the point of tension in our pursuit of character. This is where the whole thing breaks down for most of us. Fortunately, Paul addresses it in the second part of the verse: "Be transformed by the renewing of your mind." The little word *by* implies "means." In other words, the means or vehicle by which transformation takes place is the renewing of the mind. Renewal transforms us.

Notice that it doesn't say, "Be transformed by the rededication of your life." Nor does it talk about making promises to God or feeling extra sorry or praying a really long prayer or filling out a card and joining the church. He doesn't mention any of the things we typically view as catalysts for change. Instead, as the verse explains, you will be transformed by renewing your mind. This avenue leads to a changed life. It is the process that produces character.

GOING THROUGH THE MOTIONS

Developing character has little to do with what many people consider to be the usual Christian routine. This statement may come as good news. Maybe you were raised in a church, but you have grown tired of chasing the elusive spiritual highs that you experienced when you were younger. There was a time when you knew the excitement of a fresh commitment to God. But now you see little evidence that God *lives* in you. You sit in your spot on the pew each Sunday, but your interaction with God has digressed into a routine of services, programs, and obligatory prayers.

Perhaps you left the church altogether because you came to the conclusion a long time ago that Christianity doesn't work. You walked the aisle. You filled out a card. They presented you to the church. They stuck you in a class. You were baptized. When it was all over, you went back out to face the world and behave like a "good Christian." But after several failed attempts, you lost interest. Subconsciously, you wondered, *Was there something I didn't do right? Perhaps it was all just an emotional trip. Did I give it my best shot?* Christianity as you know it didn't pan out in the real world.

If this describes your experience, then I'd venture to say that you've never experienced the real thing. From God's perspective, change is not about making commitments, keeping promises, or feeling sorry. Change is about the internal process of renewal. And as things begin to change on the inside, they eventually make their way into behavior.

AN INTENTIONAL PROCESS

If you are serious about becoming a man or woman of character, you must become intentional about renewing your mind. If you are not consciously attempting to renew your mind, you are not being proactive in your pursuit of character. Renewal is your part in the process. It is your way of working with the Holy Spirit as He molds and shapes you to the image of the Savior. It is the most significant thing you can do in regard to character.

You can spend the rest of your life making promises, filling out commitment cards, feeling sorry, and talking to counselors. But Paul's words are very clear. Unless you renew your mind, you won't be transformed. In other words, if you are not renewing your mind, things will stay pretty much the way they are. Yes, you will go to heaven when you die. But in the meantime, you may not experience any abundance in this life.

THE COMMITMENT TRAP

This powerful and revealing promise implies that your transformation does not hinge on the depth of your commitment alone. This really is an interesting thought in light of the way most sermons and literature heavily emphasize commitment. If you think about it, however, the commitment to do something is nothing more than a sincere external gesture. Commitments are generally prompted by momentary emotion brought about by hearing a compelling story, testimony, or song. That is why people go back on their promises. That is why we give up New Year's resolutions. That is why married people abandon their marriage vows.

A commitment says nothing about what's inside a man or a woman. It doesn't necessarily represent the ability of an individual. Many promises are beyond the capability of the promiser. What's on the inside ultimately determines what happens on the outside. For that reason, a commitment to the process of renewal is more appropriate than a general commitment to change.

Maybe you hold the distinction of having become a Christian a dozen or more times. You know the sinner's prayer better than the Pledge of Allegiance. Not that you weren't sincere every single time you prayed it. But your Christian life is more like a roller-coaster ride than a journey. You got on board, there were a few ups and downs, and a little while later you ended up right back where you started.

Christianity is not an event; it's a continual process characterized by renewal. It's a process designed with God's purposes in mind. Through renewal, the wisdom and truth of God become the foundation of your thinking and, eventually, your behaving. Over time, a renewed mind results in a transformed life. Unless you are engaged in the process of renewing your mind, you will have no lasting improvement. Being a Christian doesn't guarantee change. Only having a renewed mind does.

UNDERSTANDING THE ROLE OF UNDERSTANDING

Your perception of reality is the foundation for all of your decisions. Your interpretation of the events around you serves as the basis for all of your attitudes. That's why renewal is such a vital part of change. In passage after passage throughout Scripture, the Bible addresses the subject of the mind, knowledge, and understanding. How you think is foundational to how you respond to everything, including God's law.

When we attempt to combine the commands of Scripture with thinking and attitudes that do not reflect reality, there is conflict. I have a card on my desk at home that says: *Biblical imperatives apart from biblical thinking result in short-term obedience and long-term frustration.*

Biblical commandments without the corresponding biblical worldview and understanding create a tension in our souls. There is conflict. God's commands don't make sense; they don't fit. Consequently, we are not motivated to follow through. We experience a sense of powerlessness. And when we attempt to follow through, our efforts are short-lived.

If you don't believe me, ask the average Christian woman what she thinks about the notion of wives submitting to their husbands. "Well, uh, I know it's in there, but I think what he really means is . . . and the exception is . . . and if a husband doesn't . . ." The *what* is clear. But submission flies in the face of common sense. It doesn't fit our culture.

But once a woman understands why God requires wives to submit to their husbands, the command doesn't seem quite so ridiculous. In fact, it really makes a lot of sense. When a woman renews her mind to what is true about her, her husband, men in general, and the ways of God in marriage, she more easily receives the command to submit.

Ask the average single Christian male what he thinks about the notion that sex should be reserved only for marriage. Once again, you'll get a kind of glazed look. "I know it is in there . . . and that's probably a good idea . . . but . . ." But it really doesn't make any sense, does it? Why wait until marriage? The prevailing reason is, "Because the Bible says so." Now that's compelling, isn't it?

But when a man renews his mind to what is true of him, sex, marriage, and intimacy, suddenly God's law makes sense. And it is compelling. But apart from biblical thinking, God's commandments regarding sex generally elicit short-term obedience and long-term frustration.

We often miss the *why* behind God's *what*. Discovering the *why* comes only through renewal. Spiritual maturity involves learning to see things from God's perspective. When you begin to interpret events, emotions, and relationships the way God does, your behavior eventually follows suit. When you see things from His perspective, His commands make sense. And your motivation to obey skyrockets.

FROM FEAR TO FAITH

An added benefit of renewing your mind is that it increases your faith in God's love and concern for your life. As you renew your mind, you will understand more and more of why God said the things He said and required the things He required. Along the way the reality will dawn on you that God's commandments are given as a line of defense against a world system designed to destroy you. God's law is given as a protective fence. You can find freedom within His moral and ethical will. The more you come to accept the idea that God is trying to give you good things, the easier it becomes to obey His commandments, even when they don't seem practical. The more you encounter His faithfulness, the less you will doubt Him. Leaps of faith will feel more like a series of small steps.

For many believers, the Christian life feels like a never-ending routine of cliff jumping. God stands at the bottom of a dark hole and shouts, "Jump! Trust Me." They shout, "Why?" But God never answers. In fact, their fellow jumpers inform them that they are not supposed to ask *why*.

For others, God is a deranged drill sergeant who gives cruel orders just to test the loyalty of His troops. He denies them certain pleasures to see if they'll keep the faith. And again, nobody is allowed to ask *why*.

Sure, in the initial stages of following Christ, there are some moments of decision that seem to parallel the cliff-jumping scenario. But after we've taken a few leaps of faith, we earn the privilege of looking back and seeing that the very commandments that once bewildered us were really some of the best advice we've been given.

CHILD'S PLAY

Every summer, young children stand nervously at the edge of swimming pools while their fathers wait with open arms, pleading for them to jump. And every summer, the results are the same. Some children are overcome with fear and run back to Mommy, only to wait another year to discover the joy of swimming. But some children stay. Carefully, they analyze the situation, looking for tangible reasons to believe that it's okay to jump. But they don't know anything about swimming pools or water. And eventually, they realize that the only guarantee they have got is the spoken word of their fathers. And they jump anyway.

At first it's a little scary. But after the initial splash subsides, they realize everything is all right, and it was fun. So they ask to do it again. And again. And again. For the children who stick it out, this faith exercise not only leads to an afternoon of fun with Dad, but it also gives them more reasons to have confidence the next time Dad compels them to do something.

Your walk with God is similar. Like the patient father, God longs for you to enjoy the freedom you were designed for and to enjoy Him. But fear and lack of faith may prevent you from experiencing the good things He has prepared for you. God says, "Jump," knowing that safety is found in His arms, not on the side of the pool. But all you see is water, unknown territory. You look around for a guarantee to boost your confidence. And after searching, the only assurance you can find is the promise of His Word. You may walk away in fear. Or you may step forward in faith.

The process of renewal gives you the ability to see that it's okay to jump. As you renew your mind, you learn about the pool. You learn about water. And most important, you learn about the arms that are reaching out to catch you.

THE POWER OF PRACTICE

As I mentioned earlier, the notion of experiencing a personal relationship with God or hearing from God may strike you as a little strange. But if you think in terms of a personal relationship with another person, the imagery changes. There is nothing mystical or strange about a friendship. And what is a friendship? It is two people who, over time, grow to appreciate and love each other as they learn more about each other's likes, dislikes, tastes, preferences, and interests, all of which require discovery. A personal relationship is the by-product of common ground and time.

Renewing your mind is the way in which you develop this dynamic with your heavenly Father. Through the process of renewal, you discover His likes, dislikes, interests, and goals. In the process you find common ground. The process itself requires time. The result is friendship.

Furthermore, when you see His principles at work in the details of your life, you can almost sense His physical presence with you. When you identify His fingerprints on the circumstances of your life, you know He is with you.

WHAT DO YOU THINK?

The best way to determine the areas in which renewal needs to take place in your life is to examine the way you respond to God's laws and principles for living. As you've seen, the natural tendency is to hear God's principles and edit them to fit your lifestyle. You rationalize actions instead of conforming to the standard. It's human nature. A lot of it happens subconsciously. But if you stop and pay attention to your thoughts and emotions in these situations, you can learn a lot. The following types of responses indicate a need for renewal:

- "I know what God says, but surely I'm not supposed to take it literally."
- "I know I should put others first, but . . ."
- "I know she (or he) is not good for me, but . . ."
- "I know I should spend more time with my family, but . . ."
- "I know I should be more _____, but . . ."
- "I know I shouldn't watch that stuff, but . . ."
- "I know I don't have any business going there, but . . ."
- "I know what God says about money, but . . ."
- "I know I should forgive, but . . ."
- "I know I should be kind, but . . ."

When an issue arises and the *what to do* is clear, but the *why to do* is not, you have discovered an area that needs renewal. In that area, you are not completely convinced that God's way is best for you. In that area, you are tempted to believe your way is better than God's. You see God as standing in the way of what's best for you. Whenever that is the case, you are in need of renewal. In such situations, commitment won't get it. And promising to do better generally results in frustration.

THE POWER OF TEAMWORK

I'll never forget dressing our son Andrew when he was a newborn. Getting his little arms through those sleeves was like trying to catch fish with your bare hands. While I held the armhole open and took careful aim, his body twisted and squirmed. I made my move, and he bent in every direction but the right one. Eventually, one limb at a time, I managed to wrestle him into those little clothes. But it wasn't easy. He didn't understand the process. Actually, at that stage, he didn't understand anything!

Then, little by little, he began to catch on. Within a few months he would see the shirt coming and lean his head toward it. Soon he was pushing his arms through the sleeves all by himself. As he got the hang of things, he made the job easier and easier. He knew what to expect. He knew where the whole thing was going.

Similarly, the process of developing character depends in part on your willingness to cooperate. God is trying to clothe you with His character. But if you don't understand *what* He is trying to accomplish or *why*, the process is more difficult and more time consuming.

THE POWER TO WIN

Like a good parent, God consistently works to shape your character. And as you know all too well, He is relentless. He loves you too much to let up or to give up. Since the day you were born, this has been His priority for your life. And it will continue right up until you take your last breath. But while God is faithfully working to produce character in you, oddly enough, much of your progress depends on your willingness to cooperate.

God's agenda for you is your character. What is your agenda for you? Is your priority for you the same as God's priority for you? Or do you give lip service to your relationship with God, inviting Him into your decisions only when you desperately need Him or when it fits your lifestyle? Imagine the potential if you worked with Him in your life rather than worked around Him. When the two of you are in alignment, it unleashes a whole new dimension of God's power in your life. As you renew your mind, you will understand and cooperate with God's purposes for your life rather than fight against them.

PREPARING TO WIN

When it comes to character, there are no quick fixes. No magic prayers. No shortcuts. Only the daily process of renewal. Renewal is foundational to character development. In the chapters that follow, we are going to take an in-depth look at the components involved in renewing our minds. Renewal moves beyond the basic devotional approach to our faith. Renewal is a systematic approach to character development. Renewal enables us to focus our attention on specific areas in our lives that need improvement. Caring for our physical bodies requires a consistent, focused, concerted effort. Our character demands no less. As is the case with most things in life, it is not enough to have the will to win. We must be willing to prepare to win. Renewal is preparation to win.

Chapter Twelve

TAKING OFF THE OLD

Being confident of this very thing, that He
who has begun a good work in you will complete
it until the day of Jesus Christ.

—Philippians 1:6 NKJV

From his vantage point on the beach, the young sailor watched as each vessel sailed out into the open sea, then disappeared over the horizon. He was convinced. The only thing that stood between Portugal and the wealth of the West Indies was a single body of water. And as he sat among the dunes, Christopher Columbus could barely contain his excitement.

There was just one problem. Everyone assumed that the world was flat. If ships ventured out far enough, they would fall off the edge. So while the open sea beckoned, Columbus remained landlocked, imprisoned by the conventional wisdom of his day.

Columbus faced untold ridicule and hardship before he was granted permission to embark on his famous voyage. The journey itself was no less hostile. Columbus and his crew overcame tremendous challenges at sea, but their greatest accomplishment was that they changed the understanding of the world.

THE CURSE OF CONVENTIONAL WISDOM

God is out to change your understanding of the world around you. Renewal is His method. Renewal is the process through which

God looses you from the conventional lies of this world's system. Through renewal, you are set free to enjoy the rewards of character.

Conventional wisdom tells us the world is flat. But that's a lie. Conventional wisdom tells us that cheating is okay, that compromising integrity will pay off, that marriage is a trial-and-error endeavor, that there are no moral absolutes. But these are lies. Lies that keep us sailing close to shore. Lies that rob us of the opportunities just beyond the horizon.

A renewed mind transforms a life in much the same way that Columbus's discovery transformed sailing. He saw the error in the navigational assumption of his day. And he challenged that error with fact. Then he boarded his ship and acted on what he believed to be true. In doing so, he changed the trade industry forever.

Renewing our minds involves challenging the assumptions and beliefs that support our attitudes and worldview. It means identifying and facing up to errors in our thinking. And it involves replacing erroneous ways of thinking with truth. Renewing our minds is a two-part process: (1) taking off the old and (2) putting on the new. In this chapter, we will examine the first step: taking off the old.

OFF WITH THE OLD

When a woman paints her fingernails, the first thing she does is to remove the old fingernail polish. Only then does she put on the new. When you refinish furniture, the first thing you do is to take off the old finish. When you repaint an old car—if you are going to do the job right—the first step is to remove the old paint. A professional sands it down to the metal. He seals the car off in a special spray booth. And right before he applies the paint, he wipes down the car with a special sticky rag to remove every speck of dust and lint, anything that might be left on the surface. Only then does he apply the new paint.

That's the process of renewal—taking off the old and putting on the new. The idea is to remove anything that will detract from a perfect new finish. When it comes to renewing the mind, "taking off the old" means identifying lies, wrong ideas, misperceptions, and misinterpretations that serve as the foundation of our beliefs and attitudes. In some cases, we have believed these things all our lives.

Columbus grew up in a day when people believed the world was flat. And that miscalculation severely hindered his and every other sailor's potential. Columbus went through a process of renewal. He recognized the error in the conventional wisdom of the day. He identified what the truth was. And then he acted on it. That is renewal in a nutshell.

CHARTING A COURSE FOR CHARACTER

The story of Columbus illustrates a vital principle: *What we believe determines how we behave.*

This principle is foundational in understanding the importance and the impact of renewal. It functions as another avenue to explain the *why* behind the *what* of our actions. Every single facet of our behavior is somehow tied to something we believe. When you and I believe the wrong thing, it works its way out in the form of wrong behavior. The opposite is true as well. Right thinking paves the way to right behavior.

That is why the renewal of our minds is so high on God's agenda for our lives. He knows that for change to take place, our minds must be renewed. The process is spelled out further in Paul's letter to the believers in Colosse: "Do not lie to one another, since you laid aside the old self with its evil practices, and have put on the new self who is being renewed to a true knowledge according to the image of the One who created him" (Col. 3:9–10).

Notice the sequence of events. We are to lay aside the old and put on the new. And notice what he says about the "new self." The new self is being renewed to a "true knowledge." Command central for the renewal process is our minds, our thinking. God is working to fill our minds with a "true knowledge," truth that finds its source in the One who created us. Filling ourselves with truth entails dredging up and clearing out the lies, the misinterpretations, the beliefs that have no foundation in fact, anything that is contrary to truth and reality.

LIES, LIES, AND MORE LIES

All our lives, we have been told lies. We live in a world that lies to us every single day. It's a consequence of living in a world that has turned its back on the Source of truth. Every day, women in our society are told in a thousand different ways that to be lovable, they must be beautiful. The message they receive is that the catalyst for lasting, fulfilling relationships is physical appearance. And although few women would admit they buy into that line of thinking, fewer still could deny having acted on it.

Men are told that the key to their happiness is a newer model that requires less maintenance. Whether it's cars or women, the lie is the same. And it is a lie we see repeated every time we turn on the television, open a magazine, or walk down the street. I've never met a man who would acknowledge thinking that way. But I know far too many who have made decisions based on such faulty presuppositions.

Single adults believe that marriage will solve their problems. Married adults believe that a divorce will solve theirs. Like flies on a windowpane, those on the inside are dying to get out, and those on the outside are dying to get in. The assumption is that marriage and divorce are problem solvers. But nothing could be farther from the truth.

Repeated exposure to the lies of this world takes its toll. Over time, these lies are woven into the fabric of our thinking. We aren't always aware that they're there. Often we are unaware of the ideas that form the basis of our decisions and attitudes. But these beliefs, whether grounded in reality or not, act as the grid system through which we interpret the data of our lives.

MENTAL IMAGES

Your mental picture of God may be distorted because of subtle messages you received as a child. Maybe your picture of God is more like a picture of Santa Claus than the God described in Scripture. You see Him as a big, jolly figure who lives out in space somewhere. And as long as you're more nice than naughty, He will be nice to you in the end. Or maybe you think God is a tyrant. No matter what you do, it will never be enough to quench His anger.

Sure, He may "love" you because the Bible says He loves you, but He doesn't really "like" you.

To some degree, all of us live with distortions like these. Our perspective can be skewed about marriage, about what a husband is supposed to be, about what a wife is supposed to do, about love, sex, money. And wherever there is a distortion of the truth, eventually, it is reflected in our behavior.

If you believe the world is flat, you are not going to sail far from shore. If you believe happiness is found in the accumulation of possessions, you are not going to be very generous. If you believe that people cannot be trusted, you are not going to have many close friends. If you believe you are less than complete without a spouse, you are going to pursue marriage at a dangerously intense pace. If you believe you can't change, you won't. If you believe God accepts you on the basis of your performance, you are going to perform yourself to death or give up altogether. On and on it goes.

This is why you can promise, commit, and rededicate over and over again without ever making any progress. Until you deal with your belief system, your behavior will never change because what you believe affects what you do.

LITTLE BY LITTLE

That being the case, it is imperative for you to begin identifying false things in your battery of beliefs. The specific changes you would like to make in your behavior and character are linked to things you believe. No doubt, you have already attempted to deal with these things at the behavioral level. And unless you have an extraordinary amount of resolve, you have met with limited success.

God's plan for change begins at the belief level. Your salvation began there, and your transformation begins there as well. Renewal requires daily, ongoing evaluation of your belief system. It doesn't happen all at once. Transformation is not a one-time event. It's a way of life. As you commit to the process, you will become sensitive to the assumptions that drive your behavior. In time you will become more discerning about the beliefs that drive your responses and reactions to the events of life.

FIRST THINGS FIRST

You cannot fill a glass with water if it is already full of dirt. You must first remove the dirt. You may use the water to do so. But the dirt has to be removed before the glass can be filled with water.

You cannot fill a mind with truth until you have identified and removed the lies. A Christian can sit for years and listen to good, sound, application-oriented messages and never change. Truth will not fill something that is already full. You cannot fully embrace a truth until you have first removed the error that stands in contrast to that truth.

A fellow who was having trouble in his marriage came to see me for advice. For forty-five minutes he told me all the things that were wrong with his wife. If half of what he said was true, he had every right to complain. He was a Christian, and he knew most of what the Bible had to say about marriage. He was especially well versed in the portions dealing with wives and submission.

When he finished, I asked him, "How can I help?"

He said, "Tell me what I should do."

I said, "What do you think God wants you to do?"

He replied, "I don't know. I have tried everything."

I said, "What do you mean you have tried everything?"

He went on to tell me all the things he had done to "help" his wife.

When he finished, I said, "I get the impression you want to 'fix' your wife."

"Yes," he said. "I do. But I don't know how. I have tried everything."

As we talked further, it became evident that this biblically astute believer was operating from several false premises. Assumptions he was not even aware of. Assumptions that contradicted several passages of Scripture he firmly believed. But the truth of the passages never made their intended impact because of the undetected, covert lies that were warping his mind-set.

False Assumption #1: Husbands have been given the responsibility of fixing their wives. First of all, he thought it was his responsibility to fix his wife. Since he believed that was true, he acted on it, which worsened the problem. The truth is, God has not called husbands to fix their wives. He has commanded husbands to love them.

This fellow could quote the verse about husbands loving their wives. He knew it. He just wasn't operating from it. He said he had tried loving her: "I've tried being nice and sweet and patient, and nothing changed!" This surfaced another false assumption.

False Assumption #2: Love is simply a tool, and if it doesn't get the job done, it is okay to use another tool. He tried loving her to get her to change. And when it didn't get the job done, he put down that tool and picked up another. But love isn't a means to an end. Manipulation is a means to an end. And when love is used as manipulation, it isn't love.

When being sweet didn't work, he tried the opposite approach. He gave her a taste of her own medicine. He tried nagging and arguing and demanding his rights. He tried the silent treatment. He didn't enjoy going home, so he looked for opportunities to stay away.

False Assumption #3: Rejection is the path to a restored relationship. Another false assumption he made was that his wife could be changed through repeated confrontation, faultfinding, and avoidance. He didn't know that was what he believed. On the contrary, he thought he believed that husbands are to love their wives as Christ loved the church. But he had never internalized that theological concept. It had never become part of his operational belief system. It was just a verse he quoted.

Rejection never, never, never serves as a bridge back into a relationship. Yet many of us respond to rejection with more rejection. It comes naturally. But it doesn't work.

So I asked him, "How does your heavenly Father go about changing you?"

He thought for a moment. "I'm not sure," he said.

"Since you became a believer, has anything significant changed?"

"Sure," he said, "a lot."

"Did God ever nag you or shame you or reject you when you messed up?"

He knew where this was going. "No," he said.

"Do you know why God doesn't resort to that?" I asked.

He stared at the ceiling. "Because it doesn't work."

"Right," I replied.

We went on to talk about how love is the environment most conducive to change. I reiterated some of the false presuppositions he had been operating from. The longer we talked, the more misinformation we discovered. There were lies and false assumptions that he hadn't even been aware of. And they kept the truth he professed from sinking in at a functional level.

THE HEART OF THE MATTER

At the heart of almost every relational problem I have encountered are lies and false assumptions. The problem is never a lack of intelligence. Generally, the people I talk to are spiritually sensitive and committed to change. The problem almost always goes back to a faulty belief system.

And understandably so. Every time you open a magazine, every time you turn on a television, every time you have a conversation at work, every time you interact with any segment of this world, chances are, you will be lied to. Over and over again, you are fed lies about what's real, about what's true, about how things work, and about what's important, about what you deserve, about how you ought to be treated. And unless you learn to recognize these distortions of the truth, you will inculcate them into your belief system.

GETTING STARTED

Some lies you believe are very, very subtle. They are difficult to spot. To get you started, I want to give you a few techniques to help you recognize the lies that have infiltrated your belief system.

A good way to identify false beliefs behind your behavior is to evaluate the things you say. You probably don't say them out loud, but you may think them. Statements like the following ones indicate that some faulty thinking is going on.

1. "I've Always Been This Way."

"Well, I know I have a problem, but that's just the way I am. I mean, my father was that way. His father was that way. In fact, my whole family has always been this way. That's just the way I am."

Okay, so I'm exaggerating a bit. But you may excuse shortfalls in your character by blaming your track record. You play the blame game. Rather than tackle the challenge of transformation, you choose to remain the same.

Two false assumptions are behind this idea. First, if I have been a certain way in the past, I must continue to be that way in the future. Second, my problem is more than God can handle.

When you point to the past to excuse your future, in effect you say to God, "I know You created the earth, the sun, the stars, and six hundred different kinds of beetles while observing the 'no two snowflakes alike' rule. I know You're the most powerful force in the world, but, God, I'm just too much for You to handle. I can't be changed."

I've never met anyone who would admit to having such a pompous belief. But without recognizing it, many do. The truth is, God has the power to overcome every flaw in your character, both known and unknown.

2. "Everybody Else Is Doing It."

The assumption is, if everybody else is doing it, God doesn't take it so seriously. You say, "But I wasn't the only one"; "Every attorney does it that way"; "But everybody does taxes like that"; or "The guy who passed me was going even faster."

Behind each statement is the same lie. Picture it. You're caught red-handed doing something wrong. And yet often, subconsciously, you offer this as your excuse. All because you believe the lie that says, "If everybody does it, God doesn't take it as seriously." Furthermore, there probably aren't any consequences.

When you attempt to justify your actions by comparing yourself to others, you make a rather startling assumption: Whenever sin runs rampant, God becomes more tolerant. The more sin there is, the more He tolerates it. If enough people fall short of God's absolute standard of right and wrong, then He changes the evaluation system to a sliding scale, and everyone is graded on a curve.

Nobody consciously believes that. But whenever you offer up the excuse, "Everybody does it," you employ the belief that the quantity of the sinners affects the severity of the sin. For a brief moment in time, your thinking is controlled by a false premise, and your behavior falls right in line with your thinking.

3. "I Can Handle It."

Another subtle, yet damaging comment is, "What could it hurt? I can handle it." The lie here is that if you can't see the harm in something, it must not be harmful. To adopt this belief is to say, "I'm discerning enough to know what's good for me and what's not. I don't need any outside input."

Of course, you would never intentionally say that because anyone can see the fallacy of such a statement. But when you encounter it in subtler forms, you may miss it. And you believe the lie.

4. "One Time Won't Hurt."

Other statements that might indicate you're believing a lie are, "I'll just try it once"; "I'm only going with those guys one time"; "It's just one party"; and "I don't usually do this, but one time won't hurt."

Behind each of these statements is the belief that there are no consequences for sins that are committed only once. The implication is that there are consequences only for habitual sins.

This lie is particularly devastating because of its subtlety. Remember, we began by identifying certain character goals you hope to reach in life. Along the way, you will encounter many temptations to veer off course. Some will be obvious. But some will seem harmless. This lie suggests that certain tangents are only temporary pit stops. And granted, the immediate effects of one-time sins may be minimal. But every habit has a first time. Every detour begins with a small course adjustment. One time will definitely hurt.

5. "Nobody Will Know."

Another common lie is represented by the rationale that says, "Nobody is going to know." This lie preys upon businesspeople who travel alone. It targets teenagers whose parents are out of town.

On the surface, it ignores the fact that nobody is ever alone. And beneath the surface, this statement assumes that as long as certain people don't find out about the sin, the advantages outweigh the consequences. It says that God's standard of right and wrong is relative, that it applies only when someone else is watching. It suggests that the only cost of compromise is the cost imposed by those who know and who hold you accountable.

Like many of the other lies you believe, this one implies that the negative effects, if any, are short-lived. It indicates a belief that the only real price of sin is the embarrassment and hassle of somebody finding out. But as long as nobody knows, no problem!

6. "But I'm in Love."

The toughest lies to neutralize are the ones linked to deep emotions. The feelings associated with them can be so overwhelming that you would rather believe the lie and suffer the consequences. In the heat of the moment, there is a sense in which you don't seem to care if it's a lie or not. But sooner or later the emotions pass. And when they do, you may look back and wonder, *What was I thinking?*

Emotions are temporary. Consequences can last a lifetime.

When someone justifies sin on the basis of love, there is a serious belief problem. Love is the antithesis of sin. To justify sinning with someone because you love that person is completely illogical. To introduce sin into a relationship is to sow seeds of destruction.

Lust is a good rationalization for sin. Love is not. At the core of this statement is this assumption: Love is more important than obedience. That is, in the hierarchy of things, when it comes down to a choice between love or obedience, love wins out. But love for another person should never take priority over obedience to God. The truth is, obedience to God will enhance your ability to love others.

FINDING THE LIES

In addition to examining the things you say, there are three other avenues for discovering erroneous assumptions.

1. Closely examine the areas of your life where you are overly sensitive. If some subjects, names, or memories create a sense of anxiety in you, a lie may be lurking beneath the surface. Your overreaction to certain situations or certain topics in conversation could indicate a false belief.

I knew a successful small-business owner who never finished college. Whenever the topic of education came up, he quickly changed the subject. His lack of education was a source of insecurity, and he was very sensitive about it. Consequently, his family and close friends learned to avoid the topic. When it did come up, he downplayed the value of education.

As I got to know him better, he eventually confided in me that he was embarrassed by his lack of education. He felt it was a barrier between him and more educated people. He was convinced that people thought less of him when they discovered the truth about his schooling.

Actually, his insecurity was the barrier. The truth was, people who knew him and did business with him held him in such high regard that his education was irrelevant. In fact, the people who knew about his lack of education respected his success even more. He was the American dream personified. His fears were unfounded. But he had fallen for the lie that his worth was linked to accomplishments.

I have talked to husbands who feel that they're walking on eggshells because their wives are so sensitive about certain issues. That's usually a good indication that an area needs to be examined. In some families, the wives and children avoid mentioning certain subjects around Dad because he will overreact. That usually means some areas need exploring. Someone needs to ask, "God, have I believed a lie? Have I been set up?"

2. Examine your strongest temptations. Temptations are always camouflaged and supported with lies. Lies make temptations appealing. The false assumptions make any temptation seem worth entertaining for the moment. Analyze your temptations. What exactly is the appeal? What is the promise of sin? What mental gymnastics do you go through to justify it? Think through the conversations you have with yourself as you talk yourself into something you know is wrong. You will discover all kinds of things that you know are not true.

3. Examine areas in which you have inordinate fears. Of course, some degree of fear can be healthy; that is, you need to use wisdom to avoid danger. But inordinate fears are fears that are not grounded in reality. You know the facts, but you are afraid anyway. Fear is often a sign that you believe a lie.

One way to track down the false assumptions behind your fears is to play what I call the what-if game.

A woman says, "I'm afraid my husband will leave me."

I respond, "What if he did? What would happen?"

"I would be alone."

"If you were alone, what would happen?"

"I am not sure."

"So what exactly are you afraid of?"

"I guess I am afraid of not being able to handle being alone."

"Have you ever been alone before?"

"Yes."

"How did you handle it then?"

"I did fine."

"Chances are, if your husband leaves, you will be fine."

This woman thought she was afraid of what her husband would do. In actuality, she was afraid of what *she* would do if her husband left her. When she discovered that, she identified a false assumption, namely, "I can't handle being alone." That wasn't the case at all.

Once she was able to pinpoint the source of her fear, she was able to deal with it. In this particular case, she was able to overcome certain behavioral patterns that were actually driving her husband away. Her fear of abandonment was causing her to smother her spouse. He felt that she didn't trust him. The trouble was, she didn't trust herself.

A LIBERATING STEP

Renewal is a two-part process. It begins with identifying the lies and false assumptions that fuel your attitudes and actions. This is not a comfortable step. It can be threatening. But ultimately, it is liberating. Take some time to evaluate your excuses. Think through your temptations. Examine your fears. Ask the Holy Spirit to reveal the lies holding you back in your pursuit of change.

God is at work in you. His goal is Christlikeness. His method is renewal. When you take steps to renew your mind, you are working hand in hand with your heavenly Father. And He has promised to complete what He has begun.

Chapter Thirteen

PUTTING ON THE NEW

What lies behind us and what lies before us
are tiny matters compared to what lies
within us.

—Ralph Waldo Emerson

By now, you have probably identified a few lies that have been rattling around in your bucket of beliefs. Perhaps you have even started to dissect your thought patterns and are uncovering false premises that you were not aware of. Identifying the lies in your thinking can lead to some powerful revelations about yourself. But that's not enough.

Taking off the old is only the first part of the process. Just as you need to be intentional about discovering the lies you believe, so you need a deliberate plan for replacing the lies with truth. Lasting change is contingent upon both parts of the process.

FINDING AN ANTIDOTE

"Putting on the new" begins where "taking off the old" left off. When scientists create a vaccine, they use the disease itself as a starting point. In the same way, to neutralize the lies that enslave you, you begin with the lies themselves. And with the lies as your road map or blueprint, you use them to lead you to the specific truths in Scripture that you will incorporate into the foundation of your beliefs. And *specific* is the key word when it comes to putting on the new.

Once you identify an error in your belief system, the next step is to find its counterpart—the truth. That means finding the specific truths of God's Word that counter the specific lies you have been told. The goal is to equip yourself to the point that you have the specific truths of Scripture on the tip of your tongue so that as you move through life and are confronted with lies, you'll be ready to counter them. That's the process of renewing the mind. It's countering lies with the truth. And it requires that you find the exact nugget of truth to defuse whatever lies come along. Specific lies must be countered with specific truths.

DIG A LITTLE DEEPER

Putting on the new often entails taking a different approach to the Bible. Finding the scriptural truths that apply to your particular situation will require some effort. And that means moving beyond a devotional approach to Scripture. You will never renew your mind reading a couple of pages out of a devotional book each day. Renewing your mind involves more than simply reading through the Bible in a year or answering your Bible study questions or filling out a notebook.

Systematic Bible study is a valuable spiritual discipline. It is part of my daily routine. I am all for books, cassettes, and study courses too. But renewal goes beyond the systematic and routine. I have seen many knowledgeable believers wreck their lives over issues of character. If knowledge was the answer to spiritual maturity, we should all enroll in seminary. Knowledge does not necessarily result in a renewed mind. Knowledge has a tendency to puff us up and give us a false sense of spirituality. Satan knows more about God than any of us. A lot of good that did him!

God wants to renew your mind with truth, not just fill it with facts. Renewal hinges on specific truths appropriate for specific issues of character in your life. You have developed a list of character goals. They are specific. Specific things block your progress. You must identify the barriers and deal with them. Consequently, your pursuit of character will lead you beyond a devotional approach to Scripture. Renewal will involve digging out for yourself the specific truths of Scripture that counter the specific lies you have believed.

FOLLOW THE LEADER

Christ demonstrated this process in a dramatic way immediately following His baptism. It is a familiar narrative used by preachers and teachers to illustrate just about everything under the sun. But more than anything else, it illustrates for us the amazing power of truth.

The story is found in Matthew's Gospel. Jesus had fasted for forty days. Don't rush by that. Forty days. More than a month with no food. Imagine the shape He was in.

Satan came to Jesus in His weakened state with three tempting propositions, each one wrapped around a false assumption. Now I imagine Jesus, being God, could have looked at Satan and said something to the effect of, "Do what? Have you forgotten who you are talking to? I created you! Get off My mountain. For that matter, get off My planet."

But instead, Jesus took the opportunity to model for us the proper response to temptation and temptation's supporting cast—lies.

Then Jesus was led up by the Spirit into the wilderness to be tempted by the devil. And after He had fasted forty days and forty nights, He then became hungry. And the tempter came and said to Him, "If You are the Son of God, command that these stones become bread." But He answered and said, "It is written, 'Man shall not live on bread alone, but on every word that proceeds out of the mouth of God.'" Then the devil took Him into the holy city; and he had Him stand on the pinnacle of the temple, and said to Him, "If You are the Son of God throw Yourself down; for it is written,

'He will give His angels charge concerning You';
and
'On their hands they will bear You up,
Lest You strike Your foot against a stone.'"

Jesus said to him, "On the other hand, it is written, 'You shall not put the Lord your God to the test.'" Again, the devil took Him to a very high mountain, and showed Him all the kingdoms of the world, and their glory; and he said to Him, "All these things will I give You, if You fall down and worship me." Then Jesus said to him, "Begone, Satan! For it is written, 'You shall worship the Lord your God, and serve Him only.'" (Matt. 4:1–10)

ROUND ONE

In round one, Satan came at Jesus with a very tempting offer. He appealed to His physical state and suggested He perform a seemingly harmless task—turning stones into bread. On the surface, that didn't appear to be a temptation. There was no Jewish prohibition against turning stones into bread. Jesus certainly didn't mind turning water into wine. So what was the problem?

The problem was that the Father had led Jesus into the wilderness. Jesus was not there of His own accord. He was following instructions. And apparently, the instructions included fasting until otherwise notified. The temptation was to put His legitimate physical concerns ahead of His allegiance to the Father. Sound familiar? Is that not at the core of just about every temptation we encounter?

Shrouded in that innocent suggestion was a big lie, namely, satisfying your hunger is more important than devotion to the Father. But Jesus saw it and responded appropriately.

WORD POWER

Now, as I mentioned before, Jesus could have responded in several ways. He could have said, "Well, you know, Satan, not only could I turn that stone into a piece of bread. I could turn *you* into a piece of bread! And so, I'm going to count to three. . . ."

Instead, the first words out of His mouth were, "It is written . . . ," not "I think," or "I really shouldn't do that," or "There is nothing wrong with . . ." The very first words out of His mouth were words of truth directed toward the specific lie hidden in that temptation. Jesus took a specific truth from the book of Deuteronomy that exposed Satan's lie for what it was. He said, "Man shall not live on bread alone, but on every word that proceeds out of the mouth of God." Paraphrased, it reads, "Life is not about eating, it is about faithfulness to My Father."

Satan was tempting Jesus to trade unbroken fellowship with the Father for physical nourishment. Jesus recognized what was at stake. It had little to do with eating. The implications of Satan's request ran much deeper. The issue was not rocks and hunger. The issue was loyalty.

That's our example. Truth for lies. And it raises a challenging question: Have you filled your mind with enough "it is written" statements that you're prepared to combat the lies you face every day? When the world lies to you about what is important, do you have a response from God's Word? When the world says you have to be thin to be lovable, or you need a certain amount of money to be respectable, do you know what to say? Is your mind so filled with "it is written" truths that as soon as you hear the lie, you can respond quickly with the truth? If not, then it is time to get busy.

If the Son of God felt it was necessary to respond to Satan's specific lies with specific truths, what does that say about us? If anyone could have overcome through sheer willpower, it was Jesus. If anyone could have reached down into His own reservoir of personal strength and experienced victory, it was Jesus. If anyone could have engaged Satan in a battle of wits and logic, He could. But instead, He reached for truth. And truth was enough. Truth will always be enough for people who know the truth. It is the only weapon effective against the enslaving lies of our enemy.

My dad summed it up when he wrote, "Truth and freedom are constant companions. Where you find one, you will always find the other. Freedom in any area of life comes from discovering the truth about it."[1]

When you address the things that challenge your character with "it is written . . . ," you wield a sword against which no foe can stand. When you quote God's Word as it applies to your daily situations, you aren't just speaking on your own. You are a representative, a spokesperson, of the kingdom of God! You're backed by the full power and authority of the Creator of the universe, the Author of life Himself. When God speaks, every other voice in the universe is rendered speechless. That's why the truth, real truth, God's truth, has the power to set you free.

ROUND TWO

But Satan wasn't finished. He dared to enter the ring a second time. He took Jesus up on top of the temple, and he offered Him a chance to prove Himself to those below. And wouldn't you know it? He used the Scriptures to support his request, as if to say, "Okay, two can play that game." Don't miss the significance of that detail. Satan knows the Scripture well. Knowledge is not enough.

Once again, a lie was fueling the seemingly harmless request. I say "harmless" in that Jesus performed miracles throughout the Gospels to validate His message and identity. What would one more hurt? The problem was not so much the *request* as it was the *requester*.

The lie was as follows: "Jesus, You have the authority to call Your own shots, don't You?" To elaborate, "Jesus, it is okay to act out from under the authority of the Father. You're a big boy. Do something on Your own for a change."

But Jesus was a man under authority. On another occasion He made that clear when He said, "Most assuredly, I say to you, the Son can do nothing of Himself, but what He sees the Father do; for whatever He does, the Son also does" (John 5:19 NKJV).

Satan knew that. That was why he appealed to the Father's promise of provision as a decoy in order to lure Jesus out on His own. But notice what Jesus did. Instead of engaging in a theological debate about the true meaning of the passage that Satan quoted, He laid out another "it is written": "It is written, 'You shall not put the Lord your God to the test.'"

Jesus exposed the lie. And He countered with the truth. That is renewal at its best. Behind it all is a passion for character. A passion so strong that it fuels a deeper discipline and devotion to God's Word. And the result is a greater understanding of the whole counsel of God.

Interacting with the Scriptures at this level sensitizes your conscience to lies, half-truths, improper uses of Scripture, and misinterpretation of events. Filling your heart with the specific truths of God's Word prepares you for the daily onslaught of error. It will enable you to recognize the lies associated with the temptations hurled in your direction.

THE FINAL ROUND

Satan was desperate, so he took Jesus up to a high mountain and offered Him immediate control of all the kingdoms of the world. All He had to do was bow His knee for a brief moment of worship of Satan.

Satan offered Jesus a shortcut. In effect, Satan was saying, "Okay, Jesus, I'll make a deal with You. I know You came to earth to redeem the people of this world. And You know that at this moment this world is my kingdom. I'll trade You what You want for what I want. I'll trade You the kingdoms of this world for a moment of Your devotion. You can act as Lord of the nations, and I will be God. You won't have to wait. You can have it all now."

What was the lie? Apparently, Satan had the authority to give Jesus the kingdoms of this world. Jesus never questioned him on that. Satan was asking Jesus to reshuffle His values. The lie was that redemption of the world was of greater value than devotion to the Father. Both were important. But one took precedence over the other. And so Jesus responded appropriately, once again right out of the Scriptures.

Jesus said to him, "Begone, Satan! For it is written, 'You shall worship the Lord your God, and serve Him only.'"

Satan offered a good thing. Jesus opted for the best thing. He saw the fallacy in Satan's logic. He recognized the lie hidden behind the offer of power. And He exposed it with the specific truth of God's Word.

READY FOR BATTLE

How well are you equipped to combat the lies you face every day? When you are offered shortcuts, are you ready with an "it is written"? Do the responses pop right into your head and roll right off your tongue? Or do you stumble through these confrontations?

Chances are, you have memorized a few verses along the way. But are you equipped with the specific truths you need to combat the specific lies? What do you say when temptation stares you in the face? What about the areas where you're overly sensitive or the situations that strike fear in your heart? What do you say then? For instance, what about your character goals? Do you know any verses about honesty, purity, loyalty, love, and faithfulness?

Most of us know some general verses about God's love, about temptation and sin, about fear. But do you have a specific verse for the areas where you're consistently under attack? This is how men and women are set free. This is where we're turned loose to reach our potential in Christ. This process turns slag heaps into mountains of rock.

Renewing your mind is the catalyst for character development. Motivation isn't enough. Willpower won't get the job done. Surrounding yourself with good examples falls short. Renewal is the ticket. Nobody plans to fail in the arena of character. But many of us are guilty of failing to plan. To ignore the significance of what took place between Satan and our Savior on that desolate mountain two thousand years ago is to plan to fail.

Are you involved in the process of renewing your mind? You probably attend church. You may be involved in some midweek program. Both environments provide you with an opportunity to gather general truth that is applicable to your general life. But are you consciously, actively, relentlessly renewing your mind? It's incumbent upon you to get involved in the process.

BEGIN WITH GOALS

The place to begin is your character goals. Each goal represents a battle line. These are areas in which you desire to make progress or at least hold your own. More than likely, your character goals also represent areas in which you will be called upon to stand against the current of the culture. These are areas in which you will face constant temptation to compromise.

The following is a three-part exercise to help you identify the potential lies and the specific truths associated with each of your character goals. It may not be easy. But it is an exercise well worth the time and effort. Work through these three steps with at least one of your goals.

Step #1: Identify Obstacles

Begin by identifying and listing specific obstacles to one of your character goals. For instance, one of my goals is to be dependable. When I say I am going to do something, I want people to feel that they can count on me. So I asked, "What keeps me from being a dependable person?" One enemy of dependability is overcommitment. I have a tendency to overcommit myself. Why? Well, for years I said it was because I had a hard time saying no.

But then I asked myself, "Andy, why do you have a hard time saying no?"

"Well, because I don't want to hurt people's feelings."

"Why don't you want to hurt people's feelings?"

This was tough for me to admit. But the primary reason I didn't want to hurt people's feelings was that I didn't want people to think I wasn't a caring person. I have a difficult time saying no because of what people might think about me. A real obstacle to my dependability is an inordinate concern for approval. I was afraid I would lose people's approval if I said no.

The obstacles to your goals may be more obvious than that. Watching television may be an obstacle. A particular relationship may be an obstacle. An event in your past may trip you up. It could be any number of things. But write them down.

Step #2: Identify Lies

The second step is to identify the things in your belief system that keep you from overcoming the obstacles in your way. Write down the potential lies and false assumptions you are tempted to believe as they relate to each obstacle.

Going back to my original example, my inordinate desire for approval was bolstered by three silly lies:

1. Saying yes wins people's approval and respect.
2. People's approval determines my worth.
3. Approval is more important than balance.

Rooting out the lies behind behavior often defuses them because, for the most part, they are ridiculous. Saying yes doesn't win long-term approval or respect. Respect is based in character, not in doing people favors. I should have known that! Besides, when I wasn't able to follow through with what I had committed to do because I was overcommitted, people lost respect for me anyway.

Why do you do the things you do? What keeps you from dealing with the obstacles that stand between you and the character you desire? Ask yourself *why*. And once you have an answer, ask *why* again and again and again until you get down to the root of why you do the things you do. And there, hidden under layers of pseudoreasons, you will discover the lies that fuel your behavior.

Step #3: Identify the Truth

The third step is to find a verse or verses in your Bible that in some way counter the lies you have been believing. And once you have found them, commit them to memory.

When I suggest this step to adults, they almost always smile and say, "I can't memorize Scripture."

I say, "That is the first lie you need to deal with. Of course, you can memorize Scripture."

"No, you see, I have a terrible memory."

"Have you ever sung along while you listened to a song on the radio?"

"Yes."

"So what you're saying is that your brain has the capacity to memorize the lyrics of countless lines from songs and recall them on demand, but when it comes to Scripture, you just don't have enough brainpower?"

"That doesn't really make sense, does it?"

"No . . . because it's a lie."

Finding specific passages for your particular issues may be challenging, but don't give up. Your character is at stake. The verse I memorized to help me in the area of dependability was the passage I mentioned earlier regarding Jesus' commitment to do only what He saw the Father doing: John 5:19.

The truth is, my primary obligation is to do what my Father wants me to do, not what everybody else expects me to do. And if I will be sensitive to His leading and say no when I know I'm not supposed to be involved in something, then I will be able to fulfill my commitments. I will be dependable. God isn't going to lead me to do more than I am capable of doing. That means He will lead me to say no sometimes. Besides, if I have the Father's approval, that should be enough.

Now it is your turn:

- Choose a goal.
- Identify one obstacle.
- Look for the lie behind the obstacle.

- Excavate the truth.
- Commit it to memory.

Go!

Chapter Fourteen

PUTTING IT ALL TOGETHER

The integrity of the upright will guide them,
But the perversity of the unfaithful will
   destroy them.

—Proverbs 11:3 NKJV

When I was learning to play basketball as a kid, I remember my coach explaining the mechanics of the jump shot. "First," he said, "place one hand behind the ball and the other on the side of the ball. The hand behind the ball will propel the basketball while the hand on the side serves as a guide. Make sure your feet are a comfortable distance apart and perpendicular to the goal. Look at the rim. Bend your knees slightly. With the ball at chest level, use your arms and legs to propel you into the air. Release the ball at the highest point in your jump."

And throughout his explanation I was thinking, *Do what?* I just wanted to play basketball. How in the world did he expect me to keep all of that straight? By the time I thought through all the steps, the shot clock would have expired.

But in time, each step became part of a natural rhythm. Before long, I could shoot a well-executed jump shot without even thinking about it. The more I played, the less aware I was of the mechanics.

GOING THROUGH THE MOTIONS

In this chapter we will focus on the mechanics of "putting on the new." They may seem awkward and cumbersome at first. You may think there is a lot to remember. But in time, they can become a natural part of the rhythm of your life. Remember the apostle Paul's sobering words: "Do not be conformed to this world, but be transformed by the renewing of your mind" (Rom. 12:2).

Transformation of character requires renewal of the mind. Renewal is a lifestyle. Therefore, it requires some new habits. New habits always feel unnatural initially. Anytime we try something new, it feels somewhat uncomfortable and possibly intimidating.

Remember turning on a computer for the first time? Remember changing your first diaper? How about that first kiss? Think back to your first time behind the wheel of a car. What about your first experience with free weights? And how about that first step aerobics class?

After my first step aerobics class, my buddy and I went up to meet the teacher. There were about ninety people in the class, so I wanted to make sure he knew he had some newcomers. I introduced myself and told him that it was my first class. He smiled and said, "I know."

STARTING OUT

As you begin to apply the principles of renewal, you may feel that the whole thing is too contrived to have any authentic spiritual benefit. After all, it shouldn't be so complicated to become a person of character, should it? Shouldn't things get better naturally?

Well, actually, no, they shouldn't. When you take into account the world we live in, the families we grew up in, the pain we have experienced, and our propensity toward sin, we have to overcome a great deal of negative inertia. Our natural drift is toward selfishness, not Christlikeness. Expecting that you can drift effortlessly toward Christlikeness is paramount to believing that you can drift effortlessly up the Colorado River. It's not going to happen.

The good news is, it will take only one or two positive experiences with renewal to convince you that it is worth the effort.

Learning to ride a bicycle is almost always a painful experience. Knees and elbows bear the marks of courage and determination. But that initial experience of freedom, that first solo flight of twenty or thirty yards, is enough to convince any kid that it will be worth the effort (and pain) in the end.

HANDLING THE TRUTH

I am going to give you four practical tips to help you "put on the new." Remember, the goal is to effectively counter the specific lies that have infiltrated your belief system.

1. Speak the Truth Out Loud

People often ask me, "Can the devil read our minds?" I don't think so. I can't read anyone's mind, but I can sometimes guess what someone is thinking. The better you know someone, the easier it is to predict his thoughts and actions as well as influence his thoughts and actions. The devil doesn't need to be able to read our minds to influence what we think.

For that reason, you need to speak the truths of God's Word out loud. Jesus felt that it was necessary to say out loud, "It is written." He didn't look at the devil and meditate. He didn't try to stare Satan down. He spoke the truth right out loud, "It is written. . . ." You would be wise to do the same.

Volume isn't the issue. You don't have to shout it. Just say it.

Hearing Is Believing

Something powerful happens when you verbalize truth in the face of temptation or discouragement because truth is powerful. Truth moves you beyond the realm of interpretation and assumption into the realm of reality. Truth takes your emotions and subjugates them to what is real. Your feelings are wonderful followers. They are terrible leaders.

This is why the psalms are so powerful. Here we find David's natural interpretation of the events and circumstances surrounding him. Included as well are all the emotions that we would expect someone in his situation to feel. Then we read as he subjects his thoughts and fears to the test of truth.

David was not content to make it a mental exercise. As a musician, he had experienced the power of truth verbalized. By verbalizing his internal battle, he gained perspective and strength. He moved the battle from the internal world of subjectivity into the realm of objective reality. Sure, his enemies were all around him. Yes, there were times when all seemed lost. Yet in the midst of all of that, David wrote,

> *But as for me, I shall sing of Thy strength;*
> *Yes, I shall joyfully sing of Thy lovingkindness in the morning,*
> *For Thou hast been my stronghold,*
> *And a refuge in the day of my distress.*
> *O my strength, I will sing praises to Thee;*
> *For God is my stronghold, the God who shows me lovingkindness*
> (Ps. 59:16–17)

Verbalizing truth reshuffles your emotions. Truth frees you to feel appropriately. It casts a light of reality over emotions that are stirred up by lies, misunderstandings, and inaccurate interpretations of the circumstances.

Truth and Character

It is difficult to be honest if you are afraid of the outcome. It is difficult to be accountable if you are worried that someone might lose respect for you. It is difficult to maintain purity if you feel that there are no consequences.

Spoken truth has a way of neutralizing misleading feelings. Truth deflates the swelling emotions that push you in self-destructive directions. Speaking the truth brings needed perspective to your panicking soul.

Sandra and I have a friend who grew up in a home where she received almost no verbal affirmation. Most of what she was told was destructive. Needless to say, her self-esteem was in serious need of an overhaul. She became a Christian in her early forties. Slowly, she began to accept the fact that her heavenly Father really did accept and love her.

Unfortunately, she worked in an environment that reinforced most of what she heard while she was growing up. Everything was negative. She was made to feel as if she couldn't do anything right. No praise. No gratitude. Just griping and complaining.

We tried unsuccessfully to help her find another job. And over time she resigned herself to the fact that God must have her there for a reason. Once she settled that issue, she began looking for ways to cope with the criticism.

I suggested she think through what was being said about her at work to make sure there wasn't something she could do to improve her relationship with the people in her office. She came up with a couple of ideas, but nothing significant changed. Next, I asked her to write down the emotional messages her coworkers were sending her. An emotional message is what we feel someone is saying about us. This is a sampling from her list:

- "You're worthless."
- "You're incompetent."
- "You're stupid."

Every day was full of rejection. Add that to the scars from her past, and you can imagine the emotional shape she was in.

Once she was able to identify and isolate the specific emotional messages she was receiving, she knew at once that they were lies. She was mature enough in her faith to know that she wasn't worthless. She was overqualified for her job, so she knew she wasn't incompetent. And she would have never gotten her job to begin with if she had been stupid.

Realizing that they were all lies was helpful. But it wasn't enough. Next, she went to the Scriptures to dig out a handful of truths she could use to counter the untrustworthy messages she was receiving in daily doses. Here is a sampling of the verses she chose:

But God demonstrates His own love toward us, in that while we were still sinners, Christ died for us. (Rom. 5:8 NKJV)

For you have been bought with a price: therefore glorify God in your body. (1 Cor. 6:20)

There is therefore now no condemnation for those who are in Christ Jesus. (Rom. 8:1)

I will give thanks to Thee, for I am fearfully and wonderfully made; Wonderful are Thy works, And my soul knows it very well. (Ps. 139:14)

All day long she would say these verses out loud, just under her breath. Every time she was made to feel unworthy: "I have been bought with a price." Every time she was made to feel stupid: "I am fearfully and wonderfully made." When feelings of rejection swelled up in her: "While I was still a sinner, Christ died for me."

For three years, that was her daily routine. Nothing in her office environment changed. Nobody expressed appreciation for her character and patience. But when God finally led her out, she was a different woman. As I listened to her share the details of what happened in her office, I often wondered how I would have responded to that much criticism. She would be the first to tell you that it was only through constant renewal that she was able to survive and prosper. Such is the power of spoken truth.

2. Personalize the Truth

Second, when putting on the new, you need to personalize the truth. This involves quoting the truths of Scripture in the first person. For example, one of my character goals is purity. Almost every day I receive an emotional message that makes me feel as if I have no choice but to entertain whatever impure thoughts pop into my mind. The passage I have committed to memory to counter these feelings is from Paul's letter to the church in Corinth: "We are destroying speculations and every lofty thing raised up against the knowledge of God, and we are taking every thought captive to the obedience of Christ" (2 Cor. 10:5).

When I quote this verse, I put it in the first person: "I am destroying speculations and every lofty thing raised up against the knowledge of God, and I am taking every thought captive to the obedience of Christ."

This is a powerful verse. The term *speculations* can refer to the "I wonder what it would be like . . ." scenarios our minds are prone to latch onto, for example:

- "I wonder what it would be like to be married to him?"
- "I wonder what it would be like to own one of those?"
- "I wonder what it would be like to watch that?"

Another verse in my purity category is found in Paul's letter to the church in Rome: "So then, brethren, we are under obligation, not to the flesh, to live according to the flesh" (Rom. 8:12).

Again, when I quote this verse, I put it in the first person: "I am not under obligation to the flesh to live according to the flesh."

3. Pray the Truth

The third way to "put on the new" is to incorporate your hand-picked truths into your prayers. As I mentioned earlier, one of my character goals is loyalty, especially as it relates to friends. One of my verses for loyalty focuses on what I say about people: "Let no unwholesome word proceed from your mouth, but only such a word as is good for edification according to the need of the moment, that it may give grace to those who hear" (Eph. 4:29).

Often, I pray, "Lord, today it is my desire that no unwholesome word proceed out of my mouth. Let every word I speak be edifying according to the need of the moment that it may give grace to those who hear."

When you incorporate these truths into your prayers, you're voicing your acceptance of the truth to God. You're embracing the truth in His presence. Your prayers become a visible and audible expression of your agreement with His plan for your character.

4. Meditate on the Truth

The fourth way to "put on the new" is to meditate on the truth. My father taught me to do this when I was very young. It is not something he suggested I do. Instead, it was something I heard him talk about. He used to say, "Andy, the last thing I think about at night before I go to sleep is the truth." He would choose a verse or a part of a verse and rehearse it in his mind over and over until he fell asleep.

King David had a similar nightly ritual. In several places throughout the Psalms, he mentioned meditating on God's Word as he lay in bed at night:

> *When I remember Thee on my bed,*
> *I meditate on Thee in the night watches.* (Ps. 63:6)

Throughout the Psalms, David referred to his habit of meditation:

> *How blessed is the man who does not walk in the counsel of*
> *the wicked,*
> *Nor stand in the path of sinners,*
> *Nor sit in the seat of scoffers!*
> *But his delight is in the law of the LORD,*
> *And in His law he meditates day and night.* (Ps. 1:1–2)

So what about that daytime meditation he noted? If you are like me, you don't have much discretionary time to sit around and meditate on anything. Other than bedtime, the only consistent time I have to meditate is in the car. I write down my memory/meditation verses on little cards and put them somewhere on my dashboard. This has been my habit for eleven years. I have memorized dozens of verses while driving. Some of my most helpful insights have come as a result of memorizing and meditating in the car.

NEW HABITS

This was not meant to be a "Four Steps to Successful Christian Living" chapter. These four suggestions are not steps to take. They are habits to develop. And *develop* implies process.

Begin by developing your arsenal of verses. Then start committing them to memory. If you are like most people, the problem is not a lack of ability. The problem is our failure to give priority to memorizing Scripture. Granted, it is not the easiest task we will undertake. But it may very well be one of the most important. If we are going to "put on the new," we need to have something new to put on.

A NEW LEVEL OF FREEDOM

Jesus reiterated the importance of having something new to put on in a discussion with a group of Jews who had believed in Him. Jesus explained the process of renewal this way: "If you abide in My word, then you are truly disciples of Mine; and you shall know the truth, and the truth shall make you free" (John 8:31–32).

An equation in this passage is so simple and yet so profound:

> Immerse yourself in My teaching
> <u>+ Discover the truth</u>
> Be made free

The English word *abide* is translated from a Greek word meaning "to remain" or "stay." It is used in other places in the Bible to refer to a specific geographical location:

And whatever house you enter, stay *there, and take your leave from there.* (Luke 9:4, emphasis mine)
After this He went down to Capernaum, He and His mother, and His brothers, and His disciples; and there they stayed *a few days.* (John 2:12, emphasis mine)

Jesus' point in John 8:31–32 is that His followers ought to "stay" or "remain" in His Word. In the same way we would encourage someone on a diet to "stay with it," so Jesus exhorts us: "Don't give up. Don't grow weary. Don't drift away. Stay in My Word!"

If we remain in His Word, we will "know the truth." Now, this is different from "hearing" the truth or being "told" the truth. And I don't believe Jesus is referring to a general knowledge of the Bible. He does not promise that we will get any smarter. He promises freedom. And freedom comes when the specific truths of His Word cast a revealing light upon the lies that support our attitudes and emotions.

MY FIRST ENCOUNTER

When I was in my midtwenties, it came to my attention that I had a habit of lying about my involvement in sports while in high school. When people asked me if I played any sports in high school, I always said, "Yes, I ran track and played soccer."

Now technically, that was true. While I was in high school, I did run around the track, and I did play soccer. What I didn't tell them was that both activities took place during PE. I was never on either the soccer or the track team at good old Tucker High School.

Every time I told that lie, I felt terrible. But I could not bring myself to look somebody in the eye and say, "No, I never participated in any team sports." The pattern had been going on for years. I would promise myself I wouldn't do it again. But over and over again, I would lie.

Finally, during my third year in seminary—of all places—something happened that forced me to deal with this character flaw. A friend of mine rushed up to me at church and said, "Andy, I think I've worked it out for you to be the chaplain for the SMU football team!"

He was so excited. And I felt like throwing up. The thought of being in a locker room full of football players terrified me. It was worse than fear. It was dread. That was when I knew I had a real problem. I saw a connection between my lying lips and my quivering knees.

After a week or so of real soul-searching, I hit upon the root of my problem. I believed a lie. Somewhere along the way I had begun believing that to be a real, respectable, worthwhile man, I had to have accomplished something athletically. In fact, as I thought through my athletic experiences in high school, a very short process I might add, I remembered an unpleasant incident that took place during my eighth-grade year.

COUNT ME OUT

I was trying out for our eighth-grade basketball team along with every other eighth grader in the school. There were three cuts. I had made the first two. On the night our coach was to make his final decision we were playing a scrimmage game. I took a shot from the corner and missed everything. From across the floor, Coach Mac yelled out, "Stanley, you've got no backbone." And he cut me from the team.

That was the last time I tried out for anything. That was the last time I ever attempted anything competitive. The emotional message I received that night was, "Stanley, you don't have what it takes to compete. Don't bother trying."

So I didn't.

Twelve years later I was still working from a script written by a coach who really didn't know anything about me. I considered myself an athletic failure based on one traumatic experience in the eighth grade. I know it sounds ridiculous. But well-placed lies are powerful. They can chart our course for a lifetime if we let them.

When I realized what had happened, I got busy replacing those lies with truth. In a short amount of time, I was free. Athletes no longer intimidated me. I didn't feel compelled to lie about my athletic accomplishments. Before long, I could laugh about my lack of athletic prowess. Years later I was invited to do a chapel service for the Atlanta Hawks. I remember walking into that room full of giants and thinking, *We've come a long way, haven't we, Lord?*

YOUR PART, HIS PART

God is going to use a variety of things to shape your character. In most cases your only responsibility will be to trust Him and remain faithful. Renewal is the exception. The principle of renewal allows you to be proactive in your pursuit of character. It gives you a place to start. Renewal is your way of working alongside the Holy Spirit as He endeavors to conform your character to that of the Lord Jesus.

You know what you want to become. You have surfaced some of the lies standing in your way. I hope that you have started developing a list of verses that communicate the truths you need to focus on. Now, start quoting them out loud. Personalize them. Pray through them. And turn off that radio and start meditating on them. And in the end, you will no longer be conformed to this world; you will be transformed.

Chapter Fifteen

UNFINISHED BUSINESS

In politics, as in life, it's better to be a skeleton in a grave, than to have one in your closet.

—Anonymous

The idea of *becoming* men and women of character directs our thoughts toward the future. It allows us to take our eyes off what we are for the moment and focus them on what we hope to become. Suddenly, change seems like a real possibility. So we set our sights on tomorrow with every intention of putting the past behind us.

Unfortunately, we can't really leave the past behind us until we have dealt with the unfinished business of the past. Becoming men and women of character involves taking responsibility for the past.

SURPRISE!

That idea comes as a surprise to some people. When you get involved in renewing your mind, you may be tempted to think only about the present and the future. You may think that God wants you to act differently now and to plan to be different in the future. But character also involves taking responsibility for how you behaved yesterday. At some point in your journey, God is going to call on you to turn and take responsibility for your past. It never fails.

Unresolved relationships, neglected debts, apologies never made—these are the things God will eventually lead you back around to. Chances are, there are things you wish you had never said. But once you said them, you never went back to apologize. In the past you have probably hurt or offended people. And many of them still carry wounds that a sincere apology would help to heal.

As you will see in this chapter, part of becoming a man or woman of character is turning back and assuming responsibility for past behavior. Character is not simply about where you are now. Neither is it only about where you are headed. Often, moving forward means going back.

GOD MAKES ALL THINGS NEW; YOU MAKE ALL THINGS RIGHT

"Wait a minute," you say, "God has forgiven me. All things have become new in Christ. I'm a new creature. God gave me a brand-new beginning. I wasn't even a Christian then."

Or perhaps you are thinking, *I was a Christian, but I didn't know any better. Besides, I don't think God wants me to get all tangled up in the things in my past.*

According to God's Word, allowing God to work in you requires having the courage and the faith to turn and take responsibility for the past. God has made all things new. But that in no way relieves you of your responsibility to make things right with people you have mistreated.

STOP THE SERVICE! SOMETHING IS NOT RIGHT!

The importance of dealing with the past is one of Jesus' themes in His famous Sermon on the Mount (Matt. 5). In this one, amazing sermon, Jesus challenged all the major tenets of His audience's belief system. One by one, He went charging through all their misconceptions about God, about worship, and about their laws. Then

He went back and put things together the way God originally intended.

In this passage, we find our instructions about how to deal with our past. What Jesus said about making things right may come as a shock to us. But it was even more astounding to the people of His day. Jesus seemed to equate the importance of being right with others to being right with the Father: "If therefore you are presenting your offering at the altar, and there remember that your brother has something against you, leave your offering there before the altar, and go your way; first be reconciled to your brother, and then come and present your offering" (Matt. 5:23–24).

I can imagine someone in Jesus' audience thinking, *Now wait a minute. That can't be! After I've walked all the way to the temple, after I've stood in line for hours, after I've gone to all the trouble of finding an acceptable sacrifice, I'm supposed to leave? He wants me to tie up my lamb or hand off my pigeon, just to make peace with someone who is mad at me?*

UNDERSTANDING PRIORITIES

That was new. Worse than new, it was terribly inconvenient. And besides, it didn't make a whole lot of sense. The Jewish believers of that day believed their relationship with God was the ultimate priority. They assumed God would be more interested in getting things right with Him than in getting things right with someone else. And if you are honest, you probably feel the same way. After all, aren't we to put God first in our lives? Isn't He supposed to be our priority? Certainly, we should be concerned about our relationships with others, but surely, it could wait until after church!

But Jesus comes along in His characteristic fashion and reverses everything. In effect He says our relationship with the heavenly Father hinges on our relationships with other people. The two are inseparable. He seems to imply that our ability to worship Him sincerely and fellowship with Him unashamedly is contingent upon our relationships with others, including people we have offended or hurt in some way.

The truth is, you cannot resolve your differences with the Father if you are unwilling to resolve your differences with others. You cannot be in fellowship with the Father and out of fellowship with others over something you have done. The two go hand in hand.

The Greek term translated "reconcile" in this passage appears only once in the entire New Testament. In other Greek literature this same word is commonly translated "change." Essentially, Jesus is saying, "I want you to leave your gift, and go and change things with the person who has something against you. Do whatever it takes to resolve your differences so that when you come back, your conscience is clear. Get things worked out with that person first. Then come and do business with Me."

"A NEW COMMANDMENT I GIVE TO YOU"

The question that begs to be asked is, "Why can't God just forgive us and let us go on?" The answer is found in a statement Jesus made to His disciples during His final moments on earth: "A new commandment I give to you, that you love one another, even as I have loved you, that you also love one another" (John 13:34).

Remember what happened when a group of Jewish leaders asked Jesus which commandment was the most important in all of Jewish law? Jesus said that the entire law could be summed up in the statement, "Love God with all your heart, soul, and mind; and love your neighbor as yourself." The practical side of character is all about loving others. The Christian faith is built on the premise of *others first*. After all, people are going to know we are Christians because of our love for one another.

It is impossible to be right with God while neglecting this command. There is something insincere about a man or woman who repeatedly tells God how much he or she loves Him while refusing to obey Him. From God's perspective, loving God with all our hearts and loving our neighbors are inseparable. To love God is to keep His commands. He has commanded us to love. And by the way, it doesn't stop with loving our neighbors. Jesus went so far as to say we are to love our enemies (Luke 6:27).

The type of love Jesus is talking about has nothing to do with how we feel. After all, we certainly can't be expected to have fond feelings toward an enemy. This is that "do" kind of love. The issue here is how we treat our neighbors and how we treat our enemies. We are commanded to say and do things that demonstrate love.

As Jesus spoke that day to the crowds gathered on the hillside, I'm sure He sensed their amazement at the new hierarchy of values. They could barely fathom that their relationships with one another were so vital to their relationship with the Father.

Jesus' audience isn't the only group that needs to be reminded of this important link. Believers today have lost sight of this relationship as well. We tend to compartmentalize our lives into categories that allow us to separate our walk with God from our walk with others. But no such separation exists. To neglect one is to hinder the other. Consequently, going forward with God often involves going back to someone in the past.

ADDICTED TO GRACE

Part of the confusion in this area stems from a misapplication of grace. When you became a Christian, you came face-to-face with the unconditional, undeserved grace of God. If you were like me, you were overwhelmed to realize that you could do nothing to earn your forgiveness or salvation. It was a gift. Period. Nothing you did had any merit. Your good deeds did not, and could not, earn you a good standing with God.

Now, that may be true as it relates to your relationship with God. But it is not true as it relates to your relationship with others. God has forgiven you, but people you have wronged in the past may not have. They may very well be held hostage to bitterness and anger over what you did to them.

You are kidding yourself if you think that all the people you have wronged have simply forgiven you and gone on with their lives. Sure, that is what they ought to do. But if you did what you ought to do, they wouldn't have anything to forgive you for in the first place.

You are kidding yourself as well if you think you have no responsibility for making restitution. The grace that was showered on you at salvation did not provide you with an escape hatch from your responsibility to others. On the contrary, the grace that was extended to you should compel you to make restitution to those you have wronged. Christ paid a debt He did not owe and one you could not pay. That kind of love should motivate you to pay the debts you can pay to those you owe.

The penalty for your sins insofar as heaven and hell are concerned has been dealt with once and for all. The consequences of your sins are a different matter altogether. You are avoiding the clear teaching of Scripture to use your forgiveness as an excuse to avoid the pain and embarrassment of reconciling with others. It is true that you can never repay God for all He has done for you. But you may certainly be able to repay in part those you have wronged.

MAKING THINGS RIGHT

One of the best illustrations of restitution is found in the story of Zacchaeus. Nobody seemed to catch on to the concept more quickly and thoroughly than he did. We usually have a cute little picture in our minds when we think of Zacchaeus. He was the "wee little man" who climbed the tree because he couldn't see Jesus over the crowd. But Zacchaeus had been a wicked man. He had wronged many people. He had a lot of unresolved relationships. And when Jesus invited Himself to eat at Zacchaeus's house that day, Zacchaeus was changed instantly. He knew he was forgiven. Jesus loved him in spite of his wicked past. Zacchaeus was given a clean slate. All things were made new.

Notice Zacchaeus's reaction. He decided to give half of his goods to the poor. And that was just for starters. He promised to make restitution to those he had cheated: "If I have defrauded anyone of anything, I will give back four times as much" (Luke 19:8).

Jesus didn't say, "Oh, no, no, no, Zacchaeus! You're forgiven. You see, old things have passed away. Behold, all things have become new. You just need to move on from here. You don't have to worry about any of that."

Jesus interpreted Zacchaeus's generosity as evidence of his conversion. Zacchaeus understood that following Christ wasn't just about the present. And it wasn't just about the future. It involved taking responsibility for the past as well.

MOVING ON

In your pursuit of Christlikeness, you will be led back to people with whom you have unresolved conflicts. That's part of becoming a person of character. From time to time God is going to tell you to leave your sacrifice, get up from your pew, and deal with your past.

A vital part of your walk with God is your relationships with other people. Part of walking with Him is making that call you dread making, setting up that appointment you know will be so incredibly awkward, writing the letter that you should have written long ago. It means humbling yourself, owning up to your part of the problem, and doing everything within your power to make those relationships right. Until you are willing to face your past, you will be unable to progress past certain roadblocks in your pursuit of character.

UNAVOIDABLE AND PAINFUL

Owning up to the past is unavoidable and painful, so painful that we are reluctant to believe that God would call on us to do such a thing. When thoughts of restitution and reconciliation start running through your head, you may blame them on an overly sensitive conscience. And they may disappear for a few weeks or a month. But then you hear a sermon or run into somebody, and suddenly, they are back.

In fact, reading this chapter may have elicited some uncomfortable memories for you. Memories you have worked hard to put behind you. Unresolved relationships that you would just as soon leave unresolved. Unpaid debts that you are sure were written off and forgotten long ago. And you may blame me or this book for bringing it all around again. But Jesus said, "Go . . . be reconciled to your brother."

Reconciliation and restitution are parts of the character-building process. Sure, they are painful. Yes, they are inconvenient. Embarrassing? Absolutely humiliating at times. But think about this. Your Savior suffered a painful, inconvenient, and terribly humiliating death on a Roman cross for the sake of past and future sins. And they weren't even His own. He took responsibility for the sins of the whole world. He died so that all men and women could be reconciled to the Father.

Let's face it. In the shadow of the Cross all our excuses, all our griping, and all our rationalization amount to nothing. We really have no excuse. His reconciling death was for our good. His instruction to us regarding our responsibility to reconcile is for our good. He loves us. To say no now is to resist the love of the One who has shown in unmistakable ways that He has our best interests in mind.

Maybe you have an ex-wife or ex-husband who calls you all the time and rakes you over the coals about several things. And most of them aren't true, but one of them is. And it's something you have never really owned up to. Or maybe on your way out of your former place of employment, you took some things that didn't belong to you. You justified your actions by the mistreatment you experienced there. Or you had a business associate, and one day you lost your temper and said some really nasty things. And everyone who heard it knows you're a Christian. But you have never apologized. Are you forgiven? Absolutely. Is it your responsibility to own up to your actions? Yes, it is.

Of course, you don't have to follow through. God is not going to put a leash around your neck and drag you into submission. But there are some stiff consequences associated with disobedience in this area.

FROM RELATIONSHIP TO RITUAL

Ignoring God's promptings to reconcile has an automatic impact on the sincerity of your worship and service. You are covering something up. You have put up an OFF-LIMITS sign. You cannot withhold an area of your life and worship God in Spirit and in truth. You cannot be the kind of worshiper He seeks while refusing to deal with the issues of reconciliation and restitution.

You can go through the motions, but something will be missing. Whenever you put up an OFF-LIMITS sign, your worship and service become superficial. You replace fellowship with activity.

THE IMPACT ON INTIMACY

Refusing to deal with the past will eventually have an impact on current and future relationships as well. I see this all the time in second and third marriages. When a man or woman moves into a new marriage without first owning up to a share of the failure in a previous marriage, there is always a price to pay.

Intimacy is always an issue in this scenario. Unresolved relational conflicts almost always affect an individual's ability to experience genuine intimacy. And the tendency is to blame the problem on current relationships rather than take responsibility for past ones.

When we harbor sin, we continually have to cover for ourselves. After all, what would happen if people knew? What if they found out? So we hide. And the walls of protection we develop to keep our past in keep others out. And often those we love the most are shut out.

"I ONCE HAD A FRIEND WHO WAS A CHRISTIAN"

Another consequence of leaving old business unfinished is that it misrepresents God to people outside the faith. Many nonbelievers have chosen to remain so because they knew, did business with, or lived next door to Christians. And the whole experience left a bad taste in their mouths.

When a believer harms a nonbeliever in any way and never comes back to assume responsibility for the behavior, the consequences can have eternal ramifications. I have met scores of non-Christians who are quick to blame their unbelief on their interaction with another Christian. Granted, the stories are generally smoke screens for a different issue. But it is a shame that they would even have the stories to tell.

Reconciliation is not limited to our brothers and sisters in the faith. It may be even more important to apply this teaching to nonbelievers. Asking forgiveness and reconciling relationships are at the heart of the gospel. What better way to demonstrate and illustrate our message?

FANNING THE FLAMES OF BITTERNESS

But perhaps the worst consequence of our unwillingness to own up to our responsibility is that it often fuels the fires of bitterness and anger in someone else's life. For many who have been hurt and whose souls are filled with the self-destructive fury of anger, a word of apology or acknowledgment could set them free.

All they would need to be released from eroding forces of bitterness is for the one who has hurt them to go to them and make it right. To say to them, "I know I could never repay you fully. I know I can't make this go away, but I'm here to let you know, I'm responsible, and I'm sorry. And if there is something I can do about it, I'm willing to do it."

TURN IT AROUND

To fully appreciate the impact of this teaching, turn it around. Just imagine how you would feel if you got a surprise visit from someone in your past who had hurt you and never made it right. Think for a moment about someone who has hurt you deeply and has never come to you to apologize. How would you feel if she walked in, sat down, and took full responsibility for what she did?

Maybe it would be your dad calling to say, "I know I'll never be able to make up to you what I've taken from you as a father. But I want you to know I'm sorry. Would you please forgive me?" It could be a former boss or an employee who quit and then trashed your name throughout your industry. It may be somebody that you have always avoided because of how angry he made you. How would you be affected if he looked you up and apologized?

Can you imagine the healing? That's exactly why God has called you to take responsibility for your past. It is possible that you hold in your hands and in your words the key to healing for a wounded soul. God's forgiveness does not exempt you from this responsibility. On the contrary, His forgiveness is the reason to deal with it. God paid a high price to reconcile you to Him. And now He is calling on you to pay the price to reconcile yourself to others.

THE HARD WAY

Not only can it be painful when God brings these things to mind, but it can be awkward, too. Several years ago I was preaching for my dad while he was out of town. I was talking about being blameless. And I said something like, "If you are truly blameless, then you can stand up to any scrutiny. The president could ask you to be the attorney general, and you'd sail through the confirmation hearings without a glitch because your record is clean."

Just as I said that, I felt as if God thumped me on the back of the head and brought an unresolved relationship to my mind. Actually, it wasn't the first time He had reminded me of the particular incident. About every three or four months I would get a gentle reminder. But that one wasn't gentle. I almost lost my train of thought right in the middle of the sermon. I remember thinking, *Lord, this is not the time!*

I made it through the sermon and then went back into my dad's office to have my usual song-and-dance prayer with God to get Him off my back. And as usual, the conviction went away—but not for long.

A few days later, I was having my quiet time. And I couldn't pray. All I could think about was a man with whom I knew God wanted me to straighten things out. I tried to resist it. I said, "Okay, God, You've forgiven me. Now I want to pray for Sandra and the kids. . . ." But that didn't work. It was as if God was saying, "Andy, you're not blameless. You're hiding something." And I remember thinking, *But it's complicated, and it was so long ago, and it is probably no big deal by now.* On and on I went. But the impression was too strong. I finally concluded that it would be a lot easier to deal with it than to continue arguing with God.

So I got in my car without the slightest idea of what I was going to do. I just had to make things right with the fellow. I drove to his house. Then I drove past his house. Then I drove past his house again. It took me a long time to get up the nerve to stop. I can't recall another time in my adult life when I have been so nervous about something. I didn't know if he would be angry or if he would think I was crazy. For all I knew, he would call the police.

Finally, I parked in the driveway, walked up to the door, and rang the doorbell, hoping nobody would answer. He came to the door and looked at me with the most confusing look you can imagine. And rightly so. I had never been to his house before. We were never close friends. And I hadn't seen him in years. "Andy?" he said. "What in the world are you doing way out here? Come on in."

I was dying. He didn't have a clue why I was there, which meant he didn't know what I had done. Otherwise he would have thrown me off his property, or so I thought. And to make matters worse, his wife was there. I was hoping I could talk to him and let him pass the news along to her. But no such luck.

As soon as I sat down, I blurted out, "I've come to apologize." He just stared at me. He still didn't know. I said it again, primarily because I was afraid if I didn't start talking, I would lose my nerve. I told him what I had done. And I told him how sorry I was.

He just stared at me. If he had stood up and knocked me across the room, I think I would have felt 100 percent better. I certainly deserved it. I told him that, too. Any response from him was totally justified in my mind.

When I finished, he smiled and said, "You know, I had a feeling it was you." His wife was in tears. She nodded her head in agreement.

Now you have to understand, I had carried the burden for years. All along, he had a hunch that I was behind an event that had caused him a great deal of pain and expense. And as long as I live, I'll never forget what the gentleman said at the end of our conversation. He said, "Andy, this makes me feel good all over."

I saw release in his and his wife's eyes. I believe they had already forgiven me. They even said so. But when I owned up to what I had done, it was as if the healing process was complete. We all had a good cry, and I left.

For someone out there, you hold the last piece of a puzzle he has been attempting to complete for a long time. He has struggled to forgive. He has tried to move past what happened. But your owning up to your responsibility may allow him to really move on with his life.

But even if that is not the case, Jesus says, "Be reconciled to your brother."

THE BENCHMARK OF CHARACTER

Daniel is a wonderful example of someone who kept his nose clean. Daniel was living in exile in Babylon, and he had become a favorite counselor of the king. The king was so impressed by Daniel, he wanted to put him in charge of the whole kingdom.

One day the king called him in and said, "Daniel, of all the 120 government officials in my kingdom, you are the most competent to rule. I'm putting you in charge of everything."

That made 119 other leaders jealous. They decided to try to dig up some dirt on Daniel to share with the king. Their plan was to sabotage Daniel's promotion.

Those 119 fellows had access to all the gossip, all the rumors, all the information needed to get the scoop on anybody in the kingdom. They split up and looked for dirt. Then they came back together, and Daniel 6 reports what happened:

> *So the governors and satraps sought to find some charge against Daniel concerning the kingdom; but they could find no charge or fault, because he was faithful; nor was there any error or fault found in him. Then these men said, "We shall not find any charge against this Daniel unless we find it against him concerning the law of his God."* (Dan. 6:4–5 NKJV)

Think of it. They couldn't find a single negative thing on him. The most influential men in the city, and they came up empty. That's the benchmark of Christian character. The only thing they could pin on him was his devotion to God. There were no loose ends in Daniel's life.

God has called you to that standard. Character is as much about the past as it is the present and the future. Your past relationships cast an inescapable shadow over your fellowship with the Father. Before you seek to take another step in God's direction, you may need to take a step of reconciliation toward someone else. Maybe the time has come to make that call, write that letter, visit that old acquaintance. And as you step out in faith and humility, know that in doing so you may be unlocking the gate that leads to healing for you and the one you wronged. Your going back may set you and others free to move ahead.

Chapter Sixteen

LETTING GO OF THE PAST

The right response can take the most painful memory and make it a blessing. The wrong response can end up being very destructive.

—Dr. Charles F. Stanley

Paris, the son of King Priam, seemed to have endured the siege. The dusty battlefields surrounding the city walls were empty. After several days of intense fighting, Troy had stood its ground. Unable to break through the Trojans' perimeter defense, the last of the retreating Greeks could be seen boarding their ships in the distance and heading out to sea. All the citizens breathed a sigh of relief.

As the soldiers stood atop the fortress, surveying the damage, their eyes were drawn to a strange object that stood outside the entrance to the city. Curiosity spread throughout the ranks as the people huddled in turrets and around portal windows to see it. It was the figure of a large animal. But what did it mean?

The High Council held a meeting to consider the matter. After some deliberation, they concluded that the defeated Greeks had left behind the large wooden horse as a gift to symbolize their full surrender to a superior foe. It was a suitable gesture, considering the casualties Troy had endured. The Greeks' visit had come at great expense to the Trojan army and Troy's citizens. They were entitled to some token of restitution. The horse was rightfully theirs.

The city gates were opened. A garrison of soldiers was dispatched to wheel the horse inside. Its workmanship was fine. The people gathered around to admire the artistry of their new trophy. It would make a stately monument to commemorate the long-awaited moment of victory. Within the safety of the walls, a celebration broke out. The people danced and feasted late into the night until their exhaustion brought peaceful sleep throughout the city.

Then the plot was revealed. In the silence of the early dawn, the wooden horse stirred to life. A secret door swung open. Slowly, a human head peered out. The coast was clear. One by one, a squad of Greek soldiers emerged from inside the horse and disappeared into the shadows of Troy. Each took his assigned position and readied for the attack.

The entire Greek fleet had quietly returned, and soldiers now encircled the unsuspecting city in full force. When the signal was given, the gates were flung open, and the attacking Greeks marched in with little resistance. A slaughter ensued. Many of the Trojan women, including members of the royal family, were carried off into captivity. Troy was ruined. The same horse that had stood as their monument of victory had become the instrument of their defeat.

STRONGHOLDS WITHIN

A Trojan horse sits just outside the gate of your heart. Its name is bitterness. It is a monument to every attack you have endured from your fellow human beings. It is a gift left by the people who have wronged you. It is a monument to the pain, the sorrow, and the devastation they have caused you. It represents the debt they will owe you until the day they are brought to justice. It is rightfully yours.

But to accept the gift is to invite ruin into your life. You see, there is more to the horse than meets the eye. The feeling of justification it brings is the deceptive artistry of a master craftsman. Though decorated with the promise of vindication, it is only a lure. The celebration is short-lived. Once inside the walls of your heart, it releases its agents of destruction. Its plot quietly unfolds from the inside out. To become a person of character, you must learn to recognize the Trojan horse of bitterness. And more important, you must never bring it inside.

STANDING WATCH

Owning up to your past is a fundamental step toward developing character. To keep a growing, honest relationship with God, you need to take responsibility for the people you have hurt. But what about the people who have hurt you? Chances are, the fallout from these painful interchanges will create an even greater obstacle in your pursuit of character. Unresolved hurt is the most difficult obstacle to overcome. It keeps sincere Christians running in place for years. Unable to make any progress, many either cling to the lie of, "That's just the way I am," or give up altogether.

In his book *Forgiveness,* my dad writes, "A person who has an unforgiving spirit is always the real loser, much more so than the one against whom the grudge is held."[1]

Unresolved hurt opens the gate of your heart to the destructive forces of anger, resentment, and bitterness. And nothing so retards the growth of character as these three things. They are hindrances that no amount of dedication and determination can counteract. You must deal with them, not compensate for them. And the only remedy is forgiveness. Anything else is an attempt to compensate for and cover up. Only forgiveness frees hurt people to pursue the character of Christ with any hope of success.

AN UNSCALABLE WALL

Hurt, rejection, abandonment, abuse. They all leave us feeling like victims. The feeling of victimization enables the harm inflicted on us by others to become an obstacle in the pursuit of character. Victims are powerless. Victims are at the mercy of others. Victims can only react. Victims are prisoners. Victims have an excuse.

As victims, we can excuse just about any kind of behavior. After all, look at the way we have been mistreated. And so pain and hurt create an unscalable wall of excuses and rationalization.

I'M OKAY, YOU'RE OKAY, WE'RE OKAY

To make matters worse, the current trend in psychology is to place more and more of the blame for a person's character deficit on our culture. Individuals are no longer responsible for their decisions and behavior. Individuals are nothing more than by-products of our society. They had no choice in how they were brought up. Consequently, individuals are not to blame for their choices. Collectively, we are all to blame. And individually, we are all victims!

The message is, "It is okay for you to behave the way you do. You have no choice in light of your background. For you, this behavior is perfectly acceptable. You are under no obligation to change. You have every right to be the way you are."

Such thinking removes all incentive to change. After all, it is always easier to stay the same and make excuses. Victims don't want to be proactive about changing. Instead, we want to be proactive about making sure that the person who hurt us pays. And so we spend our energy telling our sad stories rather than tackling the task of forgiveness.

In doing so, we open the doors of our hearts and welcome the Trojan horse of bitterness. It becomes a monument. It stands there as a constant reminder of a debt someone has yet to pay.

NO CONNECTION

Of course, not all people see the connection between their hurt and their character. They know they have been hurt. They know they have some character flaws. But they have never seen the connection. Therefore, they don't make excuses. They don't blame anyone but themselves for the way they are. However, at the same time, they can't seem to break free of the attitudes and habits holding them back.

Regardless of whether you see it or not, freedom comes through forgiveness. It is not necessary to understand the connection between the past and the present to forgive. At the same time, understanding that connection is not an acceptable excuse not to forgive. To refuse to forgive is to choose to hang an OFF-LIMITS sign over aspects of your character. An unforgiving spirit hinders the conforming work of the Holy Spirit.

Remember, your character is either improving or deteriorating. It is getting better or worse. Nothing contributes to the deterioration of character like unresolved hurt. Bitterness is like a cancer. It contaminates every healthy thing it contacts. And so your character deficiencies will eventually make contact with the healthy relationships in your life.

Again, my dad writes,

> Holding on to hurt is like grabbing a rattlesnake by the tail; you are going to be bitten. As the poison of bitterness works its way through the many facets of your personality, death will occur—death that is more far reaching than your physical death, for it has the potential to destroy those around you as well.[2]

Bitterness cannot be contained. It always spreads. Forgiveness is not optional. Relationally speaking, it is a matter of life and death.

If you grew up in church, you have heard all of this before. Since the early days of Sunday school, you were taught that the "Christian" thing to do is to forgive. But in the real world it's not that simple. Part of you wants to get even. Part of you knows you should forgive. Forgiving and forgetting made for a nice Sunday school lesson. But it is difficult to transfer that childhood lesson into the particulars of your real-world experience.

AT THE HEART OF FORGIVENESS

Forgiveness is much more involved than simply "forgive and forget." True forgiveness is more about remembering than forgetting. It involves facing the past, not suppressing it.

When you are not the victim, it's easy to give pat solutions for the pain someone else is feeling. And it's easy to take a quick look at a few Bible verses and conclude that the solution is just to forgive and forget. But the mind doesn't have a delete button. Memories don't die easily.

As a pastor, I spend a good bit of time listening to stories of hurt, abuse, and injustice. I can appreciate the sense of helplessness people feel when someone they trusted has taken advantage of them. In my heart, I often wonder along with them, "God, how could You allow such things to happen?" I can relate to their desire for justice, retribution, payback! And often I am hesitant to say to people, "Forgive . . . just forgive! Let it go. Put it behind you. Move on with your life."

It sounds so insensitive, so pat, so trite. Forgiveness seems to be such an oversimplification at times. Besides, what if they are in a situation where there are repeated rounds of abuse and rejection? When is enough, enough? How many times does God expect us to keep forgiving the same person for the same thing? There has got to be a limit—or so conventional wisdom tells us. After all, enough is enough.

COMMON MISUNDERSTANDINGS

My hesitancy to exhort people to forgive and the question of "When is enough, enough?" are fueled by a common misunderstanding about the nature of forgiveness. One that hangs people up for years in their pursuit of character. We tend to view forgiveness as a gift to the ones who offended us. We see it as something that benefits them. Consequently, we are hesitant to forgive. Why give something to people who have already taken something from us? That doesn't make any sense. They owe us. Why give to them?

But as we're about to see, forgiveness is not a gift for others. Sure, it may involve granting a pardon for an offense. But that's just the beginning. The effects of forgiveness run much deeper. For the most part, it's a gift that was designed for us. It's something we give ourselves because when we consider everything that's at stake, the one who benefits the most from forgiveness is the one who grants it, not the one who receives it.

ASKING THE RIGHT QUESTIONS

We are not the first generation of believers to grapple with the question of, "When is enough, enough?" We are not the first to wonder if forgiveness is always appropriate. The apostle Peter had the same question.

One day Jesus was explaining how to deal with some rather complicated relational issues. Peter was listening intently. The whole dialogue reminded him of something that was going on in his life. Apparently, Peter was in a relationship with someone who was repeatedly offending him. He had heard Jesus talk about forgiveness before. He understood his responsibility to forgive. But he wasn't sure how far to take it. So Peter pulled Jesus aside and asked Him, "How often shall my brother sin against me and I forgive him? Up to seven times?" (Matt. 18:21).

In other words, "When is enough, enough? How many times do I have to forgive? Is it always appropriate to forgive?" Peter wanted to do the right thing. But come on, everybody has limits. Where is the justice in a system where forgiveness is offered at every turn?

Knowing that Jesus expected more than the average teacher, he took a stab at what he believed would be a generous answer: "What about seven times?" Peter was catching on. No doubt, there was a time in Peter's life when he would have suggested "two times" or possibly "one." But he had been listening. He knew that Jesus' perspective on things was different from that of the other religious teachers. When it came to forgiveness, however, Peter didn't know just how different Jesus' perspective really was.

By asking, "How often shall I forgive?" Peter revealed his misunderstanding about the nature of forgiveness. Like us, Peter assumed that forgiveness is for the benefit of the offender. And like many well-meaning Christians, Peter was willing to stretch. He was willing to be a nice guy. He was willing to go seven rounds with the same person over the same issue. But after that or some other predetermined point, no more forgiveness.

"I'VE BEEN ROBBED!"

Of course, we can't blame Peter for thinking that way. After all, when someone hurts us, when somebody does something malicious to us, there is a sense in which that person has taken something from us. The person has created a deficit in the relationship. That's why we say things such as, "You *owe* me an apology," or "I'm going to get *even* with him."

Things are out of balance. And to achieve justice, a transaction must take place that transfers something to the victim. It could be an apology, a favor, or some other form of restitution.

For example, somebody who gossips about you steals your good reputation. An adult who abuses a child steals that child's ability to trust. A wife who runs around on her husband steals a piece of her husband's self-esteem. An employer who unjustly fires an employee steals the employee's financial security. And on and on I could go. Whenever there is hurt, there is a theft. There is an imbalance. Somebody owes someone.

Recently, I attended a support group for abused women. I was invited that particular night because the husbands of the women in the group were asked to attend. My assignment was to address the effects of sexual abuse on marriage. As most support groups go, there was a great deal of interchange between participants. About halfway through, one husband asked *the* question of the evening, "How do I forgive my wife's abuser? I feel that he has robbed us of something. He has taken away something from our relationship."

That was a perceptive insight critical to understanding the power of forgiveness. He was right. His wife's abuser had stolen something from them as a couple. There was a debt.

SEARCHING FOR SOLUTIONS

People who have been robbed emotionally are generally looking for two things. First, they want recognition and affirmation that they were, indeed, victims of a crime. Second, they want the perpetrator to replace what was taken. Unfortunately, there are significant problems with both objectives. In almost every case, one or both goals are unattainable. In some cases the victim may get unanimous public affirmation that the crime took place. But that is rare. Even more rare is a situation where a victim is paid back for what is taken. In the vast majority of cases, what was taken can never be replaced. The perpetrator couldn't pay it all back despite a strong desire to do so. Something is gone forever. You cannot pay back a relationship. You cannot repay time. You cannot pay back a reputation. There is no way to make up for years of criticism and neglect.

A "from here on out" apology is good from here on out. But it does nothing to make up for the past. The truth is, nothing can make up for the past. An emotional element involved in hurt cannot be compensated for through apologies, promises, or financial restitution. To some degree, there is always going to be an outstanding debt.

To pursue payback is futile. These debts cannot be paid back. To wait for an apology and restitution is to set ourselves up for failure. While we are waiting, the seeds of bitterness take root. And what begins as a holding pattern becomes a vicious cycle. Hurt people who hold on to the hurt, waiting to be paid back, always hurt other people. Victims become victimizers. We do to others what others have done to us. Along the way, we lose the will to do what is right. After all, look how we were treated!

NARROWING THE FOCUS

Physical pain sets us up to become self-centered. The more intense the pain, the more self-centered we tend to be. Think about the last time you experienced a serious physical injury. What was your focus? What was your greatest concern at the moment? *Pain makes you focus on yourself.* It is the nature of pain.

Emotional pain works the same way. The more intense the emotional pain, the more self-centered we become. The problem is that self-centeredness, for whatever reason, is the archenemy of character. Men and women of character are committed to putting others first. The golden rule is the standard. Self-centeredness is something to be overcome, not embraced. Consequently, holding on to hurt sidelines a man or woman in the pursuit of character.

PROTECTING THE WOUNDS

I see this cause-and-effect relationship working itself out in marriages all the time. A couple will come to my office, both parties full of anger, and each will explain how the other has inflicted pain.

So I say, "Well, this is easy. Just forgive each other and go on with your lives."

"Well, it is not that easy," one of them says. "He keeps doing it. He keeps hurting me."

"Well, keep forgiving him," I suggest.

Exasperated with the simplicity of my approach, she opens fire on me. That's when I know there is more to the situation than meets the eye. Free-floating anger, anger that can easily spill out on anyone in the vicinity, often has its roots in a previous relationship.

Upon further investigation, we usually discover some unhealed wounds from the past. Open wounds that the spouse keeps bumping up against. Wounds that are so painful that the wounded party has little choice but to protect and guard them. Often, I find that the anger in the relationship was never even intended for the spouse. The spouse got in the way of anger directed at someone else. Someone from the past. Someone who had caused a wound that had never been nursed and healed.

People who are protecting wounds always lean toward self-centeredness. Self-centeredness limits their potential for giving and receiving love. So there is conflict. And once again, a forgiveness issue becomes a character issue.

DEALING WITH THE PAIN

We all have our own way of dealing with hurt. Personally, I am prone to sitting around and having imaginary conversations with the people I am angry with. Imaginary conversations give me a feeling of power. I get to carefully choose my wording, and I get to make sure the other person sets me up for what I want to say. I always look good. In my imaginary conversations, there is always an audience present to watch me rip my enemy apart. And when I deliver that verbal deathblow, everyone listening in is in full agreement. It is a wonderful pastime, or so I'm tempted to think.

But the whole system is fraught with lies. To begin with, my responsibility is not to humiliate my enemies publicly. I am to love them. Second, the perfect conversation with the perfect one-liners and stinging comebacks would not relieve me of my anger. Once the whole thing was said and done, I would feel the same way. Ripping someone apart verbally doesn't pay me back. The person still owes me. I may feel better temporarily for having unloaded on him. But he still owes me, and I'm still angry.

Some seek satisfaction through sharing their stories with others. They look for affirmation to ease the pain. They just want to know that the world agrees that they were the victim. Some people will use just about any opportunity to tell their stories. But sharing does nothing to take away the debt.

"ANGER? WHAT ANGER?"

The other avenue for dealing with pain is stuffing it. We have all been told, "You shouldn't feel that way." As a result, too many Christians stuff their emotions. They attempt to deny them all away.

This approach generally leads to depression. Depression is almost always caused by suppressed anger. Coping with anger by suppressing it leads only to other problems that surface in the form of character deficiencies. It is difficult to be depressed and exercise self-control. It is nearly impossible for a depressed person to be gentle and kind. Depression leads to self-centered behavior. And understandably so. Depressed people are in pain. Whatever the reason, depression, suppressed anger, takes its toll on character.

CLEARING UP THE CONFUSION

I don't know how Peter was accustomed to dealing with his hurts. I don't picture him as the type of man to suppress his feelings. And he certainly didn't act depressed. Whatever the case, he was ready to draw the line with someone, and he wanted to know where the line was. "How many times shall I forgive my brother?" he asked.

Jesus responded by saying, "I do not say to you, up to seven times, but up to seventy times seven." And before Peter could respond, He continued with one of the most intriguing parables in the New Testament:

Therefore the kingdom of heaven is like a certain king who wanted to settle accounts with his servants. And when he had begun to settle accounts, one was brought to him who owed him ten thousand talents. But as he was not able to pay, his master commanded that he be sold, with his wife and children and all that he had, and that payment be made. The servant therefore fell down before him, saying, "Master, have patience with me, and I will pay you all." Then the master of that servant was moved with compassion, released him, and forgave him the debt. But that servant went out and found one of his fellow servants who owed him a hundred denarii; and he laid hands on him and took him by the throat, saying, "Pay me what you owe!" So his fellow servant fell down at his feet and begged him, saying, "Have patience with me, and I will pay you all." And he would not, but went and threw him into prison till he should pay the debt. So when his fellow servants saw what had been done, they were very grieved, and came and told their master all that had been done. Then his master . . . said to him, "You wicked servant! I forgave you all that debt because you begged me. Should you not also have had compassion on your fellow servant, just as I had pity on you?" And his master was angry, and delivered him to the [jailers] until he should pay all that was due to him. So My heavenly Father also will do to you if each of you, from his heart, does not forgive his brother his trespasses. (Matt. 18:23–35 NKJV)

DOUBLE TROUBLE

Imagine how Peter must have felt as he listened to this story. In all likelihood he was looking for an excuse not to forgive. He wanted to draw a line and then exact justice. But Jesus headed in a different direction.

As the parable unfolds, we see that God is the king. And wouldn't you know it, Peter is the wicked servant! After all, Peter had been forgiven of a great deal, yet he was demanding payment from his own offender! And then Jesus ended the parable with a stern warning: "So My heavenly Father also will do to you if each of you, from his heart, does not forgive his brother his trespasses." Paraphrased, that becomes, "If you don't forgive, God is coming after you."

At that point, Peter was probably sorry he ever asked the question. What a terrible thing to tell someone who is a victim! He must have been thinking, *Wait a minute! I've already been hurt once. I'm the victim. And now You're telling me that if I don't grant forgiveness— which the person doesn't even deserve—God is coming after me, too?*

I'm not the most sensitive person in the world. But there is no way I would ever tell a hurting man or woman, "Look, you better forgive, or God is coming after you!" Jesus' conclusion seems almost cruel. And I tend to wonder right along with you, "Lord, how can You say that? I already have one enemy. I don't need You threatening me, too."

IT'S FOR YOUR OWN GOOD

Our heavenly Father demands that we grant forgiveness. He even goes so far as to threaten us. And our negative response to that kind of language demonstrates our naivete of the destructive forces of bitterness and resentment.

As a father, I issue my most stern warnings when dealing with the things that have the potential to harm my children. When I tell my two-year-old to get out of the street, I don't speak in a calm, warm, inviting tone of voice. I'm sure I sound somewhat threatening on those occasions. But I'm not angry. I'm not displeased. My tone of voice is influenced by two things: my love for my son and my knowledge of cars.

When Jesus addressed the issue of forgiveness, two things influenced the tone of His parable: His love for His children and His knowledge of bitterness. His warning is severe because the consequences of ignoring it are severe. Anger is nothing to mess around with. It is nothing to hold on to any longer than we have to. It is not a trophy to show off. It is not a story to tell. It is poison to the soul. To refuse to forgive is to choose to self-destruct.

When you hold on to anger, hurt, or bitterness, you invite a Trojan horse into your camp. You open the door for even bigger invasions. It's just a matter of time. So your heavenly Father is going to do everything in His power to persuade you not to do that to yourself.

We all have been hurt. We all have reason to be angry. But that doesn't change the fact that holding on to the past will destroy our lives. As insensitive, unrealistic, and ridiculous as it may seem, God's threat is for our own good. He knows all too well what happens to us when we don't let go of the past. So He issues this warning: "Forgive, or I'm coming after you."

KNOW YOUR RIGHTS

God has every right to command us to forgive. Not too long after Jesus told this parable, He willingly laid down His life for you and me. And when Jesus chose to die for your sins, He chose to do so with full knowledge of your sins. He was aware of every sin you would ever commit. He knew about your broken promises. He knew the times you would fall asleep talking to Him. He knew about the periods of your life when you would completely ignore Him. He foresaw the times that you would beg Him to bail you out of trouble, only to return to business as usual once things settled down. He knew about all those things. If anyone had a right to hold a grudge, Jesus had a right to hold one against us. But He decided to forgive us anyway. In His case that meant He had to die.

We are forgiven people. How can we withhold from others the gift so graciously bestowed upon us? To do so is the height of ingratitude, the very emotion we felt when we read the story of the unjust servant for the first time. *How could he be so ungrateful?* we thought to ourselves. Jesus' point exactly.

PROGRESSING TOWARD FORGIVENESS

Several things must take place for forgiveness to be complete. I hesitate to call them steps. They are more than steps. They are more like processes.

Process #1: Charging the Defendant

If you have been hurt, something has been taken from you. To forgive, you must identify exactly what has been taken. The first process involves pinpointing what has been taken or withheld.

This is where most of us fail. We know that we were wronged, but we never quite put a finger on what we expect in return. We fail to pinpoint exactly what was taken from us. We know what the person *did*. But we don't know exactly what the person *took*.

When we don't identify what has been taken, we go through the motions of forgiveness but experience no release. I have heard it a thousand times, "But I've already forgiven him!" Usually, that phrase is spoken with such intense energy that it is obvious forgiveness has not really taken place. General forgiveness does not heal specific hurts.

Maybe you have been blamed for something you didn't do. In that case, someone took your good reputation. Someone might have robbed you of a promotion or potential relationship. Possibly, your father left you when you were a child. In that case, he robbed you of the experience of growing up with a dad who was there for you.

As Jesus illustrated in the parable, forgiveness revolves around canceling debts. Debt cancellation is at the heart of forgiveness. You cannot completely cancel a debt you have not thoroughly identified. This is a primary reason that people say prayers of forgiveness but continue to carry their anger.

Process #2: Dropping the Charges

After identifying exactly what has been taken, you must cancel the debt. You must proclaim that the person doesn't owe you anymore. Instead of pressing charges, you drop them. Just as Christ canceled your sin debt at Calvary, so you must cancel the sin debts that the other person incurred against you. It is as simple as saying, "Heavenly Father, _____ has taken _____ from me. I have held on to this debt long enough. I choose to cancel the debt. He (or she) doesn't owe me anymore. Just as You forgave me, I forgive him (or her)."

Forgiveness is not a feeling. It's a decision. You choose to cancel the debt. It's not something you have to share with the person who hurt you. And in most cases, doing so would be inappropriate. This is something between you and the Father.

You may be tempted to judge whether or not you have forgiven by how you feel toward your offender. But your feelings toward someone are not always an accurate gauge. Feelings are generally the last thing to come around. But in time, if you cling to the fact that he doesn't owe you anymore, even your feelings will change. The day will come when you will be able to respond to your offender in light of where he stands in relationship to the Father rather than in light of how he treated you.

Process #3: Dismissing the Case

The final process centers on the daily decision not to reopen your case. This element is difficult because feelings don't automatically follow the decision to forgive. Besides that, forgiving someone doesn't erase your memory. If you could forgive and forget, this whole thing would be a lot easier. But in most cases, no sooner have you forgiven than something happens to remind you of the offense all over again. And when the memories resurface, the old feelings resurface as well.

One of two things usually happens at this juncture. You take hold of the offense all over again and reopen the case, or you try not to think about it. But neither response is appropriate.

When memories of past hurt flood your mind, go ahead and face them. Allow yourself to remember the incident. It is even okay to feel the emotions that the memories elicit. If necessary, "be angry, but do not sin." But instead of reopening the case against your offender, instead of rehearsing images of retribution and revenge, use it as an opportunity to renew your mind. Pinpoint once again what you were robbed of. Then thank your heavenly Father for giving you the grace and strength to forgive. Thank Him as well for forgiving you. Don't accept the lie that you haven't really forgiven. Focus on the truth. The truth is, you have decided to cancel the debt. The debt has been canceled. How do you know? Because you decided, as an act of your will, to cancel it.

Memories are not enemies of forgiveness. Memories are simply memories. What you do with them determines their impact. Memories present an opportunity to renew your mind to what you know is true. Truly forgiving does not always entail truly forgetting. If you renew your mind, painful memories can become reminders of God's goodness and grace and healing power in your life. What were once negative memories can become sources of joy as you experience the healing power of the Father.

As painful memories become memorials to the grace of God, your character is affected in a most significant way. Don't race by this next thought: Forgiveness paves the way for you to love your enemies. And loving your enemies is the ultimate expression of character. When you find within yourself the will to love those who have persecuted you, you are expressing Christlike character at the highest level. Forgiveness makes that possible. There is no more powerful scene in all of Scripture than our Savior hanging from a Roman cross, looking up to the Father, and saying, "Father, forgive them; for they do not know what they are doing" (Luke 23:34).

BITING THE BULLET

Surgery may cause more pain than the original injury. But surgery is the beginning of the healing process. Likewise, forgiveness is often painful. It strikes at your pride. It forces you to feel things that you have worked hard not to feel. Yet it is necessary for healing. To refuse to forgive is to choose to live with an open wound. A wound that will keep you on the defensive. A wound that will be a constant excuse for your character deficiencies—your short temper, your distrust of others, your jealousy, your critical spirit. A wound that will give you every right in the world to hate those who have hurt you and despise those who have rejected you. It is a wound that will hinder the work of God in you.

Several years ago I was speaking on the subject of forgiveness. Three-fourths of the way through the message, someone in the audience started crying. It was a woman sitting five or six rows from the front. The longer I talked, the more she cried. When the session was over and everybody left, she was still there, crying. I went over and sat down in the seat next to her. "Are these good tears or bad tears?" I asked. She said, "These are good tears."

Between sobs, she told me her story. She had been through a very painful divorce seven years earlier. During that time, she sought help from a counselor. One day, after several meetings in his office, he raped her. She pressed charges, and the case went to trial. The man was declared innocent and went free. To complicate matters further, she discovered that she was pregnant from the rape. Nine months later, she gave birth to a little boy. She pulled out her wallet and showed me a picture of her six-year-old son.

After telling me the whole story, she took a deep breath and said, "You know something? For six years I have had an ironclad case against this man. I have had the support of everyone who has heard my story. While you were talking, it occurred to me that I was holding over this man's head a debt he can never repay. Even if he were to come to me today, he could never pay me back.

"For six years I have held on to a debt, waiting for him to somehow repay what he has taken from me. My anger and my resentment have controlled me. I have erected so many walls that nobody can get close to me. I have been determined never to allow that to happen again. But what you said made so much sense. If he can't even pay the debt, what's the point in holding on any longer?

While I was sitting here, I canceled the debt. He doesn't owe me a thing. I feel like a new woman."

We both sat there and cried.

If you allow them to, past hurts can put your pursuit of character into an indefinite holding pattern. But forgiveness counteracts the destructive potential of your past. Forgiveness is the avenue for the most significant expressions of character. It paves the way for you to love your enemies and pray for those who have persecuted you. Forgiveness is a nonnegotiable in your pursuit of character.

Chapter Seventeen

THE POWER OF FRIENDSHIP

Your best friends are those who bring out the best in you. . . . I have found that it is better to be alone than in the wrong company.

—John Mason

Parents are quick to warn their children against associating with the "wrong crowd." Good parents do all they can to convince their kids that their friends will influence the direction and quality of their lives. When they see them drifting toward the wrong crowd, they often panic. They understand the power of friendship. At least they understand it at a certain level. They know the power of friendship as it relates to their children. But the influential power of friendship extends beyond adolescence.

In adulthood, your friends are still powerful influences in your life. Your friends, to a great degree, determine the quality and the direction of your life. Friends can have more influence in your life than your convictions, your goals, your vows, and even God.

Chances are, you can think back to times when you compromised a conviction because of the people you were with. We have all accepted invitations to do things we would not usually do if left to ourselves. Many of the promises we have made to God and then broken were broken with friends.

I imagine that at almost every turn you have taken in life—good or bad—the influence of a friend played a part. Think about it. Whether it was something he said, a suggestion she made, or something he did, a friend is almost always involved in the pivotal decisions of life.

This truth was hard for us to admit when we were teenagers. It is doubly hard to admit as adults. We don't want to feel as if we're fourteen again and under the influence of our peers. We are adults now. We are supposed to be over that. But no matter where we are in life, friends are always going to be influential.

GOING MY WAY?

No discussion of character would be complete without discussing the dynamic of friendship. Character is about beliefs and behavior. The company we keep has a direct impact on both.

Initially, our friends impact our behavior. Our tendency is to adjust our behavior according to the company we keep. This is certainly appropriate in some instances. But as we all know, some behaviors are inappropriate regardless of who we are with. And yet given the right set of circumstances and accomplices, it is amazing what we will allow ourselves to get involved in. Not because we believe it is right or because our convictions have changed but because of who we are with. Jerry White rightly observes that "the pressure we face from others is one of the greatest barriers to making proper ethical decisions."[1]

But it works both ways. When we are with people we know to be men and women of integrity, our behavior has a tendency to shift in their direction. We watch what we say. We are more careful about what we suggest in the way of entertainment. There is no getting around it. The company we keep has a profound impact on our behavior. And given enough time, the company we keep will affect our character.

Perhaps the writer of Proverbs had these very ideas in mind when he penned these words: "He who walks with wise men will be wise, but the companion of fools will suffer harm" (Prov. 13:20).

This verse delivers a promise and a warning. If we associate with wise people, we will become wise. They will rub off on us in positive ways. As C. S. Lewis said, "The next best thing to being wise oneself is to live in a circle of those who are."[2]

But to choose fools for companions is to choose disaster. Notice, running with fools does not guarantee we will become fools. It does guarantee, however, that the consequences of their behavior will affect us.

The term *peer pressure* is often used in a negative context. But the cause-and-effect relationship of who you choose as friends can work for you as well. This character builder takes far less effort than some of the other things we have talked about. By choosing the right people to associate with, you take a step toward becoming the right kind of person. For the most part, all you have to do is show up consistently: "He who walks with wise men will be wise." That's it. In other words, anyone who allows into the inner circle a certain quality of person will be better for it.

EXITING THE IN GROUP

Through the years, I have watched scores of adults come cautiously into the church, looking for an alternative to what they have found in the world. I say "cautiously" because while they are beaten up and scarred from a life without Christ, they are not sure they are ready to do the "God thing." After all, following Christ is not a casual endeavor. It demands sacrifice. It requires a reshuffling of values. It involves lifestyle changes.

They look in from the outside and say things such as,

- "There is no way I can do that."
- "I'm not that good."
- "You don't know what I'm like."

My answer is generally the same. I say, "Look, don't worry about changing anything right now. Get involved. Give it some time. Investigate. Let me introduce you to some people who have been where you are."

Once they are locked in with a group of maturing believers, there is almost an immediate change in their behavior. They surprise themselves. And they feel better about themselves. Consequently, their motivation to continue escalates. That is the power of friendship. It has the ability to jump-start an individual's pursuit of character.

The negative power of friendship is no stranger to any of us. All of us have been its victims at some time or another. But God designed the dynamic of friendship to work for us rather than against us.

THE ACCEPTANCE FACTOR

God created us as relational beings. We long for meaningful relationships. Fueling this desire is our need for acceptance. Each of us wants to find an environment of acceptance. Our hearts are drawn in that direction. We all want to fit in somewhere. It's not a decision we make. It's part of the fabric of our souls. God designed us that way. Certain personalities have a difficult time admitting this. But it is true.

The degree to which you are aware of and driven by this need is directly related to the environment you grew up in. Rejection early in life leaves you with a more intense awareness of the need for acceptance later in life. If you did not feel accepted by Mom and Dad, you will go to great lengths to find the acceptance you missed out on. Acceptance from just about any source feels good to a person who comes from an environment of rejection. This dynamic leaves you open to being influenced by the first group or individual who expresses acceptance.

Acceptance is a subtle form of influence. When you feel accepted by someone, you are open to being influenced by him. After all, his acceptance implies that he has your best interests in mind. At the emotional level, acceptance is translated as genuine care and concern. When you are convinced that someone has your best interests in mind, you drop your guard. You open your heart. You are prone to follow. In this way, acceptance paves the way to influence.

Of course, acceptance doesn't necessarily equate with genuine care and concern. But initially, it feels that way. And the more hostile your environment, the easier it is to make that assumption. Consequently, you open yourself up to be influenced by people and groups that don't necessarily have your best interests in mind.

TWO WORLDS

Brad was raised in a Christian home where he was taught since childhood the difference between right and wrong. He was part of a strong youth group. As a teenager, he trusted Christ as his Savior.

During his college years, he participated in a campus ministry. He was a good kid with a good solid Christian background.

After graduating from college, he landed a job with an accounting firm in Atlanta. He moved to the big city with no friends and no support group. His first social contacts were work-related. Immediately, he felt a sense of belonging with the young professionals in his office. Like Brad, many of them were new to the city and were looking for a network of friends. Because of their careers, they had almost everything in common. The one exception was their values and beliefs.

Brad visited several churches after moving to Atlanta. But nothing clicked for him. He didn't feel that he fit in. He liked some of the preachers. But he found it hard to break into the single adult groups. Theologically, he was on the same page as most of the churches he visited. But socially and relationally, there was a void.

So what do you suppose happened to Brad? You guessed it. Brad never abandoned his beliefs or values. But he developed a lifestyle that was in conflict with just about everything he had always stood for. By the time he came to see me, he was a wreck. He was starting to experience consequences of his lifestyle. He was eaten up with guilt. He had developed habits that he wasn't sure he could break. But at the same time, unplugging from his social life—his primary source of acceptance—was not an option he was willing to discuss.

He was the first to admit that his "friends" were a major part of his problem. But the thought of going home alone every night after work was enough to keep him hanging on to relationships that were detrimental, to say the least. He wouldn't let go. And as far as I know, he still hasn't let go. I believe someday he will. His theological anchor is set deep. He will return to the God of his childhood but not without scars. Acceptance is a powerful force. Consequently, friendships are a major factor in the development of character.

ACCEPTANCE MAGNETS

Brad's story illustrates an often-overlooked fact. Most of us don't really choose our friends. Instead, we gravitate toward acceptance. When we sense a genuine "I'm not after anything" and "I'll take you the way you are" feeling of acceptance, we are drawn in. We don't pull out our list of friendship qualifications and conduct an interview.

You have never begun a friendship with a values clarification test. On the contrary, when you feel accepted, you will overlook character faults in the person accepting you. In the presence of acceptance, all the qualities you thought were necessary for a friendship don't seem nearly as important.

In this way, acceptance often causes you to drop your guard. Unknowingly, you allow people into the inner circle of your life who have no business being there. You invite people who operate from a different value system, people whose worldview differs from yours, people with different priorities and agendas. Over time they rub off on you. And eventually, they leave their mark on your character.

THE ACCEPTANCE HOOK

Think for a moment about some of the unwise things you have done for the sake of acceptance. This is especially true when you are in a transitional stage of life. A stage that leaves you wondering where and if you fit in. Changes in your career, your marital status, your location. These are the times when you are particularly vulnerable to being drawn into the wrong group for the wrong reasons. These are the times when being accepted by the wrong group feels a whole lot better than not being accepted by any group.

In these vulnerable stages of life, men and women are drawn into marriages that seem doomed from the start, young men and women are drawn into homosexual relationships, men and women are drawn into adultery. We are such relational beings that in moments of weakness, even inappropriate, shallow, self-centered acceptance is better than none at all.

Most of us have fallen into this trap sometime in the past. Maybe you had a mental list of what you were looking for in a spouse. But somewhere along the way, your need for acceptance lured you into a bad relationship. Maybe your friends even said,

- "He doesn't look very good on paper."
- "I don't think she is what you had in mind."
- "You don't even have the same religious views."
- "I thought you always wanted to marry someone who was . . ."

But you were in too deep. You were accepted, and it felt too good to let it go:

- "I know he has problems, but . . ."
- "I know she isn't there yet, but . . ."

And all your convictions, ambitions, and standards were sacrificed at the altar of acceptance.

CHOOSING YOUR FRIENDS

Acceptance is an integral part of friendship. But it is only one part. The critical ingredient that authenticates a friendship is love. Jesus put it this way: "This is My commandment, that you love one another, just as I have loved you" (John 15:12).

Genuine friendship goes beyond acceptance. It is characterized by genuine "I'm in this for you" and "I'll be there when you need me" love. Acceptance alone can draw you into character-eroding behavior. But acceptance coupled with love can be a powerful character-forming combination.

Notice I said "can be." It is possible to have friends who have your best interests in mind, but who don't know what's best. People who want you to do what's right but aren't sure what's right. People get themselves into complicated situations as a result of following the advice of sincere, well-meaning, unwise friends.

Remember, the person who walks with the wise grows wise. For the power of friendship to have its full, character-shaping potential, you must surround yourself with friends who are filled with the wisdom of God. These are people who will love you with an *informed love*. Men and women whose care and concern flow from a heart that has been transformed by the Spirit of God. Friends whose advice is supported by the truth of God's Word. People who can help you interpret the circumstances and events of your life from God's perspective. All of this, coupled with acceptance, makes for a powerful character-shaping relationship. That is friendship the way God intended friendship to be.

THE MEASURE OF A FRIEND

A real friend is willing to risk losing a friendship for the sake of doing what's best for a friend. The friend whom God will use to shape your character is the one who doesn't mind crashing into your life when necessary to tell you what you don't want to hear. The person would rather protect *you* than protect the *relationship*. A real friend will accept you but won't necessarily accept all your ideas and decisions.

The writer of Proverbs summed it up this way: "Iron sharpens iron, so one man sharpens another" (Prov. 27:17). The sharpening process is not always pleasant. But it is always fruitful. It is painful short term. It is preserving long term. It hurts for the moment. It helps for a lifetime. In this way, real friendships are one of God's primary tools for shaping character.

WALKING WITH THE WISE

To walk with the wise, we must be able to identify the wise. A wise person is not a perfect person or someone who makes the right decisions every time. A wise person is someone who knows the difference between right and wrong and is committed in his heart to doing what's right. The wise are men and women in pursuit of character. The wise ask at every decision-making juncture, "In light of where I want to be, in light of where I've been, what is the wise thing to do?"

The Scriptures teach that the "the fear of the LORD is the beginning of wisdom" (Prov. 9:10). Wisdom begins with the acknowledgment that there is a God, that He is the only true, living God, and that His Word is final. Wisdom takes root in the hearts of those who accept God's standard as *the* standard for interpreting the rightness and wrongness of all things. The term *fear* denotes "surrender or submission to." Wisdom is born in the heart submitted to God and His standard.

The challenge is to find, and surround yourself with, individuals fitting that description. Men and women who have recognized and submitted to the unchanging ways of God. To walk with them is to become like them. Their friendship will leave its mark on your life.

THE REST OF THE STORY

The writer of Proverbs warns us that "the companion of fools will suffer harm" (Prov. 13:20). Pursuing new friendships usually entails pulling back from some old ones. My observation as a pastor is that the difficulty of walking away from an unhealthy friendship usually keeps people from pursuing new, healthy ones. There seems to be something unchristian or un-Christlike about walking away from a friend. After all, aren't we supposed to love everybody?

Through the years, I think I have heard just about every reason imaginable for staying in unhealthy relationships:

- "But I'm her only Christian friend."
- "But he is my best friend."
- "But I'm in love."
- "But he will think I'm some sort of religious fanatic."
- "But she will never understand."
- "But he has come so far. If I walk away now . . ."
- "But what am I supposed to do in the meantime? Sit home alone?"

I have seen such statements take their toll on scores of individuals. Compassion does not compensate for the powerful influence of companions. The "companion of fools" will always "suffer harm," regardless of the reason for being in the relationship. It is a principle.

YOUR OPTIONS

When it becomes evident that a friend or a group of friends has become an obstacle in your pursuit of character, you have three options:

1. You can do nothing.
2. You can step back from the relationship.
3. You can walk away from the relationship.

Option #1 doesn't need much explanation, so let's move on to #2.

Stepping Back

Stepping back from a relationship involves establishing protective boundaries. By setting up boundaries or ground rules, you conduct the relationship on your terms.

- You choose the entertainment.
- You determine how long you'll stay.
- You drive.
- You determine how often the two of you get together.
- You make it clear that certain places are off limits.

Establishing boundaries positions you to take more control of the relationship. It positions you to become the influencer rather than the influencee. You set the pace and tone of your interaction.

Stepping back allows you to focus on and deal with the problem areas of a friendship without forsaking a friend. Stepping back creates breathing room. This response enables you to remain true to what you know is right while continuing to interact with those you consider friends.

Be warned: This approach is effective only if you and your friend are willing to respect and adhere to the boundaries you establish. And the truth is, many of your friends will not play by the rules. They will feel rejected. Some will pressure you to compromise. Others will give up on the relationship altogether.

But let's face it. Anyone who will not respect your convictions and wishes doesn't have your best interests in mind anyway. The person is not in a position to be a real friend.

Walking Away

Option #3 is to totally walk away from the relationship. With some relationships, it's impossible to set boundaries that everybody can abide by. Too much has happened. The old ways are too entrenched. If you have friends like that, then you know exactly what I mean. In your heart you know the only way to break their grip in your life is to walk away.

MAKING TRACKS

Several years ago, Sandra and I went to a birthday party at a friend's farm. We decided to take Sandra's new car. Brent, the fellow hosting the party, had warned us that the dirt road leading to the house was somewhat treacherous. He was willing to pick us up in his truck and drive us to the house. Of course, I wasn't intimidated by a dirt road. I didn't need somebody to pick us up. I could handle it. So we took off.

Things were fine for the first forty yards or so. But little by little, the ruts got deeper and deeper. And the hump in the middle got higher and higher. Before long, the grass that had grown up in the middle of the road was slashing away at our front bumper. Gravel began kicking up underneath the chassis. Sandra wasn't saying anything, but the look on her face let me know that she wasn't enjoying the ride.

Then the ruts got even deeper. The whole car was starting to bottom out. I could just imagine big pieces of tailpipe being torn away and left in the road. But it was too late to turn back.

That was when I came up with the bright idea of getting out of the ruts. I steered the car over to one side of the road and drove with two tires on the side of the road and two tires on the big hump in the middle. That way, the car was straddling the deep grooves in the road beneath us. But every thirty yards or so, the grooves widened and swallowed up the whole car, bumping us back into the ruts. That was when I would casually switch over to the other side of the road, so Sandra would think I did it on purpose. But after another thirty yards or so, we got bumped back down into the ruts again.

Finally, I had to make a drastic move. I couldn't go back. And I couldn't park there in the middle of the driveway. I pulled completely off the road and into the pasture. The grass was tall, but the ground was smooth. No ruts. No gravel. No more damage!

RELATIONSHIPS IN A RUT

Sometimes friendships are like that dirt road. The ruts are so deep that there is no way to navigate them safely. You can try to get out of the deep grooves, but before you know it, you are back into the same old routine. You promise yourself that you're going to draw the line this time. You vow not to get yourself into another situation you'll regret. But the next time you get together with your friend, it's just a matter of time before you're back in the same ruts.

That's when you need to walk away. That's when it is time to pull off the road altogether and chart a different course. There is no use kidding yourself. You just need to walk away. You have to end it. No, your friends probably won't understand. Yes, they might think you have become a religious fanatic. But your character is at stake. And to continue to compromise your character is to chip away at your ability to be a good influence in their lives anyway. Everybody loses!

You may be thinking, *But I'm the only Christian he knows,* or *I'm the only good influence in her life.* These traps have kept many well-meaning people in destructive relationships. If you're the only Christian he knows, then he is probably getting a pretty confused message anyway. If you're the only good influence in her life, then the most influential thing you can do is to demonstrate the importance of making personal character a priority. Sometimes the best way to be a friend is just to walk away.

"REMEMBER ME?"

Several years ago a fellow walked up to me after church and said, "Remember me?" I looked at him, and suddenly, it dawned on me who he was. Craig and I went to college together. He was an excellent guitar player. We would get together and play music on a regular basis. But as it turned out, our lives weren't headed in the same direction. To say the least, he was walking on the wild side.

I wasn't strong enough at that point in my life to do much influencing. And I found myself leaning more and more in his direction. Finally, I basically had to say, "It's over." It wasn't graceful. He didn't understand. But I had to do it.

Years later, Craig stood before me. I was amazed that he would speak to me. And I was even more amazed that he was at church. Then he said something I will never forget: "Andy, do you remember when you told me we couldn't be friends anymore?" I remembered all right. And the memory made me feel ashamed. I was just about to apologize when he said, "Now I understand."

He smiled, hugged me, and walked away.

As it turned out, Craig had become a Christian a few years prior to our conversation. God brought another Christian into Craig's life, a Christian who was mature enough to handle Craig's dark side. Now my reasons for cutting off our relationship made perfect sense to him. In fact, he had to go through the same scenario with several of his friends.

THE REVOLVING DOOR

I tell you that story to illustrate a basic truth: If God leads you out of someone's life, He can certainly lead someone else into that person's life. God may use your willingness to walk away from a relationship to get the other person's attention. Many times, to stay in a relationship at the expense of your character is to interfere with what God wants to accomplish in the lives of both parties. Never sacrifice your character for the sake of a friendship. To do so is to diminish the potential of your influence in the person's life and in the lives of others. Again, everybody loses.

God loves your friends. He loves them more than you do. In some cases, He loves them so much that He wants you out of the picture. And because He loves you, He may want certain people out of your life as well.

PAINFUL CHANGES

Evaluating—and adjusting—friendships is a difficult and complicated process. It takes initiative. It takes emotional strength. It takes faith. Yet getting your friendships in order is an investment in your character.

My experience and observation have led me to the conclusion that God often withholds authentic friendships until we are willing to deal with our problem friendships. The tendency is to want to hang on to the harmful relationship until something better comes along. But often God doesn't operate that way. Part of the reason is His insatiable desire for us to look to Him—and not the people around us—as the source of all things.

Your friends will influence, and in some cases determine, the direction and quality of your life. Relationships never stand still. They are always headed somewhere. Where are your friendships going? Do you really want to go there? Evaluate your friendships. Ask God to bring wise friends into your life. People who will always challenge you to stand by your convictions, not prod you to break them. Don't be content to gravitate toward acceptance. Be intentional about the people you allow into the inner circle of your life. After all, your character depends on it.

Chapter Eighteen

LEARNING TO WALK AGAIN

For when I am weak, then I am strong.

—2 Corinthians 12:10 NKJV

The story is told of an older farmer who was struggling to keep pace with the new hi-tech farms in his area. He was a staunch believer in doing things the old-fashioned way, and he considered the newfangled shortcuts of horticultural engineering to be a passing fad. Creating hardy hybrid plants and using the latest fertilizing techniques, the new farms were doubling and tripling their previous crop yields. The farmer needed a plan to compete. But rather than take advantage of the new technology, he set out to beat it single-handedly. His solution was simple. He would clear a large wooded section of his land and convert it into plowable fields. There was just one problem. Cutting all the trees would take months. And he would never get the land cleared in time for planting season. "If only I could come up with a faster way to cut trees," he pondered.

As luck would have it, the farmer stumbled across an advertisement in a magazine. It featured a new chain saw that promised to cut through a twenty-inch tree in twenty seconds. *One inch per second!* he thought. At that rate, he could clear his entire property in time for planting season. It was exactly what he had been looking for. So he hurried to the general store and purchased the new saw.

The farmer set out early the next morning to begin expanding his farmland. He selected a twenty-inch oak tree as his first victim.

With eager anticipation, he set the cutting chain against the trunk of the tree and went to work. Twenty seconds passed and the tree was still standing. He continued, reasoning that it was his first attempt and that he would get the hang of it gradually. After five minutes, with the tree still towering over him, he began to wonder if he was doing something wrong. And when a full hour had passed with only a small cut in the side of the tree to show for it, the farmer packed up the saw and headed back to the general store.

The clerk listened patiently as the farmer explained his lack of progress. "Let's take a look at it," the clerk finally suggested. With his left hand gripping the handle, the clerk braced the saw against the front porch of the general store. Then, taking his right hand, he grabbed the rubber handle on the side of the saw and gave it a quick pull. Instantly, the saw roared to life. Startled, the farmer jumped back several feet and exclaimed, "What's that noise?"

EFFICIENT CHRISTIAN LIVING

The concepts in this book may have caught your attention as the magazine ad did the older farmer. *This is what I have been looking for,* you thought to yourself. *This is exactly what I have needed.* And if you have read this far, it is quite possible that these pages have motivated and even equipped you to make the development of your character a real priority.

But like the older farmer, you may not know something essential to your success. And I would be less than honest not to mention it in closing: In and of yourself, you don't have what it takes to become a man or woman of character. You can't do it. Not on your own, anyway.

It is true that God is at work in you, transforming your character. And by involving yourself in the process of renewal, you are working alongside the Father to bring about the changes He desires. As I have said from the beginning, His goal for you is an inner person who bears a striking resemblance to that of His Son.

But sooner or later you'll discover that all the motivation in the world by itself is not enough to carry you across the finish line. Motivation won't do it. Principles and strategies are not enough, either. In addition to these things, you need power and enablement; you need help. What God has begun in you, only He can complete. Not only do you need His plan to direct you, but you need His strength to empower you.

STRENGTH FOR THE JOURNEY

In this chapter, we are going to take a look at the Holy Spirit's role in the process of character development. This is the final chapter of the book, but it may very well be the most important. Apart from the empowering of God's Spirit, your efforts will be short-lived and your progress minimal. As I said in the introduction, the Christian life is not a "be all you can be" kind of thing. It is not a self-help program. And it is not about, "Do the best you can and God will understand."

You cannot change yourself any more than you could save yourself. You cannot transform your character in your own strength. Real change involves revelations about yourself that you will never make on your own. Change requires renewal. And renewal requires the excavating work of the Holy Spirit. Jesus referred to Him as the Spirit of truth (John 15:26). Ultimately, the Holy Spirit shines the light of God's truth into the dark places of your heart.

To become a person of character, you need the enabling power of the Holy Spirit. There is nothing strange or weird about the Holy Spirit. The Holy Spirit is the Spirit of God. He is the life of God. He is the life of Christ. And He indwelt you at the moment of your salvation for the expressed purpose of empowering you to follow through with what you sense God is leading you to do.

A FINE LINE

Experientially speaking, there is a fine line between living out of your strength and exercising the strength that God gives through His Spirit. Living in your own strength is like pushing a car instead of driving it. Progress is made. But it is slow, inconsistent, and extremely inefficient. As long as you are pushing your car, you can't go some places. There are hills you can't climb. And at times, it takes every bit of strength to keep from losing ground. As long as you are pushing your car, you have no joy and no sense of satisfaction. It is certainly not something you look forward to.

Pursuing character in your own strength can be an equally frustrating and joyless endeavor. Progress is slow. You may spend years just holding your own. And when you let up for even a moment, the gravitational forces of society have the power to pull you back to where you started. After a few years of that approach, even the thought of pursuing Christlike character makes you tired. Why bother? It is too exhausting. The progress-to-effort ratio makes it a bad investment of time and energy.

Oh, yes, there is one other thing about pushing your car. The stronger you are, the farther you can push it. The stronger you are, the longer it will take for you to deplete your physical reserves and start looking for alternatives. In the same way, it takes some believers longer than others to come to the end of themselves. It takes some longer than others to throw up their hands in frustration and say, "God, I can't do this. If it is going to happen, You are going to have to get involved in a far more evident way."

A DISCLAIMER

Before we go any farther, I need to make a confession. This concept of allowing the Holy Spirit to empower us is one of the most difficult aspects of Christianity to communicate. Explaining it is no simple matter. At least not for me. It can't be reduced to three easy steps. You can't pray a special prayer and walk away changed. And reading this chapter won't necessarily do it for you, either. Like salvation, learning to lean on the power of the Holy Spirit involves the Father opening the eyes of your heart. So while reading this chapter doesn't guarantee anything life-changing, I hope that it will alert you to this often-overlooked aspect of God's character development program.

TWO SOURCES OF STRENGTH

As Christians, we operate in one of two modes: our strength or God's strength. Needless to say, there is a big difference between the two. Most believers readily agree that they have needed God's strength to get them through some trying times in their lives. They agree that they cannot overcome certain temptations and trials without help from above. Christians often ask God to provide strength for the challenges of the day.

But for too many, these are just nice things to say. Confessing dependency on God communicates a sense of humility and spirituality. Yet oftentimes there is no spiritual reality behind the words. There is no real sense of dependence. Instead there is sincere, but insufficient, self-effort. And eventually, there is a deep, abiding frustration.

These two sources of strength result in two contrasting approaches to the Christian life: the *religious* approach and the *relational* approach. The religious approach centers on your ability to do for God and His corresponding obligation to do for you. The relational approach centers on what God has done for you and what He is willing to do through you.

THE RELIGIOUS LIFE

The religious approach is somewhat appealing. On the surface it seems fair. We do something for God, and He does something for us in return. What could be fairer than that? It feels right. After all, the harder we work, the better off we ought to be. Hard work should be rewarded.

As believers, we are usually quick to reject the notion of salvation by works. And rightly so. The Gospels are clear. Salvation comes through faith in Christ. Our belief in salvation by faith sets us apart from followers of other religions in this world. And yet once we move beyond our salvation experience, we are prone to approach life religiously. That is, we measure our approval and acceptance rating with God according to our deeds. Good deeds equal approval. Bad deeds (sin) equal rejection.

If the truth were known, most people who will go to church this weekend will do so out of a sense of obligation. It's an "ought to" kind of thing. At an emotional level, they believe they will be in better standing with God for going. And if they don't go, they feel as if God might hold it against them.

Most of us get caught up in this sort of thinking from time to time. We believe deep down that if we are going to have any kind of connection with God, the connection depends on some sort of routine, some sort of ritual, or some sort of scoring system. But nothing could be farther from the truth. And nothing could be more counterproductive to our pursuit of character. Why? Because religion and self-effort go hand in hand.

Find me men and women who are attempting to win God's approval through good works, and I will show you people who are operating from their own limited strength. As long as we view our deeds as a bridge to approval from God, we depend upon our strength. God does not empower us to win His approval. We have all the approval we need. Approval and acceptance were settled at Calvary. Christ won the Father's approval for us by removing the barrier of sin. Approval is a gift to be accepted, not a wage to be earned.

The Bible has a name for the earn-your-way approach to God. It is called *walking according to the flesh*. Walking according to the flesh involves living life out of our own strength. It is a self-protecting, look-out-for-number-one, what's-in-it-for-me approach to life. The strange thing about it is that a person walking according to the flesh can be in church one minute (when that serves his purposes) and be in bed with his neighbor's wife the next.

The flesh takes its cue from the needs and desires of a man. So when an individual who is walking according to the flesh senses a need for religion, the flesh will track that down. When the same individual longs for inappropriate companionship, the flesh can accommodate that as well.

FINISH THE WAY YOU STARTED

Whereas the religious approach leaves us to do our best in our strength, the relational approach to Christianity involves a new source of strength, an ability to do what was formerly impossible to do. The best way to get a handle on the relational approach is to think through what happens when we become Christians.

Salvation involves putting our trust in what Christ did in His strength on the cross. When we put our faith in Him, He did something for us we could not possibly do on our own. He removed the barrier of sin. He took away the penalty of our sin that was looming over us. Our part was to believe and receive. We believed His promise and received His life. It was an effortless transaction from our standpoint.

Now, with all that in mind, think about the implications of this verse: "As you therefore have received Christ Jesus the Lord, so walk in Him" (Col. 2:6). Your attitude and perspective at the moment of your salvation are to be the attitude and perspective you maintain in your daily walk with God. You accepted Christ as Savior because you were unable to save yourself. In effect, you said, "I cannot. You can." Then you trusted Him to do what you could not do. And through His power, you were saved. You were saved "by grace . . . through faith" (Eph. 2:8).

God never intended for us to shift out of the "I can't, You can" way of thinking. What was necessary for becoming a Christian is equally necessary for living as a Christian. Our perspective at the moment of our salvation is to be the perspective we maintain throughout our Christian experience. We did not have the strength to save ourselves from the penalty of sin. Neither do we have the power to save ourselves from our daily encounters with the power of sin.

That childlikeness of "I need You, I'm powerless, I can't do it without You," was intended as the attitude we were to maintain throughout our lives. But old ways don't die easily. And so most of us went right back to relating to God through rituals, rules, and tradition. Granted, some of the rules were different after our salvation. And we had to get accustomed to several new traditions. But our approach was the same: "God, I'll do my best to obey You."

As we grew in knowledge, most of us were willing to accept the fact that God had an absolute system of right and wrong to which we were accountable. Our problems started when we realized we didn't have the will to follow through.

THE EMPOWERED WILL

Men and women of character have the will to do what is right. That is, we have the ability, the power, the strength, to follow through. And keep in mind, when we talk about character, we aren't talking about being nice. We are talking about the very character of Christ Himself.

The truth is, in our own strength, we don't have the will to follow through. Only one person's will is up to that monumental challenge: the will of Him whose character we seek. Only one person can consistently manifest the character of Christ. And that one person is Christ Himself. Consequently, the power of Christ is necessary to manifest the character of Christ. And that power is available to us only through the Holy Spirit.

The pursuit of character entails surrender to and dependency on the Holy Spirit. The biblical terminology for this approach to life is *walking according to the Spirit*. Think for a moment about the cause-and-effect dynamic of this verse: "But I say, walk by the Spirit, and you will not carry out the desire of the flesh" (Gal. 5:16). The desire of the flesh—desire that conflicts with the character we seek—can be overcome by walking by the Spirit. This verse is actually a promise. If we walk by the Spirit, we will not fulfill the desire of the flesh. We will be empowered to choose the path of character. We will be strengthened to will to do the right thing.

LOOKS LIKE FRUIT TO ME

Here is another way to look at it. As you think back over your list of character goals, do any of them resemble the qualities found in this list? Love, joy, peace, patience, kindness, goodness, faithfulness, gentleness, self-control. Chances are, they do. This is a list of characteristics and virtues that the Holy Spirit desires to produce through us (Gal. 5:22–23).

The apostle Paul refers to them as the fruit of the Spirit because they are produced by the Spirit. These are not qualities we can produce in our own strength. These are not virtues we are commanded to go out and attain on our own. These are characteristics the heavenly Father longs to produce through His children as we learn to rely upon and draw upon His strength. *Character is produced through us. It is not manufactured by us.*

THE CHARACTER OF THE FLESH

Despite all that, Christians who are walking according to the flesh could be easily intrigued by the idea of becoming persons of character. After all, look at the benefits. Successful relationships, the respect of others, intimacy with God. Who wouldn't want all of that? So they get busy implementing some of the strategies we have talked about.

But before too long they run into one of two roadblocks. First, the flesh is going to get tripped up pretty early in the process because of one particular aspect of character development. Remember our definition for character? The will to do what is right as defined by God, regardless of personal cost. The flesh can't deal with the part about "regardless of personal cost." That's where the pursuit comes to a screeching halt.

The second problem is that the flesh is fueled by self-effort. And self-effort is insufficient for the changes we are talking about. Self-effort cannot consistently drum up what it takes to will to do what is right. So the whole process breaks down. Good intentions, determination, preparation, strategies—these things aren't powerful enough to overcome the power of the flesh. Only the Holy Spirit can enable believers to will to do what is right regardless of the cost.

The problem isn't that you're not dedicated enough. The problem isn't that you haven't tried hard enough. The problem is that what you are attempting to accomplish is impossible in your own strength. And so God sent His Spirit to lead and empower you. The whole thing is intensely relational.

LEARNING TO WALK

When I heard people talk about the importance of walking in the Spirit, I thought to myself, *Okay, I agree, I agree, I agree. Now just tell me how to do it. I mean, I've got the* what. *I need the* how. *Give me the three points so I can put them up on my mirror, and then I'll just pray the prayer or whatever.*

I got the same feeling when I read the passage where Jesus says, "I'm the vine; you're the branch. Abide in Me." I thought, *Okay, so tell me how.* And instead He goes on to the next subject: "I have rivers of living waters springing up to eternal life. . . . You'll have life more abundantly. . . ." And again, I was thinking, *But tell me how.*

The Bible doesn't really tell us how to walk in the Spirit. It just tells us to do it. And as frustrating as that is, I think I understand at least part of the reason why. God desires a relationship. If He had given us Three Steps to Walking in the Spirit, we would have another list to follow. And lists, rituals, and routines are the essence of walking in the flesh. They don't draw us closer to God. There is nothing relational about a list. There is nothing intimate about a task. We could get a perfect score on the list and never know our heavenly Father.

Lists and steps actually encourage independence rather than dependence. Once we get a fix on "how to," we tend to take the ball and run with it—for a while anyway. When we run out of steam, we conclude the list was faulty, God doesn't care, Christianity doesn't work, and so on. Christianity is highly relational. Jesus didn't come to give us a new list. He came to give us life. God desires a relationship with you. And intimate relationships are not run by a list. In a thriving relationship, there are no formulas.

WALKING IN RELATIONSHIP

Walking according to the Spirit is purely a relational endeavor. It begins with surrender. Surrender to a person. Surrender to His standard and will for your life. *Walking in the Spirit can be defined as moment-by-moment dependence upon the Holy Spirit to prompt you to do what He wants you to do and to empower you to do what you cannot do.*

Notice that this approach doesn't compromise God's standards. It's not a license to sin. The goal is still the same—the character of Christ.

There are rules. But the rules are intended to give you a picture of where God is taking you. They foreshadow what you'll look like as God gradually transforms you into the image of Christ. Your job is not to keep rules. Your job is to walk in the Spirit. Because if you walk in the Spirit, you will not fulfill the desire of the flesh. That's the path to character.

Just as you relied on God to free you from the penalty of sin, you must now rely on God to free you from the power of sin. Your spirit is set free from the penalty of sin—eternal death—at the point of salvation. But as long as you remain on this earth, your earthly body will continue to be the target of sin's temptation and destructive power. Your pursuit of Christ's character hinges on your day-to-day dependence on the power of His Holy Spirit to empower you toward Christlikeness.

Your primary goal should be to live in an ongoing state of surrender, acknowledging that without the intervention of the Holy

Spirit, you will be defeated. If a singular theme emerges from the entirety of Scripture, it is this: *Through relationship with God, you are finally capable of doing what you were incapable of doing on your own.* That's what walking in the Spirit is all about.

FOLLOW THE LEADER

You are dependent upon your heavenly Father. We need to recognize our dependency and act on it. We ought to declare our dependency every morning when we rise. And we ought to thank Him for His sufficiency every evening as we close our eyes to sleep. Character is the by-product of dependency. For when we are weak, He is strong. And when we allow Him to be strong in us, He produces His fruit through us.

If I were to invite you to my house, there are several ways I could tell you to get there. To begin with, I could give you a map. I could say, "Here's what you do: You get on I-285 and go east to the Ashford Dunwoody Exit. When you exit, just follow this map. I'll see you at my house."

You would get in your car, you would set the map down beside you, and you would follow that map. You would do everything the map said to do. And sure enough, you would eventually arrive at my house. With this approach, you would measure your success according to your ability to read a map and follow the directions. When it was over, you would rejoice that you got to my house without getting lost. And you would owe it all to my good map and your ability to follow it.

That's a picture of walking according to the flesh. You have your instructions, you have your list, and you measure your success by your ability to execute—to do what's right. But notice where your focus is: It's on the map. And your relationship with the Father is not front and center in your thinking. Instead, it is the list—the dos and don'ts.

The other way I could get you to my house is to say, "Get in your car, I'll pull around, and you can follow me." You might respond, "But which way are we going?"

"Just follow me."

"Are we going to get on the interstate?"

"Just follow me."

"Which exit will we take?"

"Just follow me."

And so our journey would begin. When I turned left, you would turn left. When I turned right, you would turn right. And eventually, you would arrive at my house. You would arrive at the same place, by the same route, in approximately the same amount of time as you would have by following the map. But instead of focusing on a map, your focus would have been on me. Moment by moment, mile by mile, you would be dependent upon me. I would have had your undivided attention.

God's goal for you isn't just to end up at the right place. His goal is relationship. The goal is moment-by-moment dependence upon His Spirit. Dependence for direction and dependence for the strength to follow through. And when that becomes your approach to life, you will not only get to the right place, you will get there the right way. And along the way, you will know Him. And in knowing Him, you will discover His character. The very character He longs to create in you.

MEET THE KIDS

Sandra and I have three children, Andrew, Garrett, and Allie. As much as I desire my children to do what's right, that's certainly not the only thing I want for them. I want them to grow up feeling their father's love. Sandra and I are working to create a home where the dos and don'ts are presented and reinforced in a highly relational context. I don't want three children who salute me every morning and then march off to "do right." I desire a genuine, warm, unique, mutually beneficial relationship with each of my kids. In fact, I value the relational component as much as or more than the moral one. I would rather have imperfect children who feel comfortable crawling up in my lap from time to time than children who always do the right thing but who have no interest in pursuing a relationship with me.

You may think that's selfish. But I am convinced it is a reflection of the image of God in me and every parent who is in touch with God-given parental feelings. We are instructed to address the God of creation as our heavenly Father (Matt. 6:9). The term *Father* reverberates with relationship. He could have instructed us to address Him as King, Sovereign, Master, Creator, or Ruler. All of these titles would have been appropriate. He is all of these things. But instead, He chose heavenly Father.

Your heavenly Father has provided an approach to life that will not only get you where you need to be but will allow you to get to know Him along the way. He wants you to experience your Father's love. The road to character is not so much about following a map as it is walking with and relating to a Person.

THE DECISION TO FOLLOW

Of course, there is another way I could get you to my house. I could put you in the car and drive you there. And for years, I thought that was the picture of walking in the Spirit. I thought, *I'm going to grow and grow, and I'm probably going to get so committed, and so surrendered, and so rededicated that one day God will say, "Andy, you've finally made it. From here on out, it's an easy ride."*

I thought walking in the Spirit was a level we reached after years of listening to tapes, reading books, and having monster quiet times. I assumed there was a point where the Christian life would get easier. I was hoping for an infusion of willpower that would make choosing to sin out of the question.

I would hear sermons about "let go and let God." And I would keep letting go and letting go, and waiting for God to scoop me up and change me. But that's not a picture of walking in the Spirit. Because at some point in that little transfer, God would have to infringe upon my power to choose. And once He did that, the significance and authenticity of my worship and allegiance would be diminished. Freedom to choose is a prerequisite for a genuine relationship.

Still, don't you sometimes wish God would take control of your mind? Wouldn't it be easier if you could walk an aisle, pray a prayer, and push a button, and suddenly, God would take over? As attractive as that may sound at times, God doesn't want to control you. If control was His goal, He could have accomplished that long before now. Relationship is His goal. And to make that possible, He has given you the gift of freedom. Freedom to choose. Freedom to follow. Freedom to surrender.

As you follow, surrendered to His will and purposes, He empowers you to follow through on what He desires for you to do. Surrender is a sign of weakness. And where and when you are weak, He is strong. Your salvation didn't begin with a commitment to something. It started with dependence upon Somebody. And the day-to-day Christian life is the same way. It's not about committing to something. It's about depending upon Someone.

BABY STEPS

When Andrew first started to walk, we played out a scene in our house that is played out in virtually every household with children. Our precious little angel had been crawling around for months. And finally, he started pulling up and standing on those little legs. He would stand there, holding on to the arm of a chair with one hand, looking as if he was ready to let go. He had that big, goofy grin on his face, and one leg in the air.

Then the big moment. He attempted his first step. And there we were, camcorder in hand, cheering and encouraging, "Come on, come on!" Of course, Andrew didn't know what was going on. I had my arms stretched out in his direction and a big, goofy grin on my face as well. And suddenly, false alarm. He wrapped both arms around the arm of the chair and just stood there giggling.

So we did what every parent does at that point. We started bribing him. We held out toys, food, whatever we could get our hands on that would make him want to move in our direction. And then it happened. Andrew looked at Sandra, he glanced at me, and then he locked in on the bribe. His eyes grew wide with excitement. Then he dropped to his knees and crawled just as fast as he could to receive his reward.

Then the whole process began again. And once again, Andrew dropped to his knees and crawled. Now why do you suppose Andrew kept acting that way? Because crawling comes naturally to a baby. It's what a baby does. It's what he had been doing since the day he became mobile. It's all he knew.

CRAWLING THROUGH LIFE

Living life in our strength comes naturally to us as well. We have an internal propensity for independence. Approaching life from the standpoint of weakness rather than strength seems foreign; it is awkward. So when the pressure is on, when we see something we really want, even something as beneficial as character, we drop to our hands and knees and crawl.

But children were designed to walk, not crawl. And you were designed to walk in the Spirit, not crawl through life in your own strength. Learning to walk, physically or spiritually, takes time. It is a process. It begins with baby steps. It involves a series of setbacks in which you revert to your old ways of coping. And as is the case with children, to refuse to learn is to choose to be disabled for life.

FIRST STEP

For you, that first baby step may mean getting up tomorrow morning and saying, "Lord Jesus, today I cannot. But You can." Rehearse your day with Him. Pray through your schedule, review your character goals, and claim victory over the temptations you know you will face. Think through the stressful moments you anticipate. For the most part, you can predict the circumstances that will test your character. Go ahead and claim your dependency ahead of time. As you imagine yourself moving through the paces of the day, tell the Lord, "I cannot; You can."

- "Lord, I'll probably run into _____. You know how difficult it is for me not to gossip when I'm around them. I have a difficult time keeping my mouth shut. I cannot, but You can."
- "Father, I want to honor my husband. But You know how difficult that is for me right now. I cannot, Lord. But You can."
- "Today I have to give _____ an answer. I know what You want me to say. But I don't have the strength to say no. I cannot, but You can."
- "Today I will see _____. Lord, I cannot control my thoughts when she is around. I cannot, but You can."
- "This is going to be a stressful day. Father, You know I have a tendency to lose my cool when the pressure is on. I confess that I cannot handle the events of this day, but You can. Handle them through me."

Your pursuit of character is not intended to be a solo flight. It is not about doing your best. It is not about being all you can be. No doubt, you have tried being all you can be. And like so many, you have discovered that all you can be is not enough.

For this reason, God sent the Holy Spirit to live inside you. He came to direct and empower you. He will enable you to be what in your own strength you could never be—a person of character. When you can't, He can. His optimum working environment is your weakness. His primary tool is truth. His final product is a reproduction of the character of Christ in you.

So pull out your list of character goals and write across the top in big letters, I CANNOT, BUT YOU CAN. Declare your weakness. Reaffirm your dependence. And ask your heavenly Father to teach you what it means to walk according to the Spirit. For when you are weak, He is strong.

CONCLUSION

The crowd roared with excitement as the lead runner came into view. His name was German Silva. And with only seven hundred yards between him and victory, he was beginning to feel the exhilaration of the moment.

The 1994 edition of the prestigious New York Marathon had become the object of more media attention than any previous race. It was the event's silver anniversary. It featured a reunion of its inaugural runners called the "Circle of Champions." It was respectfully dedicated to the memory of its recently deceased race director. An air show was scheduled to cap off the celebration. And the circus of events surrounding the marathon seemed to pause as the eyes of New York focused on the climactic finish of the race.

Silva had run almost twenty-six miles. But that distance didn't begin to describe the route he had traveled to get there. It was the fulfillment of a dream that was born in a tiny, impoverished village in rural Mexico. Back home, his mother waited anxiously for word of his success. Back home, there was no sports coverage on television. Back home, there was not even electricity. For nearly all of his twenty-six years, it seemed Silva had been running toward the dream of something better for his mother, his people, and his village. And as he passed through the tunnel of blurred faces, colorful banners, and screaming fans, he felt closer than ever to the finish line.

Trailing close behind was his friend and frequent training partner, Benjamin Paredes. Together, they had assumed control of the race at the twenty-three-mile mark. Stride for stride, they matched each other through Central Park. By all appearances, the most celebrated New York Marathon in history was about to see its most exciting conclusion.

Silva remained confident. Having trained with Paredes, he knew that he held the upper hand. If it came down to a sprint, Silva was the faster runner. And as he neared the final stretch, he began to ease ahead of his fellow countryman. Just ahead of him, the camera car set the pace as the crew aboard captured the dramatic climax of the race and piped it into the homes of millions of spectators around the world. Physically and mentally exhausted, Silva focused on the back of the vehicle and steadily increased his lead.

With only a few hundred yards to go, the car left Central Park South and made a right turn into the Seventh Avenue entrance of the park. With impenetrable focus, Silva followed close behind. He was no longer aware of his teammate's presence behind him. His lead seemed secure. But as the cheers of the crowd suddenly turned from celebration to distress, he could sense that something was wrong.

When he glanced up at the faces along the route, they seemed painfully distressed. A policeman flailed his arms wildly and pointed back in the direction of Central Park South. Silva realized that he was going the wrong way. The car he was following had turned off the course in order to clear the path to the finish line. And by the time he got turned around, Silva had given his friend a fifty-yard advantage.

In all their years of running together, Silva had never outmanned Paredes enough to make up for such a deficit. Nevertheless, when he returned to the course, he began a feverish sprint toward the finish line. With less than two-tenths of a mile to go, Silva somehow managed to catch up with Paredes. And as the two crossed the finish line, Silva emerged with the smallest lead in the marathon's history, beating his teammate by less than two seconds.

When it was over, Silva dedicated his effort to his father, Abigato, who turned seventy the next day. "Before, he didn't want me to become a runner because the situation in my village was very hard," said Silva upon accepting the spoils of $150,000 and a new Mercedes. "Now, I think he's one of my biggest fans."[1]

A NARROW ESCAPE

German Silva narrowly escaped the sports disaster of a lifetime. He was physically superior to his opponents. He was well prepared for the race. And he was mentally focused. However, for a few critical seconds, he channeled all his talent and years of training in the wrong direction. And the error almost cost him the race.

On the brink of my most productive years, I found myself at a similar point in the race I was running. It wasn't so much that I had drifted off course. I didn't know exactly what the finish line looked like. I didn't know where to channel my energies. I wanted to win. I wanted to be a success. I just didn't know what it meant to win. I had never defined success.

You may have all the talent in the world. You may have a first-rate education. You may be blessed with wonderful opportunities. You may pour your heart and life into everything you do. But unless you take time to discover what's really important to you, until you define your personal finish line, you could find yourself winning a race you never intended to run. Years down the road, you may be looking back at a life fully invested in a commodity that did not pay the kind of return you were looking for. As Stephen Covey says, you may spend your life climbing the ladder of success, only to find that it is leaning against the wrong wall.

If you are a believer in Jesus Christ, I believe your search for meaning and purpose will eventually lead you to grapple with issues of character: Christlikeness. This is something God has called all of us to. It is what He is working to create in each of us. The fleeting and unfulfilling nature of most of our pursuits pales in comparison.

Life is very much like a race. Every day you take a step toward a finish line. Now is the time to discover exactly what that finish line looks like. And now is the time to discover what you want that finish line to look like.

God has chosen a finish line for you: Christlikeness. For this reason, your character is of utmost importance. It is one of your heavenly Father's priorities. My prayer is that it will become one of yours as well, for He is at work. He is working to shape and form you from the inside out. And as you align your will with His, change will take place. Change that will prepare you for the inevitable storms of life. And God's promise is that when the winds of conformity and compromise come sweeping down upon you, you will remain unshaken—like a rock.

NOTES

Chapter 1

1. Stephen Covey, *The Seven Habits of Highly Effective People* (New York: Simon and Schuster, 1989), 96–97.
2. Ibid., 98.

Chapter 2

1. Peter Senge, *The Fifth Discipline* (New York: Doubleday, 1990), 142.
2. Peter Drucker, *Managing the Non-Profit Organization* (New York: Harper Business, 1990), 201.

Chapter 3

1. James M. Kouzes and Barry Z. Posner, *The Leadership Challenge* (San Francisco: Jossey-Bass, 1987), 16.
2. Ibid., 17.
3. William Beausay II, *Boys!* (Nashville: Thomas Nelson), 14.
4. James M. Kouzes and Barry Z. Posner, *Credibility* (San Francisco: Jossey-Bass, 1993), 15.
5. Josh McDowell, *Right From Wrong* (Dallas: Word Publishing, 1994), 18.
6. C. S. Lewis, *The Case for Christianity* (New York: Macmillan Publishers, 1943), 5.

Chapter 4

1. Bill McCartney, "A New Season," *Men of Action* newsletter, April 1995, 1.
2. Stephen Covey, *Principle Centered Leadership* (London: Summit Books, 1991), 58.
3. Larry Crabb, *Men and Women* (Grand Rapids, Mich.: Zondervan, 1991), 65.

Chapter 6

1. Josh McDowell, *Right From Wrong* (Dallas: Word Publishing, 1994), 55.
2. Stephen Covey, *The Seven Habits of Highly Effective People* (New York: Simon & Schuster, 1989), 18.
3. The historical research for this chapter was compiled by WallBuilders Ministries, Inc.; P.O. Box 397; Aledo, Texas 76008; (817) 441-6044.

Chapter 9
1. Larry Crabb, *Inside Out* (Colorado Springs: NavPress, 1988), 31.
2. Ibid., 42.

Chapter 11
1. David Baker, *Flight and Flying: A Chronology* (New York: Facts on File, 1994), 19 and 25.
2. Samuel Nisenson and William A. DeWitt, *Illustrated Minute Biographies*, rev. ed. (New York: Grosset & Dunlap, 1964), 160.

Chapter 13
1. Charles Stanley, *A Touch of His Freedom* (Grand Rapids, Mich: Zondervan, 1991), 15.

Chapter 16
1. Charles Stanley, *Forgiveness* (Nashville: Thomas Nelson, 1987), 17.
2. Ibid., 26.

Chapter 17
1. Jerry White, *Honesty, Morality, and Conscience* (Colorado Springs: NavPress, 1978), 62.
2. Walter Hooper, ed., *Selected Literary Essays* (Cambridge: Cambridge University Press, 1979), 99.

Conclusion
1. "1994 New York City Marathon," *New York Running News*, Dec./Jan. 1995, 6–12.

ACKNOWLEDGMENTS

Six months into this project, God threw me a lifeline. It happened on a Monday night in our home. Sandra and I were meeting with five other couples discussing personality types and their impact on our marriages. A few minutes into the discussion, Ben Ortlip, one of the fellows in the group, spoke up. "Here's what I think," he said. Ben proceeded to read several comments he had written in the margin of his book. When he finished, I said, "Ben, when did you write that?" He said, "While we were talking." I was impressed.

Later that evening I approached him about helping me with this book. He graciously agreed.

Ben's participation took the quality and creativity of the manuscript to a level I would never have achieved on my own. Ben, thank you for the wonderful illustrations, the challenging discussions, the research, the drafts, and most of all, your personal commitment to the principles in this book.

I am grateful as well for Victor Oliver's encouragement throughout this process. Without his gentle nudges, I would have put this off for another five years. Vic, thanks for giving me a chance.

ABOUT THE AUTHOR

A ndy Stanley, son of internationally recognized pastor and bestselling author Charles Stanley, made his own publishing debut with *Like a Rock*. Andy currently serves as senior pastor of North Point Community Church in Atlanta. He received his master of theology degree from Dallas Theological Seminary and has also authored the bestselling book *Visioneering*. He and his wife, Sandra, are the parents of three children, Andrew, Garrett, and Allie.